Antelope Hill Writing Competition 2024
Thinking About Rome

Thinking About Rome

Fourth Annual

Antelope Hill Writing Competition

—2024—

ANTELOPE HILL PUBLISHING

Cover art by Swifty.
Contest judged by the Antelope Hill administrative team.
Editing and layout by Margaret Bauer.

Antelope Hill Publishing | antelopehillpublishing.com

Paperback ISBN-13: 979-8-89252-028-7
EPUB ISBN-13: 979-8-89252-029-4

CONTENTS

Publisher's Foreword ix

POETRY

Selected Poems by Author

11011011 3

Berry 4

Blade 5

Chris Blexurd 6

Gordon Butler 9

J. B. Camville 11

Emily Jean Crocco 12

A. J. Dachauer 14

Edward Delacroix 15

Sig Denreim 16

June Egbert 17

Kaiter Enless 19

Dominick Carmine Giannattasio 20

Harrison George Gray 24

M. S. Jones 25

Kern "Kavalry" Keats 28

Scott R. McNeil 30

Ndabaningi 36

John Oghma 37

Filip Ostler 39

João Paulo...40

Anthony Ramsey 43

Noble Red...45

Arminius Rex..46

Ethan Robert..47

Saxon Stargazer 51

K. B. Steward 53

Shannon Strix 54

Wehrwolf Tactics 57

Henri Teloz..59

Anastasia Temnikova 65

Treader...67

THVMOS 68

Poetry Winners

Honorable Mention: "Three Dives of Minerva" by Handary See......................70

Honorable Mention: "April 9, 1945" by Paul Dempsey 86

Honorable Mention: "Pietas" by John Alu 90

Second Place Winner: "I See the Marble Hercules" by Anonymous 92

First Place Winner: "The Song of Regulus" by Anon-Marie 94

SHORT STORIES

Selected Short Stories by Author

Achromous 105

Altweltaffe...112

Kaiter Enless...121

J. Ester 130

Noah Huffstutler 140

Mohammad Lonlabe...146

T. B. McGill 158

Ndabaningi 161

C. O'Brien 168

Alex Petrov 176

Francis Rockwell 184

Mark Time 193

Turn_Coat 197

Short Story Winners

Honorable Mention: "The Maker's Castle" by Vasyli Kent 210

Honorable Mention: "Denying the Purple" by Christopher Jolliffe 222

Second Place Winner: "Zeno's Djinni" by Michael Mapp 234

First Place Winner: "An Untold Story" by Michael Calloway 246

PUBLISHER'S FOREWORD

Antelope Hill Publishing is proud to present our Fourth Annual Writing Competition. Once again, we were delighted to see the outpouring of creatively in response to our theme "Thinking About Rome." This year, we intended the theme—a tongue-in-cheek reference to an online meme—to prompt participants to contemplate the perennial nature of human experiences, whether they happened yesterday or thousands of years ago, and the intersections of our struggles today and those of times long past. This became the impetus for some of the most beautiful writing we have ever published, with a wide range of styles and approaches that do credit to all who submitted to the competition.

We want to thank all those who supported and promoted our competition, and especially all those who participated by submitting their writing, regardless of whether we accepted their submission or not. Our administrative team loved reading and reviewing almost all of the submissions, and many of the ones that did not make it in this year were cut only after fierce debate. Our selection and evaluation process this year held to a higher standard than in prior years, with some much-loved submissions being left on the cutting-room floor due to lack of consensus. All participants who made it into the final print edition should hold their heads up high as exemplifying the best among the pro-White scene.

We hope to inspire more writers in our sphere to produce quality literature for our people. The importance of literature and creative writing to the survival and self-knowledge of a people is one of the perennial facts of the human experience that shines through history. As conditions in the world around us continue to deteriorate, it is all the more important for our community to create its own culture—to write its own stories, for its own consumption, and for its own benefit—because no one else will do it for us. Our small publishing house is but one part of this effort, and insofar as we can nourish a love of literature and creative writing among our customers, we will be doing our part. Perhaps the pen is not mightier than the sword, but the eternal quote by Ernst Jünger comes to mind: *"Habent sua fata libelli et balli* (books and bullets have their own destinies)."

We hope you enjoy the works in this collection as much as we have, and we look forward to many more years of sharing your talent with the world.

Antelope Hill Publishing

POETRY

Dantean Nights

11011011

The red, white, and green hangs on the wall
About to fall
Claims of all for one and one for all
Salve o Popolo d'Eroi
La nazione
From dead men, ideas have sprung free
From the Fourth Shore to Dalmatia's coast
To give their most
A young nation with much to have boast
With knife in hand, and black shirts on backs
The sticks and ax
When the Combattimento attacks
A new empire built on the ruin
Concrete festoon
From dust to dust, it too shall fall soon
Republic to Empire twice reign
So born again
With lightning rails and thunderous train
Addio, riposati bene
Presto, duce
Our time will come, we will have our day

Ancient Love

Berry

In Rome's embrace, passion's flames did ignite,
Amidst marble halls, love took its flight.
Beneath the stars, two hearts entwined,
In whispered vows, eternal bind.
In ancient echoes, our love defined.
With every caress, our souls combined.
Your lips on mine, an inferno of desire,
Our love a beacon, in this world of mire.

In heated passion, we swayed and danced,
Love's sweet music, a symphony entranced.
No words were needed between us two,
For in each other's eyes, our hearts spoke true.
We reveled in the joy of forbidden love,
And prayed that our gods would smile above.

Like all things, our time soon passed,
And Cupid's arrow could no longer last.
Our love forbidden, a dangerous game,
And soon came the day when we had to part ways.
Though miles may separate us now,
Our love remains eternal, forever bound.

So when you gaze upon Rome's sacred walls,
Remember the passion that once enthralled.
For in this city of ruins and dust,
Our love will live on, forever just.

She Whispers

Blade

Pink stained skulls, poisoned water
Creeping masses, at fever pitch
Traitors stare, from every corner
Time to summon the long lost
Witches' brew, a penny 'n quarter
Eerie echoes, a violent itch
Bastard traitors, fill their pockets
Parasite hordes, fill a ditch.
Striking hearts, across the borders
The parting glass, a wailing witch
Sparks of fury, rattle cages
She calls her sons, across the ages
Her whisper now a fury pitch!

Doll Aeneid

Chris Blexurd

Tartarus unmoved and Acheron flowing
slowly somewhere beneath her as she passes
from bedchamber to bedchamber. These
stories of men kept like obols. Hope of love
and home is more daunting than Olympus.

Indignity is all she knows of Aeolus.
Scuttled trysts, lost companions, and
a voyage begun without a full complement
remaining so throughout its course.
And the Gods are absent from every part of it.

Reverse Pygmalion

Chris Blexurd

she felt weak in my embrace
and almost warm

and I felt I could have molded
her then and there

with my hands and my lips, making
her perfect and happy

Turnus' Dream

Chris Blexurd

the range was clean and white
like a hospital or a beach or heaven or
a place you just wake up in

on strings the targets flew like ghosts
above him, taunting the silent men who
waited as ships in their bays

and when he stepped forward, it felt like
sand under his feet, the discarded brass that
spread down to the shore

it was 50 yards to the water, according to
the hash marks, to where he could bend low and
wash away the blood from his hands

there was the smell of fish and a feeling
he had seen this before, the sun just so and
the hermit crabs exchanging shell casings

Head of a Roman Patrician

Gordon Butler

I

Unmoving, patient, the old patrician watches
As tightly-controlled dartings of hammer and chisel
Liberate his marble double from the rock.
An upright head emerges, chin and jaw
Are chipped and scooped in place, a lofty brow
Is shaved alive, and there, like sentences
The deep-ploughed folds of age are written in.

Descendants, future guests will recognize
The strength that bore an empire on its back
In that stone poem, each facial line and fold
A chaos ordered, lowness raised, a border
Pushed nearer to the edges of the map.
They'll see the master's proprietary eye,
The straight-spined pride that comes from seventy years
Of ruling over men, and in the veins
Rich blood from fathers' fathers, handed down
Like a cup of precious wine. This bust will be

A testament in stone of noble stock;
Organic virtues cased in quarried rock.

II

Rome nails its downfall to planks of wood
On Calvary hill and a nation is
Abandoned by its gods.

The old stern virtues go soft
And liquify, all overgrown
With rainbow-colored rot.

Blood flows into the swelling cities,
Into the swirling brown-red maelstrom,
From a thousand muddied sources.

The gravity of the center weakens.
Far-flung provinces come unhooked,
Boundaries grow blurry and porous.

A falling empire drags him under
Into the mud, the hard marble
Sinking into a bath of earth.

Worms work around him and roots of trees
Grasp his shoulders. The turning world
Spins him senselessly about.

Sculpture becomes geology.

III

Then
An accidental spade.

Like a swimmer, he
Resurfaces
To a new millennium's light.

They put him in a fluorescent museum
In a city which was bogland when he lived.
Around him the detritus of centuries:
Utensil fragments, stained finery, barbaric trinkets.

His house, family, nation are underground.

Stranded in a bloodless, sterile age,
He keeps his arrogant frown, his senator-scowl.

Caligae

J. B. Camville

I marched with Rome, one sunlit age,
Upon the Empire trail,
Carried forth on hobnail caligae,
And beneath the billowing sail.

With scarlet standard, galea bronze,
And blade of Spanish steel,
I succored Her ambition,
And brought Her foes to heel.

I built Her roads from sea to sea,
Brought Her trade, Her Tongue, Her
  tax;
I a slave for dirt and battle,
Purple dreams upon my back.

I killed to eat across the Earth,
Blood for barley, meat, and wine,
Blue Men in Alba's heather,
And Cherusci on the Rhine.

'Twas there I made my final halt,
At the fringe of Empire's end,
Where mist engulfs the forest,
And the air the war-horns rend.

My helm now crowns a tawny head,
My sword sleeps in a lake,
My bowels hang from an oaken
  branch,
My skull from lodge-hut stake.

Mayhaps some distant future,
When my deeds and bones have gone,
Will glorify my spirit,
At some distant Empire's dawn.

They'll stand upon my unmarked
  tomb;
"He marched with Rome," they said,
But all the laurels in the world,
Won't crown you when you're dead.

The Curse of Rome

Emily Jean Crocco

The Curse of Rome has come upon us; I see it burn again,
Kindled by corrupt women and weak and evil men.
My Nation once was glorious! It brought a smile to every lip;
Turmoil has since conquered that noble kinsmanship.

When falls the Colossus, the works of old ability,
You know what is to follow is temporal instability;
For what nation can smile who tears its own dignity down,
By wild, reckless children who wear dishonor for a crown.
Descendants of great people have grown indolent through the years,
And there children are left with relics, ruins, and bitter, blinding
    tears.

Look upon what remains of greater, glorious days,
When a belief in God did guide our humble, erring ways.
Look upon our statues! Mark the genius of the hand that did this
    beauty forge,
Crumbled now by envious hands with evil hungers to gorge.

When action is not used to build great works of art,
There begins a hideous despair that makes its way into the very
    heart.
When virtue is no longer taught as the eternal, attractive design,
Then will you witness the fall of man and the corruption of his
    mind.

See now our shame; will no one come to mourn?
Once beauty and virtue were our aim, humanity we did adorn.
Witness this terrible curse: see how Rome can burn again;
Draw near this sad shrine made by the etchings of a pen.
Let this poem be a warning, a lesson and a hope
For it is often here in poetry the soul finds understanding and scope.

You have heard of our shame, and while there are
    many we do blame,
Little use is there in bickering when a ruin is in
    flame.
No. This be a time for heart, so take heart; we shall
    build our World again.
Pick up that proverbial fiddle:
Let our World be filled with music again!
Do not despair, and do not lose courage at sight of
    this formidable task at hand.
Such times you were meant for; this place of ruin
    you shall command.

Now arise Byzantium!
Byzantium, arise anew!
The Golden Age is before us;
We now must look to you.

The Arena

A. J. Dachauer

Our marble deities lay dismembered and maimed,
Just as our people, dishonored and blamed.
Barbarians envied our city's white stone;
Dazzled by glory, they wanted it gone.
Upon gleaming columns we once conquered the sky.
Like Babel we fell, because rabble can't fly.
We welcomed the Goths to plunder and loot
To the jolly wail of a Dionysian flute.
Ungrateful feet crushed the blood out of us;
They left it to ferment and mingle with dust.
Sedated by pleasures and this cruelest of wine,
Our people lost sight of the solar divine.
False emperors thrived in this castrated age
And tribunes above mocked our righteous rage.
Comfort to plebeians was the highest ideal:
"Crucify him, with the heart full of zeal!"
That crowd cheered on, for circus, for bread,
While the condemned had to kill or fall dead.
"The bleating of sheep won't lead me astray;
"I will live as a lion, if just for one day!
"So let animals maul me, let steel pierce my chest—
"I refuse to bow down, low like the rest."
Gladiator or martyr, the arena craved blood:
I gave it my all, and died as I stood.

An Ode to the Ancient City

Edward Delacroix

Oh great marbled city of the ages,
Molded and forméd by Mars' sons' strong hands,
Your glory is sung in hist'ry's pages,
Imitated by all across Earth's lands.

Senates and republics harken to thine,
Caesar's name echoed by Kaiser and Tsar,
Fasces stand proud ev'n in Democr'cy's shrine,
"Publius" nam'd, founder of stripes and stars.

'Gainst you still, Semites shout, scream, curse, and wail,
While all Evropa's proud sons with pride teem,
Your victors and heroes still are hailed
And young men on your mem'ry build their dreams.

Though the eagle has flown and Empire gone,
The brilliant brightness of your flame shines on.

Empire Collapsed and Born Again

Sig Denreim

(A diptych)

They're at the gates, don't you hear?
It is just a matter of time,
We are surrounded from all sides,
The battle is unavoidable, yes.
Their language, customs, and looks,
It might look familiar, but no,
They're not like us, no matter what,
Temple isn't made by every rock.
Resemblance exists, without a doubt,
They've studied us well enough,
To know our ways and manners,
We even offered our help.
It is going to be bloody, horrific, rough,
When gods are at war, men always die,
Only Fortuna knows who remains,
To witness the end or a beginning.
Whatever there is to lead this life,
Forces that are many and unknown,
Hold the ground firmly enough,
Victory smiles at the bold.

There's no time to wait, let's charge,
Their fear is almost in the air,
So weak and desperate they are,
This is the final hour, the last drop.
Spreading so easily has consequences,
Ideas and thoughts unroll, like it or not,
Some are good, some made us slaves,
And now comes the decent payback.
Beautiful cities they made, yes,
And temples and roads and all of art,
It went from their eyes onto the stone,
They never asked anyone else.
Decadence is the widest ideal ever,
No man easily resists,
And when enough is enough, finally,
The balance must be restored.
Winning is not easy, not at all,
Wounded beast is at its strongest,
It has to be killed in order to die,
Only then can something be born, again.

Secundus

June Egbert

My Home is so beautiful when the sun is low
Apollo, we call him
Invictus, we call him
And when he leaves, there is a shade
Diana, we call her
Caelus, we call her
When the sun is low

What did you, ancient peoples, think about?
So long before I was born?
Ancient Egyptian sand
Foregone Persian bronze
Withered Etruscan pillars
What people laughed and ate beside you?
What faces did they bear?
Did they, too, know the sun?
And the shade of the moon?

My home is so beautiful in the morning
When Apollo comes young
And the wet dew lies soft on the grass
I'm with my blonde beloved
Did you love as we do?
O ancient peoples?

I know it won't be forever
My marvelous home, this shining city
Though we reach and grab outward so far as we can
I know it won't last forever
The Eternal City, sitting on the hill

Will you know the sun as we did
O people to come?
Will you call him Apollo?
Will you call her Diana?
When the sun is low?

I hope you love as we do
Or perhaps you will fight, as we do
On the sand
With your new bronze
Knocking down my city's pillars
Will your face look like mine?

I think I would love you
You, who inherit my city
The language and ways of my Empire
I know you will build upon us
Our magic will be your science
Our brilliance, your ordinary

So even through time
Let us look at the same sun
And lie under the same moon
Because I know my city is truly eternal
In your history
In your world
In your heart
O people to come

The Citadel

Kaiter Enless

Aeneas, from dire Trojan blaze,
Midwifed by arrowtip and flame.
Sallied the she-wolf's proteges,
With bronze and lion's mane.

Iron hewn, high path to plumb,
When Alba's usurper is defied,
Drones the earth, a rubied drum,
That The Citadel will debride.

Higher swelled the garland rock,
By marbled wills of Principates,
And shadows of low Tarpeia stalk,
All thrumming, cloudborne states.

Thunder of the circus crowd,
Hero's engine as hoofs descend,
From soil unto blue Aether's shroud,
Where chariots of fire wend.

Neptune bare as arroyo Rhine,
Black wastes gleam as Persian pearl,
Stars, hills of new Palatine,
Whereat drifting forts unfurl.

Long as heard the spire's knell,
Riven by blood beyond recall,
The fair towers of The Citadel,
May tilt, but never fall.

The Forgotten Hearth

Dominick Carmine Giannattasio

Upon this darkened hearth,
Where the blood of our fathers once burned.
Lay the cold, forgotten embers. . . .
Their scornful spirits to return.

We shall surely feel their wrath,
As the centuries shall pass.
Abandoned to a lonely curse.
Stirring in their quenchless thirst.

Through the eons do their echoes cry,
Through pinewood forests and mountains high.
Over seas that roar in the frozen night;
They seek to end this wretched blight.

A memory of exalted flame,
In burning souls—ignites again.
The rightful sons with might and main,
To return with honor to their reign.

Before our noble hearth we stand,
Loyal to our blood and land.
With eager offerings in hand,
To heal our great ancestral strand.

With blood to sword we take our oaths,
And raise our banners across the coasts.
For all that we adore the most.
And for those long-forgotten ghosts. . . .

Our flame shall burn forevermore,
In songs sung and written lore.
Which tell of all who came before.
A memory once lost—restored.

These spirits now can rest assured,
That through our deeds and through our words,
No longer are we deceived and lured,
By those we have too long endured.

For now our patience has worn thin,
With love for only kith and kin.
And for the gods that lurk within,
As blood is far much more than skin.

Once more we stand before this hearth,
From whose flame we're given birth.
And give a virile Hail!—henceforth,
To the fathers of the North.

The Heart Of Ragnarok

Dominick Carmine Giannattasio

As the ashes fall upon what remains,
The scorched earth begins a new rebirth.
A long-awaited change. . . .

Sudden silence fills the air.
A thoughtful peace arises in my heart.
Through the cold, relentless wind.
A ray of light. The coming of the dawn.

Now the shadows burn. . . .

While the mountains quake. . . .

Everyone will learn. . . .

Of their great mistake. . . .

Calling out for all to hear.
For open eyes to finally see the truth.
And every light shall shine upon
Their precious lies, can't withstand the sun.

It has come.

Forward, with a hero's heart.
Strong of body, mind of endless scars.
Through wide open doors—we ride.

Until the end of time.

And so I give my life to achieve the holy prize.

Eternity divine.

Vaterland

Dominick Carmine Giannattasio

Hail to the fatherland!
From which my soul extends.
Though my eyes have never seen,
Your timeless majesty.

Where my ancestors lie. . . .
Where dreams take me to at night.
What I would not give to walk beneath your trees.

Glorious mountain sides.
Landscape of snow and ice.
Upon the raven's wings, I will fly.
Into your open skies. . . .

Manifesting light.

The solar rays of might.

Hail to the fatherland!
From which my soul extends.
Though my eyes have never seen,
Your timeless majesty.

Ravens—take me home.

Shadows Marble Casts

Harrison George Gray

Carved from stone, surviving past its mortal inspiration,
To leave a mark enduring, for all to see and witness ever on.
Faces of greatest conquerors, and creators of foundation,
Leaving such enduring legacy, upon which so many fawn.

In a gallery replete with marble visages, looming over us all.
With refined and graceful form, casting down long shadows,
Blanketing all who dare to enter their sight in oppressive pall,
To send even the most accomplished into humbling throes.

Yet, were those same past greats not in a likewise position,
Held in awe of statues of past giants, glowering upon them.
Were they not, too, measuring themselves and their mission
'Gainst victories so grand, to obscurity they are condemned.

The shadows marble casts are timeless in their impact,
And it is also timeless to compare one's works to past acts.

VII

M. S. Jones

I. PALATINVS

On moon's first baptized day, A R arrive internal *urbis*,
Where suckled, mewling babes once fed in *Lupercalian* darkness.
Grown strong the twins, the sons of Mars, both claim their right *per fortis*.
(First sacrament of Empire ends Etruscan monarchs' might).
Romulus' augury is twelve birds afar in flight.
Grammar scribed on palace walls, regards infra spectacular,
Colossal roads where courage gleams 'midst wrathful, red massacre.

II. AVENTINVS

Remus had spied auspicious flights where Numa Pompi will abide;
He saw them first, but saw the least, his brother's claim defies
Envy of his brother's count, father's day fratricide;
Romulus, eponymous confirmed as *rex*, prophetic
Diana (ancient ARtemis) effuses dialectic,
Her whining pupil takes his notes in tempered, cool alcove,
While plebeians, protest patricians' place 'neath fragrant orange groves.

III. CÆLIVS

Here *domus de* Commodus, Tullus warlike like Romulus
"First to Encrust the Walls of Rome with Marble," had his *domus*.
Mercurial, faithful Laterans mass in their rhetorical *caelus*.
Golden parks where lovers kiss, Cestius' Pyramid *gita*.
Spy *Claudium*, proud *nymphaeum* drinks Claudia's *aqua vita*.
Imperator Caesar Lucius Septimius Severus
Pertinax Augustus' wall now circumscribes *septemius*.

IV. CAPITOLINVS

Ancus' prudent soldiers under oaths sent Latins *via*.
Momentous Jupiter once out-wondered Zeus at Olympia.
Capitol anointed (*sic*) the *nouvos* heart of Roma
Ancient verdure buried 'neath arithmetic piazza,
Greedily consumed beneath renaissance architecture.
Legacies they linger still, whispers the marbled ground,
Amidst the hills, where echoes of the kingdom still resound.

V. ESQVILINVS

Hail a car, passes A R from Hadrian's Mausoleum,
To highest peak where Venus greets Adonis in museum;
Pious Pilgrims pay penance at Saint Maria *ad Niveum*.
Domus Aurea, the Golden House of Nero's grandest *opus*
Doré, me, fAR, so Latino walls adorned with golden frescoes.
Lucius Tarquinius resurrects Etruscan kings.
'Rea feels the fleeting blues, while lustful Alex sings.

VI. QVIRINALIS

From Sabine tribes upon this hill, abducted brides are stole;
Rome enforces matrimony, while Sabine men bemoan.
Royal purple clad, King Servius adds realms from *Veii's* homes.
Second founder, sixth old age king, was murdered by his daughter.
Look down upon the geometry of Pantheon, and waters
Of slothful Trevi babble on, guarding hanging lovers,
Toss wishful coins from Saturn's mint, thrown charity for others.

VII. VIMINALIS

Terminus, far o' the hills return Alex and 'Rea.
Their Roman gluttony fulfilled with history, art, and pizza.
On holy orders to return, with hope *astronomica*.
Last day of sun, all things must end. Superbus' majesty
Brought low by his own avarice, exiled by enemies.
A second birth in violet sends his kingship to oblivion;
Sans *rex*, sans wreathe, *Republica*, until *post* Carthaginians.

CLAVIS: VATICANO

Seven hills now scaled, Saint Peter's offers you a key.
A rainbow arcs above you now for those with eyes to see.
Upon the flag, the final keys unlocking destiny;
Of sacraments and virtues, sins, await to be revealed,
Weak days of man in ages play themselves upon the scene,
Seven kings with seven names, the liberal arts uncovered,
And ancient wonders wait once more, more sevens to discover.

Untroubled Troubadour Sertorians

Kern "Kavalry" Keats

Flint'd lock'd pistol pops under the Pisan sun
Atop the knoll under the call of Lord Byron's fint'd lock'd gun
Our English exiled trio, Sir Byron, Sir Shelley, and Sir Trelwany
Turns, each taking aim, at a silver piece, betwixt a stick, all in good company
They rode their horses, through the Latin groves, like the ole Equites
An atavism, of eternal Ovid's ole knight kin, over Ceres' gilded golden plains
Upon the Romulan horizons,
      glistened the glance of Shelly's Minervan *far seeing* eyes
Upon his heated and now soot-stained piece of Mars,
      Lord Byron's hand hoped with urge a future of *piracy* and prize
Upon this Saturnalian scene,
      Trelawny pondered over his long Navy service on the *cresting* steppes,
          where Neptune always *always* resides. . . .

Sea brothed and beated, the bones of Shelley found
Atop the beach at the furthest waves' reach, the skin ragged and browned
In a tempest, on a fog'd sea, in Neptune's Ulyssean animosity, Shelly hurled off
    his Ariel
After the tenth day, Sir Tre made hasted way, and found the friend's corpse, in
    need of burial
Head's skull worn river stone smooth, hands eaten away, who's man is this?
Accompanied with Shelly's Aeschylus and with Shelly's Keats. . . . Shelly's
    now on his Eleusis
Subsequent his poor sailor's fate,
      in accord to Shelly's will, his now wine and salt speckled flesh,
        prepped for beach conflagration,
          not unlike his Hellene heroes, as his friends gaze on, at his
            life's celebration pyre
Subsequent the denial of his Shelly's skull, for drink,
      in spirit of Patroclus's funerary games, amongst the sounds of the
        brain's boils,
          Lord Byron swam, in the warm Tyrrhenian Sea, 'til the limbs
            gone tire

Subsequent sealing his friend's remains for rest in Rome,
            in carrying out his Shelly's final aims, Sir Tre disassembled the
                blacked Vulcanic pyre,
                    no longer red hot, by the baked dry fame, by the drift logs' fire

Armed and loaded, The Man Who Would be King, on his own privateer
Back into the land of Hesiods' Gods, striking his Juno's Herculean fears
Stirring against the Olympian envy, where Fate's turn led to Muses' tears
Under Ottoman Yoke, the Hellene hopes, gone grounded in internal gears
Our man, Lord Byron, having led a Plutarch's Life
Came time, when still young, his struggles' end against the corporeal strife
Alabaster skin, of purest marble, despite his end-of-life
            posthumously regalled of the perennial Poet's crown
                    through eris, his lyric perennial still sung amongst men
                    renowned
Alabaster pale, Sir Tre saw his friend,
            subsequent arrival from by the side of Greek Oddyseus,
                    upon such poor misgivings, made to give the Turks back
                    some beatings,
                            to continue the three thousand years war, since
                            Aeschylus' war
                                only now, for us, to go on just a little bit
                                more…

Esprit de corps, esprit de guerre, esprit de poète. . . .

Time Corrodes

Scott R. McNeil

On my wall hangs a picture of an oak tree
That I remember planting with duty and care.
Now, that painted spot—from the window, emptiness I see,
Colored wildflowers and grassland bare.

Young shoots and leaves once bent to these fingers—
Soft green and impressionable as a newborn child—
A warm, bright feeling of tenderness still lingers,
Mingled with agony—acute then, now mild.

There was a hole I dug in black earth
And lowered the sapling gracefully in;
Candelabrum branches in a show of mirth
Seemed to nod and shake like a glad mannequin.

I recall summer heat, the cloudless day,
The fountain of the tree as it reared up its crown,
The parsimony smile of the gaunt thing in play,
Stark sunlight around it—a shimmering gown.

Water came as hot rain from yellowed squalls,
And sun from the burning, sand-glimmering sky;
The strangeness of weather-fog over the knolls
Where the scraggling pines and hedges did lie.

There was nothing special in it, no green thumb of mine
Employed to strike hardy survival
(I admit, though, I cared for it many a time,
And perhaps thus I taught it revival).

Nevertheless, one day I sat on the oak's leeward side,
Opposite the sun, when I realized I was wholly in a shadow
With the long branching blackness on the grass, me bestride,
The earth under me no longer rich or fallow.

Looking up, there—perched above me—was this:
A network of interlacing ancient steeples
Whose leaves the wind made rattle and hiss,
The nest of an elk with the voice of a people;

And the ebony branches outlined by the light
Were outreaching, twisted, gnarled, green-ravaging—
I could not discern the extent of its height,
But the oak had surpassed my imagining.

Resilient as, I think, brick must be,
I remember its branches both sequoia and white,
Drought-burned and brittle, slicked and icy,
A testament to silent might.

This oak was a fortress cresting from barren soil;
It was a solid presence here on the plain.
Regardless of circumstance, it would toil,
Clutching survival and drinking the rain.

Looking out the window now,
I gaze on the plot where fond memories wade,
Recalling the grandeur that used to be there, and how
Many a time I'd lie in oaken shade:

Moments of half-sleep, delicious bright dreams
Of dozing and waking in the crisp mottled noon,
Lying in the fork of two roots; and it seems
That I wasted much time in that singular swoon.

For the days blend helplessly together in me,
Painting a landscape in black and gold—
An ethereal hillside in my memory
Stands out in its vivid and shapeless mold;

And the curve of it like an incomplete sweep
Of an earth that is soft to my human spine—
The declivity fading indigo, never too deep
To relax my body in this respite entwine.

While the oak absorbed what it did require,
In body, from the soil and air,
It grew with an unnatural passion, a fire
That I deemed tremendously rare.

I wonder if, with the water it drank,
It somehow extracted my drive and my passion,
And stretched like a blossom escaping a rank
And odious weedbed in heroic fashion.

It devoured my love, it drank of my pride,
It soaked up the wishes I made in my head—
Copied, as it may have been, the images inside,
Embodying the fervor that it had been fed.

So it was perfect. I remember the way
That its shadow quivered in the vivid heat,
Sliding here and there to outline the day
And ending with its fingers brushing at night's feet.

I often heard daybreak singing from the boughs—
Songbirds from the distant woodlands come
To chatter and nest in the oak's lofty brows,
Their delicate flight a perpetual drum.

There was a meal, once, with my back to the oak—
Tender succulence in my mouth that I still can taste,
A fragrance of herbs in which the meal was soaked
And not a morsel to waste.

What a fool I was! I recall once saying
That this grand tree must live forever;
Convinced as I was that, by my praying,
The oak might achieve this endeavor.

I thought it could only multiply its grandeur;
I thought it could never be sick;
But the temptation was too great, it all was a lure
Whose poisoned loaf I did lick.

The oak responded, it rose to my grin,
And its forested canopy brushed at the sky—
Inevitably, though, it stretched out too thin;
The unhappy thing ran itself dry.

When the first limb came down, I was slightly surprised
To see bark decayed and blackened.
Looking up thus, I saw pending demise—
Huge trunks unreasonably slackened.

Insects had eaten them through, and the strain
Of constantly growing to sate my greed
Had spread through the wood an ebony stain—
And the rest went on with such speed. . . .

Dismally, I watched—hopeless and forlorn
As, over months, the tree shriveled and broke.
The spark of gay life it had eagerly borne
Had also been its greatest joke.

Next spring the stunted and scarred thing I saw
Out my window no longer bore leaves.
The sun and the plague had stripped the tree raw
And the bark—scattered like paper sheaves.

So standing before it, I could not believe
That the almighty oak that had once risen here
Was entirely gone, no life to retrieve
From the tree that had sheltered me year after year.

Never had I thought it could be overthrown
Or outplayed by some whim of Fate;
I failed to notice it had three times outgrown
An oak in its most natural state.

Harsh and bitter tears stung at my soul,
As though some monument had just crumbled.
Where the great oak had been, there now was a hole
Into which my emotions all tumbled.

I remember a wise friend who came to visit me
And inquired at the empty field.
I told him the truth of what he did see—
The oak had been forced to yield.

The year had grown cold, an early snow falling
While my friend and I broke our bread.
It was logic and peace for which he was calling;
Rather restlessly, I said:

"That oak was sturdier than any stone wall,
"Immovable as a mountain,
"Brilliant as a skyscraper, and as tall,
"And as luscious as a fountain.

"It could not fall, it could not end—
"I knew this for a fact!
"And now, sanity I must pretend.
"God, what did it lack?

"What was the evil stimulus
"That did my oak attack?
"What foul, dreaded impetus
"Knocked it upon its back?

"And now I must my lifestyle change,
"For days and days I spent out there
"Reclining in the shaded range
"That cooled the sun's hot glare."

My friend spent a moment in thought. I knew
That he would say something pensive
To calm my temper, to allay, to soothe
The despair I felt intensive.

"Well," he said at length, "I understand
"What sour emotions you must be feeling,
"But do not deny logic's gray demand,
"And keep yourself from reeling.

"Surely, man, you are aware
"That nothing can last forever?
"That all the world's love and the most diligent care
"Could not always have kept you together?

"Great things share the same fate as small—
"They age as the world ages.
"This oak was a book which had you in a thrall,
"But it shortened as you turned the pages.

"And for the oak shadow, branching and vast,
"In whose coolness you did the daylight shun,
"See if memory cannot be surpassed—
"Try basking in the sun!"

He spoke of lifespan unprotected,
Of impermanence and truth!
I told him I'd rejected
All that nonsense since my youth!

What valor is there in any loss,
What happiness in traditions altered?
Why should I feel aught but frost
When a grandiose thing has faltered?

Speak not to me of change or how
Even the Earth will one day shatter;
I'll cry alone, so leave me now,
To you it is no matter.

We Are All Romans Now

Ndabaningi

They sit in serried ranks,
in huddled groups,
in languid repose
We are all Romans now
They clack their prayer beads,
finger ancient amulets,
sharpen blade and spear
We are all Romans now
The horses mill about,
stand in rows,
eclectically caparisoned
We are all Romans now
Tribal chieftain, bands of kin,
haughty patrician,
long retired
We are all Romans now
Churchman, soothsayer,
literatus, bard,
healer
We are all Romans now
Armorican, Frank,
Gael, Burgundian,
mercenary, bondsman
We are all Romans now

Goth, Gaul,
Latin, Greek,
barbaritas, *civitas*, in-between
We are all Romans now
Bowman, lancer,
legionnaire, axeman,
furor teutonicus
We are all Romans now
From villa and forest,
marshland,
vineyards, meadows
We are all Romans now
Hearth and home,
church, cloister,
sacred grove
We are all Romans now
Let them come,
eastern horde, vassal men,
it ends here

OMNES ROMANI NUNC SUMUS

Anamnesis

John Oghma

I

Just ten more fucking minutes left.
God, I hate this place. I hate its walls of beige.
I hate my co-workers smiling like sour monkeys,
The stream of bullshit meetings without end.

Returning home. A starless night. The blur—
Red lights, podcasts, the smoke inside my lungs.
An owl's eyes flash. My bones whisper a prayer:
"Taste glory once before you turn to ash."

II

Ten thousand miles. The clang of weights. The pain.
I sleep in caves and roam amidst the oaks.
I sing and drink beneath great Heracles.
The spleen and shanks of deer my sustenance.

Along the banks of Fane, I wash away
Centuries of timidity and shame.
An eagle circles round the tor and dives.
I kiss the earth and hold *Cloch an Fhir Mhóir*.

III

The stench of burning cars. The sting of mace.
The haze. The march of the police. A hail of bricks.
We charge the line. Their bones snap 'neath our pipes.
Their bloated bodies fester in the streets.

Before, behind, around, the noose draws tight.
By shells, our boys are strewn across the trees.
Our mines split tanks. Our rifles crack the air.
We final few dig in and staunch our grief with rage.

Are we to die like grandmas in their beds?
To clutch at prayers until we're naught but ash?
No. Not I. Not we. Not now.
We'll charge into the fields of fame.
We'll greet our death with steel and flame
And blaze as gods beneath the sun.

IV

The bastards string my body from a yew,
But our soon triumph stays their sacrilege.
The paeans of our deeds I'll never hear
Nor see myself immortalized in bronze.

Two hundred years from now, a man will come.
His bones will tell him what he can't forget.
He'll hold and kiss these rusted hands and eyes
And know that what's within him never dies.

Metamorphosis

Filip Ostler

A statue of Ovid used to stand here.
It did stand here, but
The seagulls and pigeons used to shit on it.

The remnants of Rome's greatest poet,
Secluded, ostracized,
At the outskirts of the Empire, to witness
The barbarians
In their strange
Uncultured
Anti-Roman ways.

Yet still, the place where Ovid's statue gets
So viscerally defaced, it bears
A strange, yet so familiar name:
Romania.

The remnants of Rome
Secluded, ostracized
At the outskirts of Civilization, lay witness
To the hordes
In their barbarous
Malevolent
Post-Roman ways.

Oh, Muse! if even for one verse you could
Retell to me the fate of Rome.
Its rising, growth and timely fall
And its Rebirth, I would

Forever praise its Holy name
Where Ovid's statue stood.

The Barbarians of Our Time

João Paulo

The aqueduct sends its water to refresh Rome.
The Colosseum stands like a giant in the heart of the city.
Trajan returned in Triumph through the Avenue, bringing his spoils.
My wife wonders why I am thinking about Rome.

From the snow of Britain to the scorching heat of Syria, the legions
  march unopposed.
In silence, they prepare for battle, and with a deafening scream they
  charge the enemy.
What a frightening sight.
My wife wonders why I am thinking about Rome.

From the grassy fields of Hispania to the mountains of Dacia, the
  legions march unopposed.
Every morning, the legions set off camp, dismantling the tents and
  the walls
They carry everything they can, and what they cannot carry with
  them they set on fire.
Discipline and order are strictly enforced.
My wife wonders why I am thinking about Rome.

Envy and intrigue roam the Senate.
For a few votes and for a few coins they will stab your back.
Who can tame this den of Wolves and give Rome stability?
My wife wonders why I am thinking about Rome.

The Rubicon looks calm and idyllic.
A small, quiet, unremarkable river
Will carry the name of a decision that changed mankind.
My wife wonders why I am thinking about Rome.

The fire started soon after the feast of Nero with prostitutes.
The people believed the fire to be man-made.
As the Lord Himself they paid for the sins of others with their lives.
My wife wonders why I am thinking about Rome.

For centuries, we were persecuted, arrested, thrown to the lions and
    to the beasts.
A dream of a Cross in sky, a touch in the heart of the future
    emperor.
By the shields of Constantine we shall achieve victory.
My wife wonders why I am thinking about Rome.

The Romans sacrificed to their idols, but they never murdered
    children on the scale that we do.
They had their homosexuals and perverts, but they never gave
    hormones to children like we do.
If even Rome fell, what will be the punishment for us?

The Romans worshiped pagan gods, but they did not abandon God
    to follow their own evil desires and addictions like we did.
Nero forged currency by putting lead inside coins, and we forge our
    happiness by pretending to like our cubicles, our violent cities and
    our televisions.
If even Rome fell, what will be the punishment for us?

The Romans brutalized their enemies on a scale unimaginable to us,
But they had a mission to spread their culture, their laws, and their
    language.
What culture have we changed from their wicked ways? What
    barbarians learned anything from our wars?
The barbarians in our own country don't speak our language, let
    alone those living abroad.
If even Rome fell, what will be the punishment for us?

On the top of a hill stood a fortress, Alesia, as known by the Gauls.
The barbarians sought refuge in it to wait for reinforcements.
With two walls around their wall, Julius Cesar transformed their
    fortress into a prison.
My wife wonders why I am thinking about Rome.

The walls of Jerusalem had many layers to be crushed, and the
    defenders had confidence in them.
Titus started a competition between his men to see who would build
    the siege works faster.
Wall by wall, layer by layer, tower by tower, the defenders were
    crushed, and Rome prevailed.
My wife wonders why I am thinking about Rome.

A poet who hated his works asked his friend, Octavius Augustus, to
    destroy them before his death.
The emperor preserved his works, and Virgil remained one of the
    best poets in history.
Through his works the name Luciana and the beauty of Roman art
    remained.
My wife wonders why I am thinking about Rome.

Attila, known as the scourge of God, brought death and chaos to the
    empire.
His hordes seem infinite, his horsemen are fearless, the horses
    trample the earth like an earthquake.
The Visigoths, Burgundians, and Franks, future heirs of Roman
    culture, taught him humility.
My wife wonders why I am thinking about Rome?

If Scipio Africanus defeated an army of elephants in the Tunisian
    desert,
And if Titus Flavius managed to pierce the walls of Jerusalem and
    destroy the temple,
How would we not overcome the barbarians of our time?

If by land and by sea, the Romans threw themselves over Carthage,
And if Julius Cesar built a bridge over the Rhine in ten days,
How would we not overcome the barbarians of our time?

If the Romans with the Visigoths defeated even the ferocious Huns
    and their horses,
And if even after the fall of Rome their language, culture, and
    religion remain,
How would we not overcome the barbarians of our time?

O Roma!

Anthony Ramsey

I have seen thee, O Roma!
   There was a storm upon her height,
   The scream of the storm in the night,
   And a hallowed silence fell
   On the winds and the foaming hell
   Of the seas when I saw thee arise
   With the lure of the Gods in thine eyes;
   Not dark, as the hearts we bear,
   But enstarred, everlastingly fair,
   On the darkness, O Roma!

Thou art lovely, O Roma!
   Alone by the rocks;
   And the burning gold of thy locks—
   Down-streaming, a magical tide,
   Over shoulder and radiant side,
   In waves in whose shadows are lost
   Dead lovers, the sacrificed host,
   And in gleamings of curling crests—
   Now lift as of old our breasts
   With thy rapture, O Roma!

And we love thee, O Roma!
   Though the Spoiler is in thy hall
   And thou art bereft of all
   Save only the Spirit for friend
   That shapes all things in the end,
   Though thine eyes are a sword that has slain
   Thy lovers on many a plain
   When glad to the conflict they pressed,
   Drunk with the light of thy breast,
   To die for thee, O Roma!

Thou art mighty, O Roma!
  More rich in thyself alone
  Than the Harlot upon a throne
  Whose lure is on every flood
  And whose robes are the price of blood.
  She will pass with the shades that have passed,
  Thou wilt last with the Powers that last:
  Thou hast eaten of Bread Divine,
  Thou hast drunken Eternal Wine:
  Thou art mighty, O Roma!

In rejoicing, O Roma!
  Thou hearest the gathering sound
  Of a River that rolls underground,
  That will rise till the daylight be won,
  Till it bursts, till it foams in the sun!
  Thou hearest as from afar
  The golden thunders of war,
  The cries of thy conquering legions,
  The ringing, the singing of your regions

That shall crown thee, O Roma!

Antony in Egypt

Noble Red

(After Plutarch and Shakespeare)

. . . And the legions watered and ready to march,
Waiting on the general, waiting on Antony;
I told him, "Sir, we'll never get another one like this,
"The whole of the East wide open, half the world
"Ours for the taking, a chance not seen since Alexander";
And can you imagine what he told me?
"The East will still be there tomorrow, Enobarbus."
"Aye," says I, "but the legions won't wait forever;
"Men need an objective or they turn to mischief,
"And if you'll forgive me speaking plainly, Sir,
"If it's women that you want, there are Parthian virgins,
"Persian strumpets, Syrian sirens, all waiting for you,
"Beyond the river mud and sands of Alexandria.
"Gold and treasure, too. And crowns and thrones to boot.
"The world is an oyster, begging to be opened with your sword,
"But Fortune's tide attends on neither gods nor men."
Not a pretty speech, no doubt; I am but a soldier, after all,
But my blunt words painted true the reality of things,
And I was sure Mark Antony heard and saw, but then,
"You think," the general said, "that any woman in the world,
"Or any crowns, or thrones, or gold, or even Alexander's mantle,
"Can match the peerless charms of Cleopatra?"
And that's when I knew, for sure, right then, that we were all dead men.

War Poem

Arminius Rex

Not far from my humble abode I stand, as my forefathers stood afore me, with my beloved wife and our unborn child behind me, and ahead, a relentless adversary steeped in suffering and woe. Generations past have toiled this soil, sweat mingling with the earth, forging from barren steppe a bastion of civilization. Yet the covetous gaze of the West persists, seeking to enslave us time and again. But as our noble ancestors displayed, our spirit for freedom eclipses any fetters.

Oh, my cherished love, how I yearn for your tender caress, yet it must wait, for I cannot bear to see you endure the fate of countless others. I dwell in fearful anguish, lest you befall the tragic end of Donetsk's sorrowful father, or our child suffer the plight of Belgorod's innocent youth, robbed of their essence. Thus, I am compelled to fight, relentlessly, so I never have to gaze upon your lifeless form, as I have mournfully beheld countless others.

O Kiev, sacred city, maternal beacon to us all! Why have you forsaken your progeny? Why consign us to such woeful destiny? O Kiev, revered mother of our souls, why do you consort with those who wish us naught but harm? Where is the splendor of your storied past, the presence of Saint Vladimir, Saint Olga? Why abandon your kin, your offspring? In pursuit of the West, you barter away your finest, leaving nought but barrenness in your wake.

Here, amidst the forest's embrace, I dwell with newfound comrades, bearing cold steel when revelry beckons others. Forced to confront my own kin as if they were strangers, I stand firm, defending the same lands my grandfather once defended. Yet, here we are, reliving the past's echoes, repelling the envious foe until subdued once more. Then, perhaps, true liberation shall dawn.

Ode to Flora, Goddess of Spring

Ethan Robert

Upon an unassuming day of season's sudden turn,
Finding earthly denizens that for a springtide yearn,
Afflicted by their mortal state with branches hanging bare
Of all their lustred petals and of all their fruitful fare.
A warmth impregnates mildly so this frigid winter reign,
The Goddess she descends to garland gracef'lly our domain,
To spur the woeful crop and then to charm the humble hills,
That gently sway in her caress to grant such wont fulfilled.
Let her kiss from supple lips draw life from great repose,
Let song from cypress starlings cast new joy through olive groves,
And find first blossoms sighing forth to greet the tender vines
That venture swiftly over garden walls in swelling climbs.
And from her youthful cheeks her zephyr is not found to cease,
Not but love borne in its stride, of life she gives fresh lease.
A sentiment to wrest from ailing stems the bitter frost,
And rouse all mortal beasts with blissful scents that were deemed
    lost.

Know the wonder childlike risen quietly in our hearts,
To sense once more the tinctures of Elysium impart
The merest notes of heaven to our simple, pious lives,
As we gaze the wonders of these months at once arise.
At noon's fair crest we hear the children bounding twixt the herbs,
Chasing bees that languish florets gold with humming words,
Yet it is here they come to lay their limpid eyes upon
The Goddess who meanders with her hair adorned by sun,
With open palms that raise the solemn verdure at her gait,
And stir the fledgling birds that are forthwith relieved of weight,
Mimicked by the jealous fawns who leap athwart the banks
Of streams that run as lengths of silk through vales that sing their
    thanks.
The children, fired by such innocence of intrigue ripe,
Gaily bound in arm in arm pursuance of her flight,

And call to that pure Goddess as she dances on bare feet,
Through pastures that so twirl alike when with her aura meet,
Alas they cannot catch her for her glide is much too swift,
But rich the perfume in her wake, they settle for its gift.
The mothers, all with glee, observe their children caught in play,
Tenderly with baskets woven, pick at branches stray,
As fathers turn the yawning earth and thus begin to sow
The bread and wine of future feasts that now shall surely grow.
Flora: mother to all souls that so by her awake,
Shall egress from higher realms and in our lives partake,
Light and song bequeathed to blessed Rome from peak to shore,
Praise her sound return each year, her beauty we adore.

Ode to Virgil

Ethan Robert

When you sang of Aeneas crossing on the highest seas,
There thus was wrought a dream called Rome that came to stir this
    woeful earth,
And from it forge the paragons of men and see an empire's birth,
Yet not without the toil of a thousand battled victories.

So too you sang pastoral hymns in homage to the purest life,
That of farmhand's duty and a season's fleeting joys that urge
Not but love for one's own soil whereupon fair hearts converge,
In humblest of pursuits to seek fair sanctuary from daily strife.

Men today must gaze upon your deeds and duly from them draw
A strength of rarest virtue that so scorns the callousness of fools,
And tethers one to gloried fates that lead good righteous men to rule,
For through your lines we come to know what destiny in Rome
    foresaw.

Would you guide me in my hours when I sit so void of words?
Alike when you appeared to noble Dante in his fervid quest?
And offered ripe your charity at no doubt graceful god's behest,
To steer the weary poet from the wretched and hell bound human herds.

Assuredly it was dear Apollo who did come to rightly grant
That verdant garland to your youthful brow with but a tender reach,
Thus epochs Augustinian found your honored hand beseeched,
So bestowed upon you was the legacy that so enchants.

Centurions recalled your verse, decamped beneath the Pleiades,
On embers meditating, there a fire antecedent climbed,
Drawing forms of eagles that with honored souls at once did bind,
Progenitors of Europe's might—Prometheans! Let flames proceed!

Sonnet to Augustus

Ethan Robert

Guided was the dawn to might anew,
Risen by great gesture of the hand,
Of poise in straight arm thrust, to fingers spanned,
His providence at once beheld in view.
Let mankind come to know his actions true,
Witness his great empire expand
To harmonize discordant foreign lands,
And thus one finds the faith of Rome renewed!

Appearing there before Europa's sky,
Was ushered in a beast of ardent cry,
A feathered breast caught gilded by the rays,
Ascension that near blinds horizon's gaze,
Aquila! He is birthed once more in flame,
Augustus! Sing his glory, speak his name!

Horizons on the Edge

Saxon Stargazer

What causes Man to be in search of yonder Plains?
To cap Mountains tall and search peerless Deeps—
Cross Badlands swaths and brave Tropic rains
Pave Tundra paths and muster on the Beach

"O! Something calls me onward, I dare not do less!"
God made Man to labor, fill full all of Earth
Plant Promethean fire in every empty breast
Sow Gardens East of Eden; Mankind's rebirth

Fields proffered bronze—Tubal, Cain's delight
The nations they were filling so Men by ship took flight
Hellenes concentrated upon the former coast
Lands not remembered led Alexander's eternal boast

Rome's spear laid Athens down (but took its soul to keep)
New blood came to worship at greater conquers' feet
Yet even all the mighty fear domains to tread
"*Non plus ultra*" the Pillars of Hercules said

Greater flowers fed from Empire's molted flesh
Letters, tongues, and arts peoples soon threshed
Fractured minds uncommon into new directions press
Isthmus of Gibraltar the Spaniards crossed due West

Albion drove still further in peopling the globe
Creating stations all around and paying back the loan
King Arthur's former sword now in a new land sheathed
Equipped Colombia abroad to foreign places reap

As long redwoods tower their siren cry will call
Pilgrims far to marvel at frontier culmination's squall
Only lastly did the winter poles softly glitter
Adam's seed vainly hoping for a fruit not yet bitter

Their pallor faces bled tears hopelessly sordid
Until they craned their necks and a better view accorded
The Space above the Sun is horizonless expanse
Recondite path of Man—a liminal romance

A fork in the soul now decides the marked of Cain:
Perchance heads bow low and no greater care is fed
To endless limits breach than we are naught but dead
Fetters of clay will catch us—our labors run with rain.

But on the rocky lane there is room enough still
To house the hopeful watchers and nourish iron will
If we stick to venture our sure destiny we'll fulfill
To join in the Lord and build the City on the Hill

: *Horologium Hominum*

K. B. Steward

Dust
Raised from the Earth
Bound with blood and bone
A new clay molded to live freely
To serve as witnesses to His love

Sand
Endless dreams sift through man's fingers
Fortitude for the mightiest
Weaponry to those most tenacious
Acclaim unto he who captures His glory

Ash
From the fires of their iniquity
Evidence of once great ambitions
Remnants of life carried off by the wind
Such is destiny for all who kindled His anger

Residing all together in mortal confinement
Flowing along an empty strait to familiar ends
Once the final grain proudly rests atop the pile
He extends His hand to invert the vessel once more

The Crone

Shannon Strix

Lilies, violets, and petunias are what she adorns her crown,
My princess who I'd smite the world if a thorn had made her frown.
Eventually, she will bloom and flower for another,
And my perceived selflessness will be tested as a mother.
Though mother and daughter are bounded by blood to Mother Earth,
Mothers must kill her egoic self to allow a rebirth.
But after aging past maiden and mother titles of mine,
What was Ceres to do after letting go her Proserpine?

My tale starts with recalling her picking flowers in the grass,
But now she carries a bouquet in a church made of stained glass.
She walks the aisle to a man with big career plans to leave,
To go far away from our hometown and strand me to bereave.
I understood that they must move to where they both could find jobs,
But my daughter being ripped from my breast caused my jealous sobs.
Daughters still need their mothers to make their new home, I implored,
And despite my pleas she said texting is all she could afford.

I gave her a small, inherited home when she was a maid,
And gave her dozens of acres, and it's where she should have stayed.
My grief curdled when I thought of my snubbed generosity,
It was this rootless new son that drove my animosity.
I knew she would find a mate, for her face would lure any man,
But in my matriarchal world, he must live close to my clan.
And with my wrath at his disrespect for tradition and taboo,
I would use my job position to ensure boys get their fair due.

I went to my grade school class with plans for boys that were uncouth,
For I chose a meager teacher job since my daughter was youth.
Now, when a boy acted out or was too rambunctious to learn,
I'd banish him from the group until he begged me to return.
Ungrateful boys, for which I have taught you basic skills,
No more shall you long to roam; I will calm your nature with pills.
Their mothers blindly trusted me and fed their boys Adderall;
The young boys became quieter, broken, and lost overall.

A new school year started, and my new class felt hopelessly gray;
I had the reputation as witch, which had spawned their dismay.
But one child stuck out to be a most challenging student;
He was exceptionally nasty and the most impudent.
I held a meeting with his guardian for his attitude;
His grandmother showed up, scantily clad, practically nude.
The mother was gone, and his grandmother acted like a tramp,
Clinging to long gone maidenhood, she ignored the poor scamp.

Laughing at her painted face, fake tan, fishnets, and miniskirt,
But her familiar eyes made me stop and feel disconcert.
Gray hairs and wrinkles between both of us made us the same age,
And both of us fixated on reviving a past life stage.
In a world where the maiden and mother are celebrated,
How to be a wise crone has been sadly annihilated.
Most of my life takes place after my looks and fertility.
Perhaps all of these years are to wield a new ability?

I could not go on punishing boys for their virility,
For their castration will lead to gender instability.
And I could not carry every girl, so she avoids any stone,
For perception comes from tripping so she becomes a wise crone.
The first usage of my new mindset was applied at my school,
To make class interesting and memorable rather than cruel.
Class became interactive rather than lectures out of spite,
And the once gray children became clever, disciplined, and bright.

My philosophy was truly tested when my daughter came home,
A short trip for the holiday; it was all their work would loan.
The first thing she said when just us two were at last together,
Was to weep that her life was like existing in the nether.
She blamed her beloved for bringing her to such a poor state;
She wanted home and to leave her husband she began to hate.
Wiping her tears, I held her close, soothing her state of distress,
But my next words cut us like a thorn, despite my soft caress.

"You do not hate him, you have told me so, and he still loves you,
"You made a commitment and a vow that you must carry through.
"Hold yourself accountable for choices that you made or make,
"Once you take ownership of your fate, your Will will never break.
"You've nearly met your initial goals that you set beforehand,
"But you must complete your quest to return to your promised land.
"I surprise myself by not taking you back in a heartbeat,
"But renouncing my wants will make us women that are complete."

Sighing at my answer, she wished I was more sympathetic,
Though she joked that her stubbornness is most likely genetic.
Agreeing with my view that their financial goals were almost met,
And in a few years, they will buy the house next door with no debt.
Winking at me, she hinted at children when they can move back,
And they will need a wise grandmother near to help with the slack.
For she had learned that just a wife could not run a home alone,
While the man had his role, childcare was aided by the crone.

After many years, my daughter and new son returned for good,
To live across the street so she could embark on her own motherhood.
And after retiring from my long teaching profession,
Hundreds of past students wrote letters, thanking my impression.
Now surrounded by dozens of faces that seek my advice,
I maintained all our traditions, all due to my sacrifice.
So to all the women that yearn to cling to what was before,
Embrace the changing phases and your past wisdom evermore.

Roman Echoes

Wehrwolf Tactics

From Trojan walls asunder, born on the gods' good will,
The noble sons set sail then, their fate but to fulfill.
"Hail!" cried Aeneas, on the prow boisterous and tall,
"One day Rome's eagle shall be mightier than all!"

Young Romulus and Remus then suckled wolfish might,
And gathered round them comrades who slew in every fight.
"Hail!" cried the founders, reveling in the brawl,
"For here Rome's eagle shall be mightier than all!"

To Carthage, Greece, and Britain the legions then went forth,
And no man could oppose them, o'er seas or in far north.
"Hail!" cried Africanus, and Caesar then from Gaul,
"Now see, Rome's eagle is the mightiest of all!"

The Empire, thus ascendant, grew fat and tired and glad,
Its citizens grew foreign and its emperors grew mad.
"Hail," slurred great Nero, as crimson flames rose tall,
"No fear, Rome's eagle is still mightier than all!"

Through borders, never greater, pored decadence, despair,
And disputes over laurel wreaths on fine perfumed hair.
"Hail," wrote Aurelius in his meditated scrawl,
"Why must Rome's eagle stay the mightiest of all?"

The Empire moaned in chaos of an endless civil war
Oriental cults and worshippers deigned ask, "Whatever for?"
"Hail!" ruled bold Constantine, triumphant over all,
"With Christ, Rome's eagle now shall never ever fall!"

Barbarians came on, endless, and stormed into the gates;
They killed and burnt in solemn streets, blasphemed the gods
    and fates.
"Hail!" mocked Attila, as survivors groaned in thrall,
"With Christ, Rome's eagle now shall never ever fall!"

From distant Eastern waters watched Byzantines the end
Of Western Roman dominance on which they, too, depend.
"Hail," from Constantinople, yet shielded from the fall,
"Why must Rome's eagle stay the mightiest of all?"

Indignant, tired scholars then wrested from the tombs
Of ancient Roman warrior kings the stories of their dooms.
"Hail!" cried the Renaissance from Italian marbled halls,
"No fear, Rome's eagle is still mightier than all!"

Through printing press and rapier the Roman stories spread,
And all the European stock honored their ancient dead.
"Hail!" said Holy Emperor, proclaimed by musket ball,
"Now see, Rome's eagle is the mightiest of all!"

Then every nation's capital was built of columns white;
They carved fasces and Latin script and eagles taking flight.
"Hail!" cried new senators from every nation's halls,
"For here Rome's eagle shall be mightier than all!"

Now every Western citizen can gaze and ponder long
On their own Roman heritage, proud and deep and strong.
"Hail!" cries an inner voice, powerful if small,
"One day Rome's eagle shall be mightier than all!"

Through Modernity's Inferno

Henri Teloz

I

At a headstrong age of ten plus eight,
Dario Fante walked his capital streets quite late,
In old Rome where statues looked down upon,
A twilight of a glory now far gone,
Where brick and stone and flesh was laid,
Where its debt to Greece was fully paid,
At the headstrong age of ten plus eight
Dario Fante would walk and wait and wait.

Headphones in ears and phone in hand,
He walked with gusto across that same land,
Where chariots raced and gladiators fought,
Where senators argued and philosophers taught,
And all basked together in the ancient Sun,
At the height of a vital glory second to none.

But Dario knew of some obscure location,
That could bring back the fathers of his declining nation,
And he knew of an ecstatic time,
In which life still mattered, which felt sublime,
Yet its voice was now little more than a whisper,
A low hum in the night, a small speck in a picture.

II

In an old alley where rubbish was strewn but fountains still flowed,
A rip in spacetime would loom, see how brightly it glowed,
A time where men lived, spoke, and breathed a lofty air,
A place when no true man could stand to be elsewhere,
And through this glowing portal, a figure would slowly emerge,
As the times of the past and the present magically converged,
In that alley where rubbish was strewn but fountains still flowed,
A man in eternal resplendence was suddenly shown.

This man blinked and stared with an impenetrable scowl;
Dario panicked and thought, "What must I do now?"
He'd brought him here from beyond, yet without a plan,
And knew not what to expect from this here ancient man.
The man did not budge and with one hand grabbed at his toga,
And with one swift movement threw it over his shoulder.
The man blinked and stared with an impenetrable scowl;
Dario wondered if his plans had gone afoul.

"Virgil!" he cried. "Is it really you here?"
The man smiled and took the boy near.
"'Tis I," he replied, "and who might you be?"
"I'm Dario Fante, born in this city."
"And this city, boy, does it have a name?"
"Why its Rome!" he exclaimed. "You must see its decay!
"But Virgil!" he cried. "Is it really you here?"
"I've told you it is I, now what is the year?"

"Two millennia have passed since you wrote your poems,
"And things now move fast, beyond everyone's knowing,
"But you all were the apex, you were the peak,
"Now everything's worse and we've become weak.
"Take a look at this city and see what we've become,
"And with your ancient wisdom, tell us what can be done!"

They walked out the alley without muttering a word,
The boy and the Roman, a sight so absurd,
But Dario was committed to proving his point,
And hoped this noble poet would not disappoint;
There were no wise men nor guiders in this entropic age,
No man to act as a philosopher, guru or sage;
Beyond time, they entered the street without muttering a word,
So Virgil could see what since his epoch had occurred.

And now the first and nearest location,
Was Termini, Rome's central train station,
Which connected all the country like veins to a heart,
Where mothers happily greet and lovers sadly depart,
And the chance for the noble poet to see with his own eyes,
The degradation, now custom, but once a surprise,
And now at this first and nearest location,
Virgil could see what had happened to his civilization.

"I have something to show you," Dario said,
As the two walked and Virgil nodded his head,
And Dario explained to the poet about cars and trains,
And computers and cell phones and bars and planes;
Before long they'd arrived at Roma Termini;
"What you'll see here will hurt you to see."

And at the entrance the pair walked steadily over;
The first terrible thing they noticed there was the odor,
A strong stench of piss, musky and humid,
A gang of loud Africans and a gypsy well-suited,
But that same gypsy concealed a knife in his pocket,
And with a slash from an old lady stole a locket;
The Africans shouted and an Arab did spit;
At them one threw a bottle which them almost did hit.

"See!" screamed our Dario, in complete exasperation,
"Look how they destroyed our grandest train station."
"Yes, 'tis strange," Virgil solemnly conceded.
"A clean up 'round here is quite sorely needed"
But the poet was not as outraged as Dario wished for,
So he took him 'round the back, to show him some more.

In dietro the situation was yet even worse;
Behind Termini station was if struck by a curse;
Criminals and lunatics from all the wide world,
Made the place prohibited for any young girl;
And for any man too, one would take a big risk,
If one must walk there, one would have to be brisk.

"They've destroyed it," the young man said to the poet,
And another place, come here, I will show it.
"Wait there young man," Virgil replied,
"I've seen all this nonsense, now show me inside."
After Virgil saw these new modern wonders,
He left the station and again they did wander.

Soon they arrived at a spot on the Tiber,
And Virgil felt a twinge in his very fiber,
To see an Albanian dealer get up and spit,
And throw two beer bottles right into it,
And his friends did scream and laugh and cheer,
While our drug dealer snatches another beer.

On the bridge our Virgil began to feel quite ill-at-ease,
As an African gang extort money from some passing Chinese,
Then they blocked another girl's path, not letting her through,
And slapped her frantic young boyfriend who came to her rescue;
On this ancient bridge across sacred water,
Virgil's stoic visage did almost falter.

"That's not it," said Dario. "There's still much to see.
"We must go to the ancient quarter of our fair city."
And with that they headed off and picked up their feet,
Past graffiti on the walls and feces on the street,
And Dario did look with a satisfied eye,
At the old poet's shock at the people they passed by.

In modern Rome there was so much to which he was not accustomed,
A woman dressed as whore but berating her husband,
A gang of foreigners playing music and making a ruckus,
A man dressed in leather displaying his buttocks,
A general sense of disquiet and decay,
A group of people with neither direction nor stay.

Finally their descent through modernity's ravages,
And introduction to whores and perverts and savages,
Would come to an end, quite thankfully,
At the ruined remains of that great old city;
At last they arrive, at that old Roman Forum;
Overcome with emotion, Virgil almost lost his decorum.

That old city, once grand and vibrant and hopeful,
Left in ruins from a rot that indeed might seem almost total.
"What do you say, now I've finally taken you here?"
He saw down Virgil's stern cheek shed a singular tear,
As Virgil looked upon the half-standing pillars and columns;
Remembering how they once stood, made him feel deeply solemn.

But before he could consider his loss and face it,
An African shook his hand and forced on a bracelet;
He then demanded money for this unwanted present,
Upon hearing "no" said something unpleasant,
But Virgil's eyes of fire burst out from glare,
And he slinked away from this fiery stare.

Around the Forum, once shining, exuberant and bright,
Stood an unceremonious culture unaware of its plight;
Poverty stood out against what was once rich,
While fat American tourists whined in high-pitch;
Men from across the globe with faces both weak and empty;
A culture so impoverished but that thought it had plenty.

III

Dario looked up at the poet from far long ago,
Content that Virgil had seen all that he could show.
"There's much more, oh Virgil, and its worse all the time;
"This city's nothing but litter and foreigners and crime,"
Dario breathed out, feeling finally satiated.
"In your day nothing like this would've been tolerated."

Virgil thought for a moment but he thought with intensity.
"Times are bad indeed but we ourselves write our own destiny;
"We cannot lament our place in this Great Cycle;
"A Roman man accepts his fate without becoming suicidal;
"Knowing that bronze and silver and gold and rust all comes again,
"All interlacing and repeating, beyond even pleasure and pain."

Dario blurted, "But you've seen this decay, weakness, and crime."
"Yes, I will report to great Augustus what I've seen in your time;
"Perhaps from tomorrow we'll create an age so Golden,
"That when one recalls it their heart and soul is emboldened."
But Dario seemed somewhat disheartened,
And tried to get more from him before he departed.

"I shan't lie that this poor future left me shocked and surprised,
"But here is still much raw matter than can be utilized,
"Because what was once done can again be redone,
"And for those men who seize, the world can be won;
"For Glory and Homeland, in which we feel eternally at home,
"This is all that we think of, when thinking of Rome."

Behemoth, Slain

Anastasia Temnikova

Behemoth, shining—
The heir to Mars and Venus: monster, sired by demigods;
His stately countenance of bronze catches the sun as gold;
His stony veins flow crystalline to sate his reaching limbs,
Claws confident they can restrain the river's rushing whims.

Behemoth, sprawling—
The distant lands submit themselves beneath his sinewed gait,
Feed him with blood, and feast too off his bounty; hear his rage
So great we animals all tremble at his feet and bite
Our malice down; fear not his greatness, but our lacking might.

Behemoth, stretches, slumbers—
Spoils.
He has consumed the fruit of every bended branch,
Has glut himself on foreign fare;
But what he did consume now lives within;
And what it is, he cannot stomach;
And what it is, it will not stomach him.

Come, look on the body, come look!
Come climb the spine protruding from the dirt,
Come write your name in chambered organs, long run dry.
Then let's move on, it's boring here—

What hero dealt this Herculean blow?
What cruel chimera rent the beast in twain?
What greater horror can we know than this:
What gods created; men have slain.

Thinking of Rome

Anastasia Temnikova

Thinking of Rome, as Romans thought of Greece;
We are eclipsed in mind and monument,
As Caesar wept at Alexander's deeds;
Their pantheon glimpsed in our firmament.
As skillful Time, the sculptor, smooths each flaw,
Strips gaudy paint from perfect marble planes,
Rome shed its birth, begot of crook and whore,
To cloak in lavish myth its blemished reign.

When a millennium had lapsed, and half,
Since Rome had ceased to stand, the Greeks sailed then
To unify, and met with kin, who laughed:
There are no Greeks here, we are Roman men.
Now cast we Janine eyes on what has passed,
And forth, to wonder: what of us will last?

Wayward Ways, or The Crumbling West

Treader

Winter whistles and wretched winds wash away warm words of worldly wisdom; a whisper through webs of wary and worthy, who worthlessly whimper against wills of the wicked.

Worst, whence wages are wrought, with wild weight of wasted wings, woe the Watchman! The Warden! Awake He will! Witness He'll bear with wist of West still;

No warrior without, no weapon to wrest, no wit left to whet, no watchword attests.

Within? They wax, witch-weasel and wraith; the Wolf to whine, wretch-writhe, and wane.

With whittled wealth from wayward twining, what wrath can withstand he, so weathered and wav'ring?

Awoke, "What's won?" said wallowing, weary. His own weakness worn, wreath 'f whither, of worry.

Worn hollow was the Roman, weaved by His own wrongs; the widowed West wails, forever withdrawn.

Post Scriptum,

Rome was not built in a day, nor did she fall in one. Such was the fate of the Western Empire; so too may decay be ours, should one do nothing.

Memoria Romanorum

THVMOS

I can hear it, thundering from the land laid with cobblestone,
the sound reaching out and touching far off lands unknown.

I can see it, streaming in hues of crimson and gold,
a tapestry of valor, tales of the bold.

I can smell it, the fragrance of laurels and wine,
wafting through time, a scent intoxicatingly divine.

I can feel it, the touch of marble's cool embrace,
in columns and statues, each bearing grace.

With senses attuned, Rome's essence we embrace,
in every sensation, its spirit we trace.

A whisper in the breeze, a distant chime,
echoes of greatness, once so sublime.

Through crumbling ruins, it softly calls,
recalling the glory of ancient halls.

In fleeting moments, it comes alive,
a timeless tale that will forever thrive.

As it once was,
so it is again.

Three Dives of Minerva

Handary See

I. Introduction

On Mount Olympus, all gods slumber deep
But one, whose works on earth are all awhirl
The owl Minerva, perched on sacred bough,
Peers down, the arrow of her ancient sight
A'piercing through the silent shallow depths
Of water flat and still as its stone font,
Which crumbling and lushly seam'd with moss
Fits firm, and not the slightest out of place
Amid the stolid ruins that surround.
What spies Minerva on the water's face?
An old man seeing hist'ry lit anew?
A weak man faced with what he might have been?
A rural man, his faith in weapons seized?
Not one can say, but something locks her gaze
And silent as the dead, but thund'ring swift
The echoing voice of Rome in earthly ears,
Three fated times, her wings against her sides,
Down through the shallow depths, Minerva dives.

II. The Boomer

One evening as the dusk rose in the sky
So also rose a man of wobb'ling knee
Stair by marble stair he inched along
And muttered evil grievance as he went,
"I'll reach the top, no matter who it kills,
"And give no thanks to my ungrateful kin
"Deserting me, like sight and sound and health,
"And leaving me to tour my last alone.
"My wife sweats not, preferring souvenirs
"And taking in the numbers on the tag.
"My daughter dear would sooner die than pay
"Respects to men in white immortal stone,
"So built, she claims, by black and beaten slaves.

"And so I heave these shallow breaths alone
"Eight-five, eight-six, eight-seven, eighty-AGH!"
His foot struck air where he thought one more stair
And forward fell his back upon the stone
Groaning out his words of inner pain.
"What good is life, this death delayed so long.
"I thought by living with it out of mind
"My end would rather catch me by surprise
"Not mock and stab me ever in my sight."
But pausing thus, and finding no bone broke
Felt reassured to double his complaints.
"So what, I'm fine, and what a merry thing,
"That I should outlive all my dignity
"'Tis soon I'll fester in some foreign home,
"Some child, one hand pinching shut her nose
"The other feeding, cleaning, wiping down
 "This body she'll detest as much as I.
"To what great end go these unworthy means?
"The dream of life eternal ends like this,
"Confusion welled in slowly drowning screams."
Relieved of his curmudgeony exhaust,
He rolled his head to see half graying sky,
And half a warm lit marble roof, which shrugg'd
Off gravity atop a colonnade
Like mighty tree trunks grasping at the sun
So that's what framed his irritated view
And paved the scene for passing of an owl
Soaring, silent, through the colonnade
Into the great white megalith it made,
This silent sight hushed back the old man's cries
And served to rest his eyes back on their aim.
So hobbled he back up, and did pursue
The owl into the most magnif'cent room.
Dead slow was his approach, which deeper dug
The trench of his once fleeting shallow awe
Passing breath between two rows of four
Ionic columns, this the inner room
Lit nobly, like a candle at a desk.
Then took him in the sight of human stone
So massive, and imposing, yet relax'd

He wondered how the sculptor dignified
A face between such elephantine ears
"'Tis good to see you, Abe. I trust you'll have
"No trouble hearing all my troubled thoughts."
But saw he then upon the statues' arm
Or rather on his cuff, that great gray owl
Which soared above him only moments past.
The owl looked at him sharply, then looked down
And back again, and forth as if to point,
The man's attentions to the ground,
Or not the ground, but just the arm supports
Of Lincoln's massive white imperial throne.
And ho! What's on those such same pillars which
The Great Emancipator's hands do rest?
"The Fasces, sans the axe." The old man mouthed.
"What circumstance brought this before my eyes
"Which easily I think I could have missed.
"A symbol of authority of Rome.
"What business ye in these United States?
"How badly aged in light of what was done
"In Italy till nineteen forty-three.
"But then, look round, all's Roman that's in here
"The floor, the wall, the pillars, and the chair,
"The founding fathers really were not shy
"In staking claim to Rome's antiquity.
"How strange to think, that they once long ago
"Would aim to make this land a great New Rome.
"Could any land be further from the claim?
"When youths look at their phones instead of work
"And serve no god, but worship idle hands
"The better prey-things then and to become.
"Technology is ours, but discipline?
"No sacrifice too small for them to shirk.
"But honest Abe, I'll honest with you be,
"Imperial dressing suits you very well.
"It fits that you who kept the union whole,
"By force of war, fought common man to man
"Just like so many twigs snapped underfoot
"But bound together now, and some say gagged,
"But strong, and everlasting all as one,

"So fits that you should bear the fasces now.
"I wonder now, if your commands had had
"The self-same unity of which you preached
"And not been hacked apart by voting hands
"To schizophrenic cuts of compromise.
"If Caracalla Lincoln freed the slaves
"Then where would all those free men be today?
"Linconia, of course, if not where first
"Intended, then at least in Africa,
"Or maybe in a southern U.S. state.
"Since you insisted black and white could not
"Beneath a single roof of laws be free.
"How greatly diff'rent would the world be then?
"The world would change, but not this building here
"And better its surroundings it would fit.
"What think you, Abe, of all that's come to pass?
"Thy legacy is half-baked unity.
"Some young still praise you, knowing not your way,
"'I can not tell a lie' you'd say, what jest!
"Now not a word of truth can pass your lips.
"But still, you did your part, Abe, that's for sure.
"You trusted those who follow'd do what's right
"But here we are, and where did we go wrong?
"Us founding fathers, wasted on the young."
As if in answer, crept a beakish rat
So comfortable, to fear not human feet
Did scurry 'cross the stone and up the throne
To gnaw and gnash the lash'ed stone fasces
The man looked on amused for just a bit
Before his eyes grew wide with sober shock
"Does tooth of rat carve straight through solid stone?
"It looks as though white leather on white beams
"Is loosening with every scrape and chomp."
At last the rat broke through the topmost cord,
The bundle widened, looser at the top,
But not that greatly changed in all its shape.
The rat moved down and started chewing up
The next among the two remaining cords.
"No more, rat, what's the point to doing this?
"What sustenance in statues can be found?

"What gain you wearing thin the social cord?"
Gnawing, clawing, 'nother cord did snap.
The bundle fanned out wide,
Dry bundle of spaghetti in the hand
Now greatly chang'd in function and in shape.
The rat moved down to cut the final cord.
The old man spun his head and spied the owl,
Still sitting, all the stoic, on Abe's cuff.
"And you, what kind of owl sit's idly by,
"Too full? Too sick? To rid the world of pests
"So careless that they show you their own back?
"Now dammit, eat the thing or it's too late."
The owl cared not, and stared him the abyss,
'Til sudden rang the final sinuous snap,
And all around him fell the great stone rods
At two men tall, the width each of an arm,
And thirteen in their number crashing down.
Now nowhere could be seen the busy rat,
The owl took off, the old man flail'd in tow
As fast as wobb'ling knees could carry him.
Loud shouted he for help from any man,
But none were 'round, so bound he for the stairs.
And strangely, where that step had failed to be,
That felled him on his way to see the stone,
A step right there there really must have been,
To hook the old man's foot, and bowl him down
That flight of eighty-eight, dead to the ground.

III. The Tranny

An anxious, nasal voice, inside a car,
Did fret to read the text sent from a friend
And wondered 'loud if friends were friends at all
Who flake and strand you at the outlet mall.
"The one day that I feel well myself,
"So good in fact, I'd looked ahead to this,
"And now I have to brave the aisles alone.
"Or plod home drenched in mis'rable defeat,
"But no, I'll not well handle that much shame.

"Today my stars align, if not my plans,
"So in the store I'll go if it's my last
"And fye on any thoughts that bar my way.
"Today is an adulting kind of day."
So walked the nervous twenty-something in,
Relaxing at the calm familiar sound
Of automatic doors and welc'ming bell.
In truth, even relaxed his neck was tight
And tunnel-narrow was his line of sight,
To 'void the prying sidelong glances, yet,
All sounds were magnified against the will,
So every moving mouth spoke mockery.
He moved along the aisle, found a skirt
And holding up to waist, uncertain match'd.
Eyes darted, hunting over all the shelves,
For somewhere one could better see oneself.
A curiosity then caught the eye,
An oddly realistic looking owl,
The kind they put in gardens to scare pests
Sat quaintly on a battered wooden desk.
There, just beyond, not far, the mirror hung.
Approaching close, the frame came into view.
Corinthian columns stood on left and right,
Their florid ends flourishing floor and crown,
All plastic, all spray-painted tacky gold.
"Oh dear, how gaudy can a mirror get,
"Produced en masse, a cheap, presumptive piece
"To mimic all the opulence of Rome.
"That ball of dung that over free men rolled
"Amassing soul by soul, sold cheaply for
"A dream to be the biggest roundest dump.
"Let's credit them where credit's surely due,
"The echoes of Rome's scent still carry strong,
"So now I see it manifesting still,
"A mirror suited well to wannabes,
"Who wish, like many rulers here today,
"To mask their ugly, hateful, grand designs
"By framing them within antiquity."
And then the twenty-something shivered deep
Rememb'ring just what he were here to do.

"It's just a moment, nothing all that hard.
"I'll look down at the skirt and look away,
"No need is there for me to see my face
"Which, being beautiful and feminine,
"Could never be unpleasant were it seen,
"But merely my unearned anxiety
"Afflicts me with an over-careful eye.
"Like painters who disown their greatest works
"So I can't bear to see my naked face
"For I and I alone know what's behind."
So glancing low the mirror, thought he that
The skirt was cute, but better off than on.
When suddenly he caught sight of the owl
Which seemed to stare right through his very soul
Though ricocheting off the mirror's edge.
Unsettled thus, the twenty-something's eyes
Did dart about unbridled for a spell,
And stuck to what their master most forbade.
But 'lo, far from the face he feared to see,
A handsome youth with chiseled jaw appeared.
A glorious sight in banded metal mail.
Before the scene could fully register
The odd reflection's oddness multiplied
When suddenly, in English plain, it spoke.
So this is what you do on better days?
Pretend to better Nature's master plan,
By donning some immodest uniform,
Not fit for either gender, least for thee?
At this the youth was taken quite aback
And red-in-face, and looking round to make
Sure none could see or hear this odd exchange
He whispered full of anger his return.
"Dear mirror, whose opinion wakes my dread,
"I've plenty critics without counting you.
"But who exactly speaks to me this way
"I've never seen this handsome lout before."
I wouldn't look too fondly on my face
If I were thee, a sad Narcissus we.
I'm you but stronger, if I may be terse.
For wasting words is not the Roman way.

And certainly a waste those words would be
Expelled on such a hopeless case as yours.
"Do tell me what dishonor did I give
"To now be so ungraciously received."
Dishonor you do to us every day,
By choosing to be other than ourself
Content are you to be this spineless wretch?
What pleasure's worth defacing us in garb
That only serves to emphasize one thing,
That either man or woman thou art not.
Why scribble thee outside of nature's lines?
Accept the post the gods have put on you.
More joy'd the one who greets what comes their way
Than one who tries to turn the gods to slaves.
"But all my faults will soon be remedied,
"If not this generation, then the next.
"Technology parts every sacred sea.
"Old creeping Nature, that foul dinner guest?
"Man walks him out inside a little cup.
"Soon medicine will fix us 'fore we're sick.
"Weak evolution's grip will fin'lly slip.
"And sex and gender, flipping at a switch.
"That day, what man calls righteousness will die
"And evil, less its fangs, will joyous rise."
When nature's gone, and gods are left no say,
The only beauty left is man's design
And when that's so, you won't be there to see
How ugly man has made himself to be.
A woman will you never ever be
A sickly man is not her recipe.
The great lesson of history is this,
That Power is a burden, and the fool
Destroys himself and all who gave it him.
So much the worse for modern man today
His mastery of Nature, stolen sips
Of liquor from the cabinet of the gods
And waters he them down to hide his crime
Till vanished is all flavor from the world
And this the gods see punishment enough.
Best not mistake for weakness, holding back.

They're giving men like you the rope you need
To hang yourself, example for all time.
Man's sun of power's setting as we speak.
Grim nature cometh soon to cull the weak.
"Then what pray tell, should I do in my stead,
"Who holds out hope for tech's eternal reign,
"Since I see routes obtaining what I want,
"And unproductively you say abstain."
Now you and all your kind do play at gods
Ye cage your haul in, fatten them with grain
Deny your catch to live their wild ways
And in so doing cause them to be sick.
A sickness that then passes on to you.
Now sacrifice a portion of your stock,
Not very much, but just the seeming best,
The same will bathe in blessings so divine
That nothing would he miss from what he gave.
That's what it means to leave room for the gods.
Begin this now, and spare yourself the rod.
"Leave room for gods, you say? How false a creed!
"One engineer 'leaves room for gods' and lo'
"The rocket bursts in flames, her crew entombed.
"'Tis not for gods, but gremlins, leave ye room,
"'Tis cruel, uncaring chance, which grits the road
"Whereon the wheel of evolution turns.
"And crushes it the weak, to make its way,
"And crushes it the strong another day,
"But ever cares it not for human ways,
"So turn our back to Nature, this I say!
"'Twas thirsty work it carried us this far,
"Step off your chariot and drive a car.
"Unjust is nature, so unjust is man
"Until he takes the world into his hands."
It's not that nature's gods are made unjust,
But see they through the justice wrought by man,
Which changes least as much as godly wills.
Gods stage the world as fleeting beautiful,
Which tops off every man's cup to the brim,
And one who's filled the cup too full with sin,
Tastes nothing but the liquid he put in.

The liquor of the gods surpasses sweet,
'Tis fine to drink it mixed, but better neat.
"Your rhetoric is losing hold of me,
"I'd sacrifice all beauty in the world,
"To make it just, for just the world should be."
Is that quite so? Then tell the very truth,
Why hide you from the mirror at the first?
"That's simple, mine's the worst of every world,
"'Tis ugly, whether looking out or in,
"The chance for justice passed when still a kid.
"Technology's advanced not to the point,
"Where sex and gender misaligned can be
"Restored as by the flipping of a switch.
"It's risky, costly, wholly incomplete,
"Unless the process starts in early youth,
"And yet, who lets a six-year-old decide
"Decisions that determine their whole life?
"And so, most every manlike girl like me,
"Must shoulder flesh whose seeing makes them sick
"Until eighteen, when last adulthood deems
"Us culpable to make our own mistakes.
"But then, the latest treatments come too late
"A lifetime lived in some sick stranger's house
"Leaves body, mind, and spirit not untouched,
"And being pulled all life toward being man,
"No medicines or surgeries suffice
"To bend the bones to where they should have grown
"Or replicate one's missing childhood.
"It's sad to bear this burden but I do,
"With hope that someday others won't have to."
Oh woe and tears! Some martyr think you be?
How far human control has now advanced.
Appearance, well as health, now you command,
To such extent as only seen by man.
To criticize you, call you what you are,
A special class of crime denoted "hate."
And yet, poor goblin, not enough for thee?
Just how much power's needed, do you think?
Must more than every mouth, but every mind,
Confess that you're a girl, as dare you say?

Perhaps you'd wish no people there at all,
But simulacra, scripted with thy praise.
I've warned you that this end won't satisfy.
And one more thing I really ought to say,
That Rome atop her height of tyranny,
Had liberty to spare compared to thee.
"How futile to have talked some sense to you,
"But trying as you might to light my gas,
"You can not wrest me free from what I know,
"The one who lusts for power isn't I,
"But you, foul colonizer of the earth.
"Too weak am I to stomach what you say,
"But luckily too smart to hold in sway.
"Begone now, thou expansionist asshole!"
Then make me, thou asshole expansionist!
And then the glass was shattered all around
The twenty-something's fist all streamed with blood
And jutting through the mirror on its stand.
And every eye within the silent shop
Rest wary on the girlish looking beast,
Who tearing up tore sobbing from the store,
The mirror's laughter haunting evermore.

IV. The Libertarian

What's not good for the hive, Aurelius writes,
The same is surely not good for the bees.
"For shame, ol' Marcus, always so on point
"But stumbling at the end when most it counts.
"The last of five good emp'rors, all since you,
"Above yourself, let nepotism rule."
One Midwest Summer, humid, hot, and bright
A father rocked his porch and read his book
A long-dead leader's meditations that
By circumstance still live with men today.
He looked up from the page and took the view
Of acres green and pastures roughly sown.
His daughter laughed a child's laugh and chas'd
A lolloping path barefoot toward the dog

Who'd go and stop to keep her in the game.
"Contrarily, Aurelius, if you
"Could see these sights, I'm sure that we'd agree
"Though rotten is man's bee-hive in the world
"It really makes no difference to this bee."
And glancing over briefly to his side
He looked with fondness on his Remington,
Now leaning up against the window sill
Accessible to greet unwanted guests.
"A house, a fam'ly, land, and last, a gun.
"The man with these is nothing short of king.
"If any knave should breach these castle walls
"He'll find hot lead and death wait here for him.
"Though addicts, fiends, fanatics rule the earth,
"Though base and violent races flood the streets,
"'Tis not my place to bring the fight to them,
"For theirs is freedom just as much as mine,
"And none may know which creed survives its time.
"But one day when foul Satan foots my mat
"These iron sights will with his eyes align."
And that was when ill omen cracked its grin.
As if to punctuate his monologue,
A winged creature perched the porch's rail
And to the man's surprise it was an owl,
A barn owl 'wake and active at midday.
Though new to him, he'd heard it not that strange,
Some owls are apt in daylight hours to range,
And was about to turn back to his page,
When fierce and angry barking took the stage.
"Hey Daddy! Barney found a dang'rous thing!
"I picked it up but dropped it when he barked
"He's growling at it now! Come see! Come see!"
With one more sidelong glance upon the owl,
The father stood and ran to join his kin,
And what he found on joining with the group,
It curdled all the blood beneath his skin.
"A needle" he remarked, at first unsure
Then rallying his wits, "Get in the house.
"Take Barney with you, look before you step."
The needle, clearly used, was weather worn.

Imagination raced, *How many times*
Has my dear faultless daughter gone to play,
And only chance has turned her foot away,
From falling, bare upon this poison'd point.
What if there's more? I'll have to scan it all.
But then, whoever left it might leave more!
Ought I to make my daughter run in boots?
Or keep her stuck inside until some day
When time restores the safety of my land?
But why? Why shoot up here before my house?
Do more ill-doings pair with this ill sign?
Need I to be alert for walkers late,
Who patient at my daughter's window wait?
Uncertain of the future, of himself,
The father took the needle in his palm
With every milligram of caution kept
To aim the naked point away from flesh.
Then ripping through the sky, a screeching tore.
The man looked up, and looking down once more
The needle in his palm was now transformed.
With violent shakes he whipped it to the floor.
"A SNAKE!" he yelled. "A god-forsaken SNAKE."
The same recoiled to its favored stance
Through slitted pupils stared, and chose to kill,
So rearing up, it bared its fangs and hiss'd.
The man sprang back, and made as if to run,
But held his watch just long enough to see
A winged beast descend upon the snake.
At first he thought for sure it was the owl,
But blinking twice, an eagle seem'd it now.
With fierce impressive talons, waging war
Upon two fronts. One set assayed the head,
The other pinned the body to the earth.
And talon versus fang the creatures sparred.
Which one are you, the eagle or the snake?
This uninvited thought then crossed his mind,
The battle seemed to slow, and clear became
his mind, and answered he the best he knew.
"I am of course the eagle, proud and free,
"The patron of this most industr'ous land

"And yet. . . ." then memories cascaded forth,
Of every threat he'd faced, and backing down,
Retreating from the city, from the town,
Allowing every evil to abound
And sail the silent waters in his wake.
"Perhaps I'm not the eagle, but the snake.
"Not soaring free, but belly to the ground,
"A coward, hiding in my borrowed den,
"A single deadly threat my sole device
"To keep the booted heel off my head.
"And just my head. 'Don't tread on me' implied,
"Like Gadsden, that I'd strike when too encroach'd,
"But now there's venom dripping from my lawn
"And see I now the line was long since crossed
"But craven my inaction paved the way
"For evil to pollute the very air
"And weighted down the quality of life
"With all our daily armor forced to don.
"In this way was I most like serpentkind
"Who spill their eggs and never thence return.
"For forfeiting the fight beyond my door,
"Not even could I guard her here at home.
"My efforts and beliefs were all pretense,
"In truth I left my young with no defense."
The snake and eagle, locked in battle still,
Split ways at last when talon latch'd on jaw,
And now, held in two spots, the eagle with
No great exertion ripp'd the snake in two.
The head fell void of life, the tail limp'd,
The eagle beak'd out strands of tender meat
And feasted on the carcass, fearing none.
The danger gone, the father heaved a sigh
And blinking saw vivid scene depart
As quickly as the vision first had come.
"Daddy, Mommy's bringing you the gun!"
His little one yelled, running from the house.
But seeing that the husband was now calm,
The wife and daughter traveled without rush,
And making sure to look before they'd step.
"The snake escaped," the father said at last,

Uncertain how to share what he had seen.
"Don't fear, it got a most impressive scare,
"And surely left to stake a claim elsewhere.
"But now I've need to well dispose of this."
And picked the needle up, which now was two,
The plastic in the middle snapp'd, the point
Facing askew, a vintage burgundy
Now glisten'd on the tip like morning dew.
He turned to face his daughter and his wife,
Looked sadly at his Remington, so clean,
Beyond them at the house, and all his land,
And further still, the town in which he lived,
And last, the rolling hills that cupped them all.
He sent them home, and walked his slow way back,
And muttered to himself what now he knew.
"Perhaps the last good emperor was right
"In one case, if all others he was wrong.
"The hive's own sickness trickles to the bee.
"But unlike bees who sting and lose their life,
"And unlike snakes who hold their ground and bite,
"What's needed now's an eagle's warrior pride.
"The talon's free of venom, but commands.
"The talon knows the fang's blind from the back
"And takes its victim, time and time again.
"It's time I whet these talons of my own
"And take this fight beyond my meager home
"To hold men to account for all their vice
"If with our honest lives, they won't hold stride."

V. Outro

On Mount Olympus, all gods slumber deep
But one, whose works on earth for now are done
The owl Minerva, wings a'fanning wide
She soars out from the fountain soak'd in pride
And once the water's ripples do subside
Her talons clasp the sacred bough astride,
A stillness falls that freezes all entombed,
Her solitary sentry reassumed.

H ONORABLE M ENTION IN P OETRY

April 9, 1945

Paul Dempsey

I

Such is the end of all,
The end of all, of all.
Houses bombed, torn
Apart, ripped,
With people inside, outside
In the basement,
Embracing one another,
Holding tight.

There are no thoughts in your head
When bombs are falling.
Only endure, endure
And pray,
Prey.

Your eyes will burst
Like those windows.
Your bones will be crushed
Like those walls.
Pregel will overflow
With blood.

Lonely does the city stand,
Once so full of people,
Laughter, joy, and grief,
A safer grief, retained,
Guarded by the city's watchful forts,
Soothed by the homely sky.

Now,
No one can hold so much pain.
It breaks the gates,
It foods the plains,
It even pierces time—for you
To remember once in a while
In a park of bare trees growing on ruins
Or going by bus
Down the crownless castle hill,
 Or at night,
Unfashed yet by bombs
(Remembered and feared by the city,
Who flinches when fireworks go off),
Remember—and choke.

II

Barbarians have come:
They are at the gates.
Leave your solitary outpost,
Save your soul.
You heard it? Lasch has surrendered
Königsberg.
No point in standing ground, Hans.
Let barbarians
Reap, rape, rope.
We have no business here
Anymore.
After all, barbarians
Will have the city,
Live the city,
Breathe the city
And then, perhaps, love it as we do.

Save your soul,
Don't leave it here,
Under rubble. Take
It with you
To our new home,
Wherever it will be.

We'll be exiled. Exiled, Hans!
Not executed.
And we'll start anew,
As our fathers did before us.
But the city will stay, will stay,
As you cannot exile cities
Like you do their people.

Our houses—or perhaps only mine or yours
Will remain, become home for people.
After all, barbarians are also people,
They need homes.
And even if nothing stays, the sky will,
Reminding no one now of how we
Loved, danced, and died
Under its low ceiling.
It is so low here you could touch it—
Perhaps touch it we will soon, perhaps
It'll fall on us.

Hans? You hear me? Hans!
Why turned you into stone?
Your red hair became tile
And your body bricks.
Where will I find you, Hans?
You've become home for other people.

Pietas

John Alu

Grieve not for forlorn Ilion. Such doom Destiny decrees.
All consumed within a cruel crucible;
Both iron and flesh like ephemeral dross in a moment unmade.
Her hallowed stones shatter, mortal memory renders to myth.
Their fleeting image is mixed with dust and
Scattered by callous winds across the Scamander Plain.
There, prostrate amongst the ashes of his forefathers,
Sifts Aeneas for but one ember yet glowing,
The last numinous spark of Tros' once lofty heirloom.
A grain of burning gold, treasure most bittersweet and pure.
Taking up that faint cinder,
Fragile as a newborn, he bears it near his breast.

I See the Marble Hercules

Anonymous

I see the marble Hercules,
The soldiers marching on parade,
The battle on the ancient frieze,
The masterfully crafted blade.

By these the world is well-adorned.
Was Adam not for "valor form'd"?
It is no accident that brawn
Is beautiful to look upon.
The man who stirs the maiden's heart
Is he best shaped to hurl the dart.

A world at peace would have no place
For specimens of noble race.
Some men must do each other wrongs,
Or bards will have no battle songs!
And who would thrill to hear a tale
Of concord in a quiet dale?
The faint-of-heart cry "War is Hell,"
While heroes strive to perish well!
So grant me the courage and mettle of yore,
And let me not wish for a world without war!

Nor let this spirit ever wane
Through peril, suffering, and pain.
The sting of honorable strife
Is better than an empty life.
A world where no one ever bleeds
Is one without heroic deeds.
With nothing endured, there's no glory to gain,
So let me not pray for a world without pain!

Will I regret these words one day,
When struck by loss I dare not say?
I loathe to think that I'd succumb
When that exacting day has come.
I know the price of dignity
Is torment, grief, and misery.
So brace my resolve till I draw my last breath,
And let me not beg for a world without death.

The Song of Regulus

Anon-Marie

Across a shining sea of ships
The Romans went to war
   The sea we call the Roman sea
   Was not so through all history
   When Rome was but a polity
Upon a river shore

And all around their little boot
A merchant empire spread
   On all shores of the Middle Sea
   Save for the shores of Italy
   Was spread the desert devilry
Whose god on infants fed

The Roman gods were human gods
   With faces like our mothers
The god of Carthage was a beast
   Who feasted on our brothers

Against their fleets in Sicily
The Roman consul sailed
   To fight them on the Roman sea
   On which through all our history
   Our Lady Queen of Victory
Has by her prayers prevailed

He smashed the fleets of Carthage
   Off Sicily's bright coast
Then marching into Africa
   He led the Roman host

And they fought a giant serpent at
Bagradas River Gorge
   Our ancient enemy whose coils
   Led our race to grief and toil
   Whom we have fought in knighthood loyal
From Adam down to George

And so true sons of Roma
   Remember thus your call
To crush the heads of serpents
   And cut the horns of Baal

Now Regulus was hated
In all that Southern land
   For in each desert town he took
   The temples of their god he shook
   To rubble lest his men must look
Upon the devil's hand

And now again Bagradas sees
The muster of the fight
   And with the hosts of Carthage fought
   The mercenaries they had brought
   From all the world, and there they sought
To wreck the Roman might

There underneath the elephants
Like giant moving hills
   Our men were crushed as trumpets roared
   Throughout that massive, trampling hoard
   While on white tusks our men were gored
Like rolling slaughter mills

Yet the Roman host stood fast to see
The overwhelming odds
   And the prophets of the Siren's song
   Of gold would then have got it wrong
   That the Roman host would not for long
Endure the desert gods
For they who thought the world like

A pay-for-service top
    Were greeted by a grim surprise
    From legions of aquiline eyes
    That that for which a Roman dies
Might spinning worlds stop

And thus there passed a triduum
As though all earth stood still
    And every life that Carthage drew
    The Romans sold most dear for two
    As brothers into death they flew
Phoenician blood to spill

And the rich will tire of riches
And wisdom will tire the wise
    But ever til the day of doom
    Though darkness over Earth shall loom
    The sight of home and childhood room
Shall lift the Roman's eyes

For no man dies for money
But a man might die for love
    And the little gods of hearth and home
    The virgins and the mother's womb
    Inflamed the hearts of the men of Rome
Though the sky grew dark above

But the die was cast against them as
The third sun went to set
    And their army dwindled two by two
    As side by side the Romans drew
    For death, and though defeat they knew
Surrendered they not yet

But when the third sun fell away
And on them fell the dark
    The consul looked around to find
    His stubborn, straggling battle line
    And all to bitter fates resigned
Regrouping on his mark

One last great charge the Roman led
Against the desert power
  And Carthage could not comprehend
  What drove the Romans to the end
  For though their battle line did bend
It broke not for one hour

And two by two the Romans fell
  From heat and loss of blood
Til two were left surrounded
  And all alone they stood

And now proud Carthage captures
  The Roman and his band
And back to Carthage they must march
  Across a sea of sand

And there they made the Roman swear
To delegate with Rome
  And if he did not bring them pax
  He would return in chains and locks
  Where they would shut him in a box
To die far from his home

And so the consul homeward turned
To look once more on Rome
  But to the Senate he forbade
  For peace with Carthage e'er to trade
  And captive to the oath he made
He turned at last from home

For naught on Earth could make the Roman
Break his solemn vow
  Not the unknown death he feared
  Though visions of cruel tortures reared
  Not even his own country dear
Could turn him from his plow

And so we honor Regulus
   From that age until now
Who once returned to Carthage
   To serve the Roman vow

And when again the consul came
To where his death was sure
   They locked him in a box to die
   As nails pierced his tawny hide
   Yet not once did the Roman cry
From the tortures he endured

For Our Lady came to comfort
The consul in his hour
   As every son who keeps his word
   As she once kept the Holy Word
   She knights with her heart's holy sword
And with her blood-red flower

And thus the Roman consul showed
The Earth the Roman way
   That Roman oaths nor break nor bend
   But stand like stone until the end
   Until the Son shall come again
Upon the Judgment Day

And the memory of Regulus
Still spurs the Roman breast
   And after passed a hundred years
   Beyond the wisdom of all seers
   There came to Rome the news and cheer
"Carthago Deleta Est!"

But every age has Carthage
And every age has Rome
   And we must fight as Roma fought
   To guard the land our fathers bought
   With blood and toil lest we be caught
Estranged in our own home

So remember sons of Roma
As the call comes once again
    As Carthage round about us runs
    With lies and financiers for guns
    Remind them that the Tiber runs
Within the hearts of men

Remember sons of Roma
    Remember lest it fall
That we crush the heads of serpents
    And cut the horns of Baal

S HORT S TORIES

Exsanguinate

Achromous

A silvery vapor clung to the horizon, trees motionless in the chilled air, the leaves having long since turned and fallen. Each aspect made the day's appearance all the more dismal.

Upon this solitary land was a house of withering brick and iron, the majority of the windows having been walled up. The courtyard beyond the gate was paved, yet grass grew wildly from every crevice. Cold winds seemed to blow colder there than outside the fence walls, accompanied by a shrill howling in and out at the openings of the neglected quarters.

The passages of the home were dark, necessitating the boy of the house to have left a candle burning on a table in the foyer. He took up the light, and solemn features were made apparent. The face was in want of tenderness: hollow cheeks accompanying dry lips and a gravity in the eyes rarely seen in youth.

The boy moved through the passages and ascended the disheartening staircase. At the end of one corridor, the outline of a door gleamed with light beyond.

He took the opposite hall and made several turns before coming to a locked door, which he opened with a small key concealed in his boot. Within was a bedroom which had remained undisturbed for years, left to dust and vermin. He closed the door and locked it behind him. At the wall near the bedside hung a likeness, the only object cleared of dust. A small plate of metal at the painting's frame held the name: Peter Gauger.

No matter how early he had to rise, or how late into the night, each morning and evening the boy went to greet his father's portrait. When the boy turned to the bed where his father had departed, he could always clearly recall the sickly man's pale and motionless form. For many long days and nights before, Herr Gauger's health had suffered a slow decline of body and mind. Though possessing fleeting reason in the later days, the father's clouded thoughts seemed to clear for brief moments preceding his end. This the boy was certain of, for a sorrowful awareness came into the father's eyes. Herr Gauger had often had bouts of fancy and unconnected speech, but his final moments were not a fit of a diseased mind. There had been something the father desperately wished to profess. His eyes had filled with agony as he willed his voice in vain.

"*Lütje!*" a coarse woman's voice suddenly yelled from the outer corridor.

The boy quickly made his way out of the room, locked the door, and returned the key to his boot. Though he bore the name of *Ludovicus*, he was as yet a small fellow, and his late mother had christened him *Lütje*.

It was the young Esther Gauger who had called, standing in the hall with all her haughtiness, the light of the distant room at her back. Her beauty was of a voluptuous nature, accustomed to flattery. She looked down her nose at the boy who stood before her and demanded her late husband's room be cleared of any personal artifacts. At this, Lütje looked her in the eye, aghast at the command. Instantly she struck him across the face, for she despised the resemblance to his mother, and perhaps his very bones for no other reason than he was not inclined to adulation or the enmity inherent in her family. Indeed, he was the antithesis to their belligerence and misanthropy.

"What am I to do with them?" Lütje asked simply.

"Throw them away, burn them, only be rid of them!" Subsequently, Esther took her dress's train in hand, gave a dignified flick of the head, and returned to the lighted room where the two voices of her progenitors could be heard murmuring beside the crackling fire.

In the darkness, Lütje looked at the strip of light around the door and wondered, as he often had, what his father had seen in such a woman. Perhaps Herr Gauger had not seen at all. Consumed by the sudden death of his first wife and the loss of his family, he had sought any solace, no matter how unworthy. Before Esther and her parents had come into the house, it had been full of warmth and peace. Since the coming of the three Holzheims, suspicion and loathing had degraded the home and name. The servants had all been dismissed and the old Herr Schröder with his bent back was put in their place. Schröder, with his scheming eyes and leech lips.

Lütje made his way to the parlor where Herr Schröder partook of what remained of the aged wines and brandy. Once consumed, the bottles were tossed aside or broken with a mirthful laugh, accompanied by a song which could hardly be understood and was in a dreadful key.

Lütje had long since lost his fear of the old man's temper. The boy endured the harsh words and unsolicited beatings with a soundless clench of teeth and hardened brow. Schröder would often say the boy was better for the brutality he received, that it *would make a man of the spoiled child.*

Once this was settled, Schröder gave the boy a key to the "dead man's" room, expecting its prompt return.

With such indulgences in drink, women, and other substances of an impairing nature, one may imagine it would have made the skin leather and cause the liver to surrender. Yet, Schröder held all the vigor of a man in his prime. A similar condition could also be observed in the three Holzheims. The parents had been nearly in the grave when they initially entered the house, yet as time passed they appeared to have drained the life of the home into themselves.

Begrudgingly, Lütje moved his father's personal effects as Schröder deemed, for the old devil was the Holzheim's personal servant. Most were burned or destroyed with delight. That which was of worth or could not be reduced to ash was set aside for future profit. To see Schröder spinning the father's silver watch by its chain as if intending to throw it made a deep loathing simmer in the boy's heart.

Intentionally, Lütje left his father's portrait for last, hiding it beneath the mattress. Lütje knew evening had come when the lighted room had gone dark, and the family retired to their bedrooms, which housed the remaining comforts.

Having toiled into the late hours, it was nearly morning when Lütje found a moment to quietly head for his father's now spartan chambers. Carefully he took his father's portrait under his arm, the chamberstick in his other hand, and made his way silently past the boards which would have creaked. He stopped when suddenly he saw a candle's light flickering around the corner ahead. Quickly he doused his light and retreated as far against the near door as he could. Daring to glance around the edge, he saw the Holzheims with the mother at the head of their procession. Never had the boy seen the family awake at such an hour, and making their way as if they did not wish the walls to hear them.

Finding their attitude curiously nervous and expectant, Lütje clutched the portrait under his arm and followed at a distance.

They would venture underground into depths Lütje had never known, where the air was stale and cold, with wooden doors and stone walls of a time long past. All concealed beyond lock and key.

After descending the spiral stairs, the ceiling rose in great vaults upheld by towering pillars. In the small light of the candles and lanterns carried by the family, one could barely discern the decaying grandeur. All appeared to have once been above, now sunken into the earth by force. Winding throughout the ground and stone could be seen strains of tangled roots, devoid of greenery. They had sunk the structure and presently held it together below the surface. Below the windows were great shards of shattered glass, the floors cracked or crumbling where the roots had tunneled.

As they went on, the bramble grew thick and concentrated about one of the far walls. Concealing himself behind one of the great pillars of stone and marble, Lütje saw the family pause before a mangled form resembling a man, which the roots had strangled and contorted, digging beneath dry flesh and penetrating into its bones. The form did not breathe nor gave any sign of life.

Frau Holzheim raised her lantern and with irritation bid her daughter to hand over the dark bottle she carried. In the light, Lütje distantly perceived the entangled man's flesh appeared to have rotted away and been picked clean by rodents and pests. Only the teeth remained immaculate, long and savage while the rest of the body was frail and decayed. Upon the head and jaw was hair as wretchedly tangled as an invasive ivy.

Frau Holzheim put the dark bottle to the parted teeth and poured a small portion of its contents. The jaw cracked with discontent when deprived of further nourishment. For several minutes the family simply stood back and waited, watching the creature with impatience. "That is time enough," said Herr Holzheim, expectant of what was to come.

With haste he took a knife from his pocket and a tin cup from the other. Swiftly he sliced at the creature's neck and was careful to catch every drop of blood in the cup. At this action, the creature grinded its teeth but could not shift its head in the vise of root and stone. It was not long before the gush of blood slowed to a drip and ceased, the cup filled to half its capacity. Herr Holzheim greedily drank, his wife and daughter moving near. His wife tapped at his shoulder violently and snatched the cup for herself as her husband took a breath of satisfaction. After each partook of their portion, the youngest receiving the least, each reveled in sensation. The blood softened the harshness of their countenance, cleared the eyes, and filled the bones with renewed vigor. However, it would not turn back time for them, and in their dissatisfaction, they repeated the process once more.

With a mind for self-preservation, Herr Holzheim warned against his wife taking more than her share, for at a point the blood would go beyond remedy and become poison if taken in too great a quantity. This they had observed in a previous servant who had crept into the dark chamber alone to take more than was allotted. It had polluted his mind and body until he was more ghoul than man, a wretched creature to be put down by Herr Schröder.

Not wishing to observe further, Lütje clutched the portrait and turned from the scene, his back at the pillar as he closed his eyes. When the lights of the family had gone, Lütje quickly followed behind its dim remains, but the way was shut, and he was left to the dark, among the whispering of wind and the shifting of the unknown.

Unsteadily digging into his pocket, he found the matches and alighted his candle. With the image of his father under his arm, he walked the path the family had taken to the creature. In the dim light, Lütje looked upon the entangled form. He saw the withered and torn rags had once been fine silk, leather, and lush fur about the shoulders, now dry, cracked, and broken. If any gold, silver, or jewels had been about the man, they had been torn from him.

Though bound, the cracking of the creature's jaw below empty eyes made

Lütje widen the distance between them. With the remaining light, Lütje followed along the walls until he found several doors not blocked by root or rubble. One had been locked, but the other appeared to have had its handle broken away, and the door could be pushed open. Within was a shallow room that appeared to have belonged to a scribe, its books and parchment thrown about and the desk toppled over. Most appeared to be several generations old, but there were trails of melted wax which must have seen use within the last years and parchment which had not yellowed and was clearly of a recent make.

Crouching to the floor and gently setting aside the portrait, Lütje recognized his father's writing upon the newer parchment. Holding the candle near, there could be no doubt it was his father's hand. Judging by the notes to the side of the page, it appeared to be a translation of older writings. Gathering up several others by his father, he found they were translations of letters and historical records of several men who appeared to have no relation. However, it was concluded that the men separated by decades or even centuries were in fact one in the same. The last translated letters were addressed to *"His Serene Highness, H. Silvanus."*

As the wax of the candle was nearly spent, Lütje glanced about to see if a wick remained among the candles cast aside and was relieved to find light would still be allotted to him by a lantern which bore oil.

He continued to read of the immortal below his home. After the original owners of the house had perished, their secrets with them, the creature was long forgotten, until Lütje's father had stumbled upon the door and had fashioned a new key. Before the father, others spoke with the creature and had offered the blood of animals. While the offerings had given it energy, it was not long before the creature's health was supped away by the roots. If cut, the roots only grew again and entangled themselves further. The last page ended abruptly, on the day Lütje's father began to fall gravely ill.

Rising, Lütje silently went before the creature, his hand tight at the lantern. "Can you . . . understand me?" he asked, holding his breath as his heart pounded in his ears.

There was no response.

Lütje swallowed a portion of his fear and repeated the question.

There was a minute shift of the creature's head, as if it were then regarding the boy, interested in the young voice it had never heard. It attempted speech, however such an effort had not been made in years and its mumblings were unintelligible. With aggravation, it took several moments of silence before it forced the skinless mouth to render speech. "I . . . understand thee. . . . It wast a predecessor . . . who did impart unto me thy tongue. Yet . . . vague is the memory. . . . Through time, that which was once whole hast decayed. . . . And those above taketh much . . . for perhaps a great many years. . . . They pine for what runs through these veins. Were I free . . . and my strength renewed . . . the blood would bring unto them an end. . . . Alas, frail have I been. . . . Long have I remained *host to the parasites*," he finished with contempt.

Lütje was at a loss.

"What ist thy name, child?"

"Lü—Ludovicus Gauger, though all call me Lütje," was the boy's quiet reply.

"Gauger. I recall thy father. . . . Dost thou know what became of him . . . ?"

"He has passed on."

"Alas, yes. . . . Yet, dost thou know the circumstance?"

"He. . . . I was told he had some disease of the mind."

The creature gave a low laugh at the throat. "Liars are they! It wast not the mind, dear child, but that which accompanied his sustenance. . . . Slowly, it burned from within. . . . With gluttonous rapture did the parasites speak before me of their deed, and those likened to it."

"Then . . . you say they were poisoning him. . . ." the boy's voice trailed off. A fresh sorrow came to his heart as he recalled his father's sufferings, and a hatred for the culprits.

Suddenly, Lütje dimly heard the voice of Herr Schröder. Instinctively flinching, he dropped the lantern and it rolled across the floor. He rushed to stop it before it reached the bramble, but it tumbled below the roots and upon crumbled stone. Its glass shattered and the dripping oil ignited.

Seeing the slowly building flame, Lütje glanced at the bound man. There was no aid he could give. Running for the exit, he was caught at his collar by Schröder, who flung him to the ground with curses and accusations of thievery. Without having seen the building fire beyond, Schröder furiously dragged the boy by the arm to one of the locked doors and threw the boy into the dark room, locking it firmly. Lütje pounded his fists desperately on the door, but his pleadings fell on deaf ears.

While the family above moved about without care or worry, the fire seared the roots below. They clenched and spasmed as if in pain, reduced to furious embers whipping at the walls and floor. When those among the walls cracked and turned, the very foundation shifted. The pillars below were struck by the enflamed roots in their frenzy, causing the ceiling to weaken under the strain. As they burned, the roots loosened their hold upon the creature.

Unnerved by the rumbling below, the family had all come together in the parlor, ordering Schröder to locate the source and put a stop to it. With hesitation, he did as he was bade, but upon reaching the bottom of the stairs below, he could only stare in awe at the spectacle of light and motion before him. Schröder had not long to spectate, for the mangled creature seized upon him as a wild animal starved to madness. Its teeth tore and gnawed at his flesh until little remained.

Feeling the heat behind, the eyeless creature turned its head back, having felt only the chill of the sordid air for many a year. Now life rushed through him. The throat which had long been parched was relieved. Flesh which had long dried and rotted was slowly regaining its form. Yet this meal was not enough.

To the side was heard the pounding upon a door and the coughing behind it as smoke seeped its way in. Still deprived of sight, the creature felt along the walls of distant memory and crawled its way to the steps it had long dreamed of ascending once more. The Holzheim family had been gathered together not far from the entrance to the cavern, and the creature found the meal it craved. One by one it assailed them. When Herr Holzheim fled, the creature pursued him along the floor and caught him at the leg. It pulled him near, and its teeth tore into the throat, silencing Herr Holzheim's feeble cries.

When the frenzied mind had begun to clear, the creature looked back at the steps where it could smell the burning air, the steps leading to where it had been confined for many years, smoke now crawling along the ceiling.

*　*　*

It was a fine room; the ceiling above was of a deep mahogany. Light streamed through the windows, where beyond a choir of birds were at their morning work. Too haggard to move, Lütje's weary eyes looked down and saw he lay in a comforting bed with soft sheets and a finely crafted frame. At his bedside, reclining upon a simple chair, was a man of noble baring, with hair of a deep red, the eyes a striking steel blue. The pale eyes which had long been sightless were enamored with the scenery beyond the window. The face which had long been thin and frail, was now sturdy and defined by age.

Seeing the boy had awoken, Heimirich Silvanus gave a subtle smile. "A great wonder is the day. The sun's light and all-encompassing warmth wast long absent from my mind's eye. . . . Once thy health hast been restored, thee and I shall set forth into the world, *Ludovicus*."

The Roses of the Emperor

Altweltaffe

"I want to drown my guests in rose petals. I want a flood of pink and white and red to come down on them like some sort of fruity play on Old Testament punishments by God himself. I want people to literally drown in a mass of flowers."

"That's kind of decadent," the event manager remarked. "We were going for more of a laid-back kind of thing so far, don't you think?" I eyed her with all the aristocratic condescension I could muster, which is a decent amount, if I do say so myself.

"It's supposed to be dramatic, unexpected. Violent, even." I had to interject, before she started talking again. I understand that you employ practical minded people because that is the kind of attitude that will move and shake what needs to be moved or shaken. But one does wish, occasionally, for a poetic vein to innervate the minds of these drones. At the very least it would improve the flow of communications.

"Can't you see that this is decadent already? Half the guests are flown in by helicopter from the international airport, for heaven's sake. The roses should wake them up to the fact that all of their tasteful suits, their select topics of conversation, their dear charities, are not fooling anyone. Why do they act like accountants when they have a seat at the emperor's table?!"

"Alright," she conceded, and made some hectic notes on her tablet, the manner in which she hammered her pen on the thing conveying clearly that this was a concession against her better judgment, "I guess you will want everybody to gather in one room for this. What should be the excuse? Do you want to give a speech?"

There was sarcasm in this last remark, and I do think people should not be sarcastic to their employer, at least when their wages exceed a certain amount. I wouldn't chastise my gardener for being sarcastic, I reckon, should I ever happen to speak to him.

"A speech will do just fine, thank you. Don't you know that Wagner used to lull his audience to sleep with dainty passages only to wake them up with the kettle drum? How did that make them feel? Don't you think they were annoyed?"

She replied she wouldn't generally try to annoy her guests, but that she could see the appeal. Her sarcasm was here to stay, it appeared.

"They should be annoyed at themselves! Annoyed for having been caught in a pretense! Annoyed for having believed that anybody could mistake them for anything else but the class of people who go to the kind of party that gets flooded with roses. In any case, I'll leave the details to you, but I'm thinking, some sort of decorative sheet that looks like it hides the ceiling, but actually hides a ton of rose petals. A literal metric ton. Make it so I can hit a button for the release. With my foot, maybe. Or a small remote in my pocket, yes."

"There may be some legal concerns as well. People may have rose allergies." I was glad that she was now thinking about the feasibility of it all, but I grimaced nevertheless. My event manager was unperturbed.

"If somebody literally drowns in rose petals, you may also want lifeguards on notice. And the flowers will have to be cooled between delivery and the party. We're going to need a trailer for this in the lot, specifically. I will send you a proposal tomorrow at the latest."

*　　*　　*

"When you hear of the falls of some empire, you think of razed buildings, burning cities, tumbling pillars and the cries of innocents. But empires don't really crash down like towers. The crux is that we fixate on these material signifiers: castles, gleaming weapons, a crown. But the empire is not really a palpable thing. The figures in the ledgers that trace the movements of goods and people over continents and centuries, they describe a succession of men working toward their own goals, that happen to contribute to this rough shape we so readily recognize as the empire. Think of a river! It starts humbly, drops of cold water from a thawing glacier, running into a brook. But the brook runs ever downward, and meets others, and they unite with others again, until you have a stream! Each brook is still somehow in there, contributing, never relinquishing its guiding principle, the hungry quest for the low energy state. Together they shape the land! But at some point, the energy is spent, entropy raised beyond some critical point, and we arrive at the delta. The river breaks up into egoistical, meandering, and stagnating divisions that swamp the land. Pointlessly, you might add, because they all end up in the sea anyway, mixing with the salt water and losing their identity irreversibly." We were strolling along the beach in the last light of the day. I was glad that I had been able to dismiss the event manager; she was grating in the peculiar way of competent women. At my side was a trusted security guard, who was as good a listener to my spare thoughts as was the surf. "That's where we are now. In the delta. Men using the last energy of the stream to pursue their own goals, as did their predecessors. And we sit on the banks and wonder why their efforts don't accumulate to a landscape-shaping, boulder-moving force. It's because the force is spent upstream, up the river of time. You look at it from the other side as well, and say that the landscape upstream is such that rivers form there, while they can't in the flat lower lands. So to speak, our times are not conducive to the emergence of greatness. Maybe. I believe this to be two sides of the same coin."

"What is an emperor, then? In your view, the emperors of old bundled the self-interests of the smartest and strongest under his purview and found some compromise between their goals and the emperor's own. But today, what use is it to bundle the efforts of men of purpose, when it all pours into the ocean? It leads nowhere, and there is not enough overlap between the different factions to bundle anything together, anyway. If you think we're in the delta, in the dispersion of the empire, you're saying the empire has fallen already."

I had not expected him to reply to my monologue. I was slightly taken aback, as one tends to be, when people hired for their readiness to follow orders prove to have a mind of their own. I humored him nevertheless.

"It has to start over. The emperor should be the germ. What is low has to be lifted up again, and the cycle started anew. But it won't work if all they do is look down. These are brooks that hardly remember the days of crystal-clear glacier meltwater, muddied by all kinds of silt. To them, oblivion in the ocean is release, deliverance. Maybe they're right even, in some twisted kind of way. But in the end, this is just a metaphor, and they're people. They need to feel in their heart of hearts that power is attainable. Have they no desires, beyond comfort?"

"Is that where the roses come in? Is that another metaphor, being smothered by luxury? I'm just curious," he had to add, remembering his station.

"Yes, but so much more is contained in my little plan. Shock and awe! They need to be reminded of their mortality in the same swoop as they come to realize that they have power, that there is actually power to be had, to be attained. I want to shake them awake! Who will be cowardly, when the moment comes? Who will be valiantly heroic? Most importantly, who will see the opportunity for action beyond the moment; who will see that at a time when people drown in roses at parties, anything goes? I intend to give the broadest hint: it's all up for the taking, and fortune favors the bold."

*　　*　　*

There is always a feeling of being superfluous in your own home when a large party is being prepared there, at least in my experience. A lot of people show up to do work that are at best superficially aware that I, fundamentally, am the reason they were summoned. So they bustled around me, displaying polite annoyance that I was standing in my own hallways. Naturally, I tried to be out of the house as much as possible during these times. When returning from such an escape trip, I had to wait for a trailer that was being maneuvered into the delivery parking lot, where many of the workers had already parked and taken up space. On the side of the trailer, there was a childish semblance of a flower to be seen. I understood that my roses had finally arrived. I felt some excitement rise, and repressed it. I decided that I would go and inspect my arsenal.

*　　*　　*

The florist opened the trailer, and we stepped into a cooled atmosphere. On shelves lining the sides rested heaps of rose petals of predominantly pink color. Their fragrance was strong, and I wondered if that would give my guest an ominous feeling, to smell flowers where none could be seen. I dismissed the thought and did a quick mental mapping of the shelf space in the trailer onto the floor space of my atrium. "I assume that this is the first of several such deliveries. When will the rest arrive?"

The florist was perplexed. "This is the full order. If you need more, we would have to go to different suppliers, too. This is a lot, to be frank."

I asked her to follow me and brought her to the atrium. "I need this room to be flooded with roses. Certainly the front of the room, where the high windows are."

"You'll want a lot more roses than what you ordered."

I waved my hand impatiently at this, as I felt my wealth earned me the right to not be bothered with the mundane affairs of numbers.

"A whole lot more. This hall is pretty large. The amount of roses you have ordered now will give you a light drizzle of petals, not a flood. But that was also what she said—your event manager, I mean. She said you wanted rose petals to lightly snow on the heads of your guests."

"We call it the Atrium. The hall, I mean. Because of the large skylight in the middle of the room. In any case, that's preposterous. I want people to swim in petals. Think of literal flooding. Monsoon of flowers."

"What about wind machines, then?"

It was at this moment that I considered making her my new event manager. I made it clear to her that this novel avenue of exploration interested me strangely and strongly.

"Less people are going to stand at the sides. We could drop more roses there and blow them inwards."

I barely heard her anymore. Storm of Roses! Hurricanes, typhoons, tsunamis. Forces of nature that move men! Had I set my eyes too level, had my vision been

115

too timid? No, the impression will last. If the violence is not subtle enough, if the pain it causes is altogether too physical, their focus will latch onto neurotic themes of injury and recovery. Suffocated by roses, on the other hand, that would get them.

"There's also a type of canon that can shoot large loads of confetti." She was evidently only warming up.

"Let's keep it at the original arrangement." I made a mental note to see my event manager about subverting my wishes. This was a most unusual situation.

*　　*　　*

I met her two days later, in the parking lot, where by now, cooling trailers for roses had replaced almost all of the worker's vans that had populated it before. She had been avoiding me, and I only caught her, I assume, because she had been trapped in a discussion with a rose farmer (or rose breeder? The particulars of rose agriculture evade me). He had a poor grasp of English and gesticulated wildly, while my event manager was trying to get him to understand that she had not ordered that amount of roses. I stepped in before she could resort to any kind of physical violence against this helpless man. He took the opportunity to scurry away.

"It's quite alright—I amended your order the day before yesterday. Whoever did the calculation for you must have been off by a couple of zeros! We're lucky I happened to run into the florist."

"You can't be serious about this." She dispensed with niceties right away, apparently. So much for decorum. "Somebody is going to get hurt! I can't in good conscience let you do this!"

"If that's what it takes, so be it. Breaking eggs for omelets, et cetera. And who are you, exactly, to tell me what I can and cannot do?"

"Clearly, I'm the voice of reason here. These are people we're talking about! I should alarm the authorities about your plans. In fact, I will, and I will warn your guests as well!"

I raised an eyebrow at this. "You would spoil my surprise? I'm afraid that would rather dull the prospects of our future collaboration; I hope you can see that. Apart from violating the NDA you signed, of course."

"Please, we can find some better way to do this. I don't know what you hope to achieve, but we can do it without breaking the necks of your guests with an avalanche of flowers. Couldn't you settle for a fog machine, like we did on your birthday?"

I shook my head. "My wishes are clear. There will be a reckoning, and it starts with the roses."

Her expression became hopeless. "In that case, I really don't see how I can continue working for you. This is a horrible idea. People are going to get hurt, and you should see how wrong that is, for some erratic fancy of yours no less."

"People getting hurt is the point of the exercise, to some extent. If you're not going to help me, you should focus your efforts on making the rest of the party go smoothly. I will engage your florist to assist me in this matter."

"I refuse to—"

"Then your services are no longer needed."

Without any further objections, and almost imperceptibly, she nodded. I was not even certain if that meant that she accepted being fired, or that she accepted that she couldn't change my mind. I determined that it didn't matter, as long as she didn't interfere any further.

*　　*　　*

"What is an empire, then?!" I felt their eyes on me, felt them occasionally dart to meet each other, ensuring themselves that this was not normal, waiting for the punchline, the comic relief. "What is an empire then, if it is not ruled? Who rules, when nobody claims its power, when nobody claims its treasure? It is but a piece of land. And you are not a ruling class; you don't look for any kind of power at all. And when you do, still, you would never do it in your own name. You look to distribute it instead, to make it pointless. We used to warn of the barbarians at the gate, of the foreign, those who might upturn our order. You have long become the barbarians within, completely foreign to the order that you usurped. It's no use being afraid of any kind of invasion; any invader would find himself unable to plunder what has long since been emptied." I looked to the waning sun on the horizon as if it could supply the next words to me. I was making a practice run for the big speech. The few bystanders took my pause as an opportunity to gracefully move to different parts. The less fortunate group toward which my words had been directed looked uncomfortably down their flute glasses, at the ground, or, in the case of a few more steadfast men, at the horizon as well. None met my gaze, into which I attempted to pour magmatic fire. I emptied my own glass.

"Why would we be fit to rule, exactly?" He said it while keeping his eyes fixed westward, where the sun plunged into the sea. He might have been an executive of some company that did business with me or an official of some sort. "We have not attained this status by force, or by cunning. We played by the book. Maybe the book wasn't written according to your liking, or maybe you think that now we have the means to impose our own ideas on those who come after. But isn't it so that everybody who is here, at your party, in these circles, is only here because he conformed? In the end, it's impossible to come into money or fame without it, because surely these things only exist in relation to conformity. How could you be rich, if you were an outsider? You'd just be some guy with a lot of money. How could you be famous, if you were an outsider? You'd just be known to many people, a feat achievable by a singer, or a hooker. It's that force that holds us together. We don't punish non-conformity. It punishes itself. Wealth is within; poverty is without us. Thus we never craved wealth; we craved the approval of those whose proximity promised the fulfillment of our desires." He turned toward me at this point, bearing an expression of utter boredom. "We are not the ones you seek."

*   *   *

I had his words in my mind as I pushed the button. It will sound contrived, but time slowed down for me as the roses fell. The audience, though much larger than at my dress rehearsal outside, mirrored the one there. Inasmuch as they had been listening, my wild words of empires and power, of will and might, had disturbed them. Their expectation was that whatever followed would make my performance fit some formula, would make it digestible and presentable in a retelling to a third party. So when the flowers fell, I'm sure, for a second, many thought that this was it—relief, release, the end of the tedium. I agreed with them. This was it. I saw skinny legs in linen trousers buckle under the impact of the wave. Men and women brought to their knees. Hands waving, golden bracelets clattering, reaching for something to grip and hold in the sea of petals. And yes, here and there, I saw laughter, as some were left standing who were missed by the heaviest loads. Disbelieving smiles on their faces as they watched white and pink petals float down slowly behind the vast bulk that had already dropped. Then, a long moment of silence, before the moaning started, the chattering rose up, the disoriented noise of people who were unsure of protocol. People were shaking themselves free of the petals, leaving valleys in their wake as they pushed toward each other. In places, the surface of the roses stirred, but nobody emerged. And then, cries! I became almost ecstatic at the sensation. Islands of alert movement, angry glances shot in my direction. Somebody stepped close to the podium; I recognized him as the disillusioned man from before. He was brushing rose petals from his hair as he moved toward me.

"We have different ideas about the dance of conformity, it appears." He was hiding rage behind a performative cheeriness. "Maybe you think us sycophants when we attend your parties and listen to your speeches, but if you want to be an emperor, I wonder who should fill your court but us. And your disregard toward us makes it very clear: you can't be our emperor. We are upholding an order here; you spit on it! You liken us to barbarians when it's you who's declaring his enmity to civilization. I don't see how proximity to you can be anything but toxic to our ambitions."

He had come close enough to grab me by the collar of my shirt, at which point, my bodyguards swarmed him. I removed myself from the atrium.

*   *   *

From a balcony, I was watching the lights of the last ambulance recede, casting a colorful play of dancing shadows onto the hills. Below, I saw the distraught florist guide workers who were pushing barrows loaded with large garbage bags full of rose petals. Curiously, my event manager came out to join me. For a while, we looked out into the night in silence.

"I know you technically already fired me, but I wanted to give you my notice in writing." I took the letter she handed me; it was a common enough procedure after all, even though I was rarely bothered with paperwork nowadays. "This might not impress you greatly, but the talk downstairs is that you have lost your mind. I have overheard several groups openly discussing how they can use this to dispossess you of your wealth. To speak of outright rebellion would be an understatement. You really buried it all in one night. Buried it under your silly roses."

I didn't think it was a good moment to repeat my thoughts on the matter, again. I was not surprised by anything she had told me; I had planned for it after all. I was quite satisfied. What was left to be seen was, had I only planted seeds of discontent? Or had I shaken their golden cage, shaken the stage set to make it clear to the last one of them what was real, and what wasn't? Would they conspire to conserve the status quo? Would their shock cause all of them to bury their heads in the sand even deeper? No, at least one of them must see: if an emperor can fall, so can everybody else; and if he can be made to quit, if he can be replaced, if his spot is up for grabs, then everything is up for grabs, really. You rulers of the world!—all you have to lose is your chains.

*   *   *

I never saw the event manager again, but I wonder if she'd be content to know that, in material terms, I was heavily punished for my fanciful misdeeds. I pondered this question now, briefly, as I looked upon my new "event manager." He was a different creature, in appearance and outlook. He was waiting for instructions, and I gave them thusly:

"I want to drown the population of this city. I want a flood to sweep the slums, to wash all the scum out into the sea. I want you to demolish the dam and let the

119

waters of all the little tributaries come down on them in an instant, an Old Testament punishment by God himself."

"That's . . . feasible," the soldier for hire remarked. "It would have some dramatic implications down the line, don't you think?"

"It's supposed to be dramatic, unexpected. Violent, even."

The Star of the Lost Gods

Kaiter Enless

He ran and the beast followed. Its four legs drummed dusty earth, fur drab as caustic wastes surrounding, unsated jaws slick with crusted blood of hapless prey, and yellow eyes wide with dire intent. The man recognized it as a procyon, a descendent of what had been called wolves in the days before The Parting. He knew from his time at Haeru's Keep such creatures were carnivorous, communal, and typically hunted in packs. This one, he thought, must be abnormally self-reliant, and so, particularly dangerous. He glanced fearfully to his pursuer as he crested an obdurate rise which plummeted to a sheer arroyo at least sixty feet deep. Perceiving the dead end the predator bristled its back and snarled. The man drew his thick cloak up like the wing of an enormous bat, palling his front from nose to boot. He hissed, raised himself to full height, and felt a surge of confidence, for the monstrous canine shrunk back, ears flat to pate, lips curled. His elation evaporated as the feral pursuer regained its courage and launched forth. As it sprang, he wrenched the cloak free, flung it, and dove in less than a second. Tangled in risen cloth which obscured the decline, the beast hurtled over the precipice and spilled into the ravine. A shrill and terrible cry lit up the sun-sucked stones, and thereafter all was still save the thrumming of the man's heart and the quickness of his breath. He drew his left leg up from where it dangled over the abyss and lay upon his back, panting and counting clouds. One drifting column appeared as a serpent with mouth wide, another as a young woman with long hair and gentle guileless features. He thought of Verity and her plight, rose from rain-starved perch, and trekked round the edge of the canyon until irradiated ground afforded a manageable descent. Above the flinty furrow, heaving clouds slithered and the near old star slouched below horizon's brand. He passed curious effigies of recent construction, of twined hair and chiseled bone, some bestial, some human. Whether warnings, waypoints, or shrines he knew not. He drew a map from his pocket, studied it 'neath a raw gale and moved on from the grisly totems, deeper into the desolate rift where a narrow fissure in an elevated portion of the left-side cliff opened into a spacious cavern. Inside it, sitting beside an unlit firepit, a disheveled man in dark blue cloth. The blue clad man studied the traveler a moment and spoke. "You Dyak?"

The wayfarer inclined his head. "You're The Archeologue."

"Armin." He studied his guest a moment before intoning with practiced fluidity. "Bright is the furnace."

"May it wax by our kindling," Dyak replied, his voice low and solemn. Armin beckoned the man to sit adjacent him. Dyak did so and looked to a hopper that hung on a spit above the cavity. The Archeologue placed his right gloved hand upon a stack of dried wood in the pit.

"What are you doing?"

"Channeling the spirits." The Archeologue chanted gibberish and turned his palm up as the tinder sparked to life, as if commanding the flames to rise.

Dyak crossed his arms and smiled. "It would be a neat trick if I didn't know you wore a burner gauntlet. The Mechanikos' design."

The Archeologue dropped the burning wood into the shallow depression and looked to his companion with approval. "A Haeru man. How fortunate. I feared The Ordinator would send another pageless mercenary to spite the Mechanikos."

"He's not so petty. Tell me, Armin, do you think the Mechanikos is right? Can such a device have existed?"

"His findings, fragmentary though they be, suggest it does. You are probably too inexperienced to have been permitted into the inner archive."

"I required a final proving."

"Well, I have seen the records. The myths carried some truth. The technology was lost after The Parting. Only the schematics remain." He leaned over the sparking pit and his eyes flashed with audacious fervor. "And they're here. In this ravine. Once we have them, it will change everything." He shifted the wood and flames lapped toward the skinless hopper. "Bitter times near an end."

"An engine that produces a nascent star. Sounds of something from a mummer's tale."

The Archeologue chuckled. "When you put it that way I suppose it does. I confess I didn't believe it either, until I saw Haeru's proofs. But imagine what could be done with such a device. We could find our scattered brethren and all they have built on yon planets. If we can retrieve the schematics. The tribe of this valley—"

"The Scald."

"Yes. They regard our forebearers as gods and maintain the schematics as holy relics. As The Ordinator probably informed you, one of ours who escaped them saw the designs in one of the old transport ships the Scald use for shelter. From what the poor soul relayed, they don't understand what the structures they inhabit were used for and so inhabit them as a convict would a barrow. A pity they haven't the technical knowledge to evaluate the true worth of their inheritance."

"The Mechanikos told me the Scald are abnormally violent."

The Archeologue shrugged. "So are you."

Dyak dropped his gaze, his visage momentarily abstracted.

"Oh in the name of The Strayed, don't look so forlorn. You're not one of those sensitive, weepy types are you? Breast clutching to pitisome poems at midnight?"

Dyak chuckled. "I promise I'll not mangle your ears in such a fashion."

The men talked with warm regard over roasted meat, slept on fur cots, and departed the cave at daybreak. By midday they reached the mechanical midden to which The Archeologue had alluded. Arrayed about scorched reddish stone were large nautical vessels, bent and bowed, like enormous bludgeoned whales beached in some seismic calamity. As the men wound between the abraded odd angled hulls, some festooned with wreaths of desert flowers, The Archeologue pointed skyward. "Will be a blood moon tonight."

"Why does it turn red this time of year?"

"During its orbit, our planet blocks light from the star which would normally strike it. Only light from the planet's atmosphere meets it, and as the waves are stretched in the process, a reddish hue is achieved. You see—"

The man's oratory was beset by a cry from above. Dyak sprang aside as a crude wooden spear pierced the cracked earth beneath his feet, it clutched by a dark-skinned and fur-garbed man who had leapt from the prow of the ship the seekers idled beneath. The assailant released his armament, drew an antiquated blade from hide wrap at waist and lunged at The Archeologue. The dark warrior's ingress was obstructed by Dyak's powerful arm about his throat. Struggling against the shackling grip, the would-be slayer twisted the dagger round and drove it toward his binder's skull. Dyak caught the warrior's hand, hauled the man off his feet, and used the momentum to plant the blade hilt deep in its owner's heart. Dust settled with blood, and The Archeologue looked on in horror as Dyak rolled the corpse from his body and sat upright with deep breaths. Wind groaned and vultures cawed from the cliffs as if in delight. After several seconds Dyak spoke.

"He was following us, but not for long."

"Why do you suppose that?"

"If he had shadowed us before we slept, we would be dead."

The Archeologue nodded and helped his companion to his feet. "I owe you. Are you alright?"

"Fine. Help me move him."

They hauled the dead man into a clastic incurvation and looked down at the silent form with mournful expressions. With deft hands, they entombed the body with stones, that its repose might be undisturbed by beak and fang.

"I don't like saying this, but if this is the Scald's customary way of greeting outsiders, the chances of your woman being—" He broke off, unable to finish the cruel sentence.

Dyak's face went soft with anger then hardened. "Whatever happens, I won't hesitate."

They left the makeshift grave and followed the shade of derelict watercrafts, senses primed for hiss of breath and patter of feet. Several miles ahead, the canyon widened and fires and dusky forms rose up out of the blurry heat. The Archeologue pointed through the fevered carnival of the desert lesion to a massive anvil-prowed freighter that matched the description of the man who had escaped. Their prize was close, and they stole toward it along the left-side canyon wall, under cover of invasive fog as Scald watchmen leaned upon their spears and smoked pipes of clay. The marooned seacraft, unlike the other detritus, remained evenly erect, and a rope ladder dangled portside. The Archeologue gestured to the cliff-face adjacent the ship, where weathering had carved steeped depressions that formed a thin, natural stair. Like shadow puppets who held their own strings, they clambered up the rise until they stood in slanted blackness even with the ship's starboard. From the bracing elevation they noticed a peculiar statue upon the prow, in the likeness of a great winged beast and a man upon it holding a star in one hand and a scroll in the other; both visages were fashioned from a single aged piece of metal. Before the curious totem, a Scald woman, swaddled in elegant dyed garments, knelt, head bowed, as if in prayer. Up from the bowels of the dilapidated machine, a retinue of Scald men came bearing burnt offerings of herbs, and behind them slaves of various races followed with somber eyes. Dyak focused upon a woman among the back of the throng whose hair was covered and skin darkly tanned. Despite the alterations, he recognized her and straightened with wide eyes.

"Verity."

The Archeologue placed a steadying hand to his companion's chest, fearful he might bound from the escarpment.

"Not yet."

As Apophis' maw swallowed the sun, the men watched the curious rite that was as the echo of some primordial custom. The robed woman lifted her hands and lowered her head and raised a chant, and the men chanted after her as if in response. If whatever they beseeched heard their orison it gave no reply. One of the men, smaller and fiercer than the rest, remained aloof from the ceremony and shook his head as the chorus soared. After the ritual reached its apex and the crowd returned to the darkness of the hold, the silent watchers leapt from the prominence and landed upon the deck, as drops of blood from a rusted blade. Both rolled to a crouch and listened. It was only the groaning of the wind through the gutted gash of earth that sounded as the bellowing of some blood-starved monstrosity set to devour them all. They briefly inspected the fetish and discerned a scrawl in their own tongue upon the base. "In memory of the intrepid men and women of the *Megalopsychia*, our first home beyond this sphere." The Archeologue ran his hands across the inscription, and his eyes widened with apprehension.

"This is—"

"Armin, we need to hurry."

The Archeologue nodded, and together they snuck below the deck of the ship become a fortress. A rough iron stair terminated in a wide and darkened hall at the end of which stood two fur-wrapped natives, conversing in barking patois. The air was thick with incense, rust, and more faintly, the odor of flesh and flame. No ornamentation adorned the walls, and the four doors stood stalwart. Swiftly, the men ducked into the near leftward portal and found themselves in a storage room filled with dried vegetables on antique metal racks and salted meats packed into crates. Dyak locked the door as Armin moved to a threshold at the opposite end of the room from which the men had come. The door opened, and a young woman entered and stood staring at them with the fretful doeish eyes of one who has seen the dead.

"Verity," Dyak whispered. The Archeologue held a hand to his lips and beckoned the woman to close the door. She did so, bolted the latch, and clutched at her hair, then rushed to Dyak's arms.

"I thought. . . . It is shameful to say. . . . I thought you had abandoned me."

Dyak shook his head. "Neither I, nor the Mechanikos. It was he who discovered your whereabouts. I would have come sooner, but I didn't know where they had taken you." He inspected her and discovered lashes about her arms. "Damned brutes."

"I tried to get away. They would always catch me and whip me. But the lashings were nothing to the thought I might never again see our Keep. That I might never again see you."

"Girl," interceded The Archeologue, "we have another task. I would ask two things of you." She swallowed her fears and straightened with attentiveness. "Are there any plans on this ship? Schematics? Old ones, from before The Parting?"

Her brows knitted. "Yes, there are a number outlining the construction of an ancient machine. The Oracle keeps them."

"The robed woman on the prow?"

"You were watching?"

"From the cliff."

"You were most sly. I didn't notice you. She thinks they're inscriptions from the gods. As do most of the Scald."

"Where are they, these divine inscriptions?"

"In her private quarters. She sent me to fetch some herbs. I must be back soon or she'll send an attendant to retrieve me."

"Then go back."

"Certainly not!" Dyak protested, trembling with wrath.

The Archeologue held up a hand in entreaty and spoke gently. "They're lax enough to let her wander on her own. Who is better positioned to seize the plans, you, me, or her? If"—he focused upon the woman, whose whole body trembled with the magnitude of coming events—"you are willing."

"I am a woman of Haeru. I am willing."

"I don't like this. Let me go. Take her from here and let me grab them," Dyak protested.

"No, he's right. It's the safest way. There isn't time to argue."

Dyak looked between his expectant companions, brow furrowed with the weight of the decision. "Very well."

She guided the men to a cabinet where long-hooded cloaks of beige hide hung and instructed them to don them so as to render themselves less conspicuous should a Scald stumble upon them. With their hooded garments they determined they could pass as locals if viewed from a distance and bid farewell to Verity, who slipped from the room. Agony built with minutes and made both bodies its exclusive domain as a sharp knock sounded upon the door from which they had entered. The men tensed. Came then a call in a foreign tongue.

"What are they saying?" Dyak asked.

The Archeologue listened and spoke. "One of them asked if anyone is inside. Another wants to know why the door is locked."

"We have to get out of here."

"No. Their search for the key will alert others. We'll let them in."

"Even if they're fools, they're recognize the game immediately."

"Of course. But we can't let them away. We'll bind them."

"Are you mad?"

"You told me you wouldn't hesitate."

The words sent tremors of ire roiling within Dyak's mind for hypocrisy was baleful to him. He steeled himself, seized an iron pan, moved flat to wall, and gestured to the door. When The Archeologue opened the portal, the jabbering ceased and for a moment none spoke. One of the Scald stepped through, peering with perplexity at the shrouded figure before him. The entrant's voice resounded suspiciously, a demand backed by violence stark in mangled brow and coiled sinews. The first Scald was a large, powerfully built man with braided hair and a necklace of human teeth. The speaker's companion, a short, fat man adorned in feathers, filed in, whereafter Dyak slammed the door behind them and struck the recent arrival upon the crown with the flat of the pan. The little Scald went down without a cry as the braided man hissed and lunged. The two tangled and crashed into a near shelf, spilling utensils and spice in their wake. Cookware clattered to the floor as the Scald drove fists into Dyak's face with furious abandon. The relentless assault was broken by an empty sack secured about the Scald's throat. With Armin's aid and a supreme exertion, Dyak pried the man off him with a knee, finding sufficient distance to drive his elbow to the Scald's brow. Disoriented and roped, the tribesman was hauled backward, arms writhing vainly as Armin tightened his hold. With a growl, the Scald swung side to side, as some mad kenneled hound, and shucked the old man free. The Archeologue scrambled for the pan. The Scald ground his left heel to the elder's knee. Armin loosed a moan of agony and drove the pan to the leg that pinned him—once, then again more viciously. The Scald mewled, paralyzed by pain, and fell. Poised to pounce upon The Archeologue, the Scald was waylaid from behind by Dyak, who fixed a vicelike hold about his throat. Swiftly, the broil subsided, along with the Scald's consciousness, and when he lolled, Dyak released the man and helped Armin to his feet.

When Verity returned she found the men tying the unfortunate Scalds by wrists and ankles. A fearful expression dominated her features, and in a quivering voice she gestured to the portly tribesman upon the ground. "That's Dancing Horn."

Dyak spread his hands in puzzlement.

"He's expected to officiate the night ritual. They'll be looking for him."

"Do you have them?" The Archeologue demanded, bounding toward her with blazing eyes and searching hands.

She smiled proudly and drew a heavy lambskin envelope from the folds of her cloak and passed it to the man. Without inspecting the contents, he slipped the prize into his satchel as a furious thrumming resounded, followed by Scald exclamations. All three shifted to the hall-facing door.

"I told you they'd be looking for him."

Scarcely had the words left her mouth then pounding and chatter reverberated from behind. Their eyes met. They were boxed in with no clean escape. The Archeologue turned to the woman, gripping her shoulders tightly. "Let them in; distract them. Once you have their attention, we'll fall on them and run for it."

"But—"

She swallowed her words under his desperate gaze, lifted her head, and strode to the hall-side door as the men melded with the adjacent wall like trained assassins. Moments after the Scald entered, vicious blows rained and a chorus of pain filled the scullery. Seconds later the trio burst through the hall, up the stairs and out onto the deck. All inwardly groaned as they realized the rope ladder had been retracted and lay knotted around the portside railing. Dyak's hands had scarcely set upon their means of flight when numerous Scald armed with wooden spears poured from the interior and surrounded the trespassers. The men parted, and The Oracle moved between them, no longer garbed in her resplendent robes, clad only in a simple gown of roughened cloth and a diadem of flowers. Dyak sprung forth, placing himself between the encroaching tribesmen and his companions. The Scald footsoldiers leveled their spears at him, but The Oracle gave an order and, hesitantly, they retracted their weapons. She cast a discerning eye between the trio, reserving exceptional ire for Verity, and spoke officiously, gesturing toward the statue upon the prow.

Dyak looked to Armin. "She said we have violated hallowed ground. She wants Verity and the relics, that is, the schematics, returned."

"Tell her we came for Verity, and we'll give her papers back if they let us take her."

Armin relayed the massage without argument, and The Oracle listened and shook her head. She extended a hand and waited. Verity stepped forth and some of the Scald hissed at her.

Verity spoke and Armin translated. "These are my people; they have been searching for me. I didn't ask to be brought into your village."

This outburst strained The Oracle's patience. "Cease this foolishness. The Scald have claimed you with five stone of gold."

"My people don't measure life by rocks."

"If it is gold they desire," Dyak said. "I shall oblige."

He moved his left hand to a pouch at his waist and raised his left hand in appeal as The Oracle's retinue readied their armaments. When they relaxed he removed a large chunk of solid gold from the pouch and held it aloft; with his free hand he extended all five of his fingers and pointed to Verity with his chin.

"Tell her our people will come looking for us if she should refuse. Tell her there needn't be enmity between us." Armin did as instructed, and for a long moment The Oracle gave serious consideration to the proposal; but before she could answer, the cruel-faced Scald who had stayed aloof from the ceremony intervened.

"Why listen? They invade and strike. Let us kill them."

"He offers more than what we bought her for. Surely," The Oracle replied, "they will offer as much for others of their number. This is a sign from the Far Ones. Can you not see, Keen Jaw? Our prayers have brought prosperity to our door." The faces of the Scald guardsmen formed a tapestry of inhibited doubt and excited affirmation.

Keen Jaw motioned to Verity. "That one is mine."

"I have already told you this is the Far Ones' providence. You deny their grace?"

"I deny you."

Keen Jaw shoved the woman to his soldiers and her protestations were swallowed by the hum of the crowd. A few shouted at the usurper; the rest expressed approval of the coup and turned feral eyes upon the wayfarers. Keen Jaw extended a hand for a spear readily supplied. Realizing the horror at hand, Armin leapt forth and shunted Dyak aside as the lance sailed through the air. Dyak tumbled and turned to find his companion pierced through the gut, his hands upon the protruding haft. The crowd murmured and Keen Jaw smiled as Armin lurched into the shrine. Before Dyak could draw the blade he had taken off the felled tracker, Armin braced himself against the altar and raised his voice. The Scald looked on, unapprehending until the old man lifted one of their floral offerings from the bowl before the statue. He spoke again and Keen Jaw scoffed. The mirth died as the sacerdotal tribute ruptured in flames and danced in Armin's palm. From behind the dark cloak of the sky, the moon shone red as bloodied bone. Scald screamed, and The Oracle fell to her knees gibbering. Keen Jaw's eyes flew wide and he barked for another spear, and when none responded, turned and found his men fleeing, some into the bowels, others, over the sides of the ship. Keen Jaw howled with rage and hefted a discarded polearm which he raised toward the injured Archeologue. Dyak and Verity prepared to intervene but found all preparation vain, for The Oracle rose and lunged, driving a dagger into the recusant's spine. He screamed and turned to the woman with abject perplexity swiftly replaced with rage. He shoved his spear into her chest as she raked at his face like some wild raptor. Both rocked in fatal embrace and fell dead upon the deck, crimson by satellite and blood. Dyak and Verity rushed to their companion who lay upon his side beneath the shadow of the shrine, still and slick in his life's water. Unlike the Scald leaders, whose death masks were fixed in terror and pain, the old man's unliving visage bore a languid smile. "Old fool," Dyak muttered bitterly. He felt Verity's arm and his tone softened and trembled. "What did he say to them?"

"He told them their Oracle was right, that the Far Ones had returned. That he was their envoy and you and I offspring of the gods. He said they would behold a blazing judgment and that the heavenly spheres would run red with the blood that was to be spilled."

"So that's why he burned the offering. They had never seen a portable combustion unit before and thought it some divine power. Come, help me with him. We shall not leave him here."

They secured the body by way of one of the rope ladders and lowered it to the ground, followed after by another. The boat town was deserted, and where the Scald had fled neither knew. Stillborn was all lamentation, viced in the adamantine gauntlet of resolve. They buried The Archeologue at the base of a low hill beyond the ravine as distant worlds burned in the oppressive blackness above. Worlds the interred had opened.

Child's Play

J. Ester

A story about the founding of Rome

The past echoes through the dreams of the young. . . .

As soon as the din of the engine died down and the car had come to a halt, two boys stumbled out and dashed across the parking lot, their father's voice fading into the distance.

"I will pick you up later. Have fun!"

Ronan and Remi did not acknowledge their father. The sounds of the surging waves beyond the tall, dry grass and the salty air, mingled with the scent of seaweed, captivated their spirits and urged them on. The boys leapt into the sand, flung off their sandals, and continued running along the dunes. Though the beach was largely deserted, with only a handful of people basking in the morning sun, there was only one spot that captured their attention.

After a few minutes of running, it finally came into view: a secluded cove, shielded from the world and cut off from the beach by imposing rocks. No local had claimed the cove yet, leaving them in solitude. Each grain of sand, from the rocky shore to the limestone cliffs looming above, was theirs. It didn't belong to them by conquest, legal right, or sheer luck, but rather the boys had always felt it was theirs by destiny.

Ronan noticed a small crab scuttling in the sand.

"Our loyal subject."

Remi chuckled.

"What is a king without his citizens?"

"We shall strive to protect him!"

Carefully navigating around the crab's home, Ronan headed toward the sea, with Remi in tow. Dropping their shirts and sandals, they plunged into the warm water, letting it enfold them. The boys raced to see who could swim the furthest, but the longer they swam, the more they found that the water had begun to take on a life of its own. They found themselves enveloped in a fine mist. The cove disappeared behind the veil, and soon the boys could see nothing but themselves. They tried to swim back, but the mist only seemed to grow thicker with each stroke. The world around them continued to dissolve; the sky turned black and the water took on a wine-dark shade, as if the heavens themselves had opened up and decided to merge with the sea. Tired, the boys desperately looked around for a sign.

Their wish appeared to be answered by a flash of light, barely visible in the distance and hovering high in the sky. The boys gathered all their strength and swam toward it. The light's glimmer quickly overpowered the mist and revealed a small island with a hill in the middle of it. The boys looked up. Perched on the hill was a fortress, and behind its walls, reaching high up into the sky, stood a white marble tower with a lit pyre on top of it. The strength of its flames reached far and wide, and the boys were unable to look at it directly, hovering their hands above them in order to shield their eyes.

Contrasted with the surrounding darkness, the fortress and the fire within it appeared to be the only thing holding up the sky and stopping it from crashing into the sea. As soon as the thought entered the boys' minds, something seemed to grab their legs from under the water. It pulled them down into the deep dark that even the light from the fortress could not penetrate, and as the boys were forced to let out their last breath, everything around them went silent.

Ronan and Remi woke up on the shore of their cove. They looked at one another and, without a word passing between them, at once understood the charge they had been given.

They wasted no time and set about their task. Digging out a small pool and heaping the sand aside, they did their best to recreate the island. Remi dropped clumps of mud in the middle of the pool, building up the hill, while proudly declaring the necessities of what he thought would exist behind the walls of their own fortress.

"Homes for our people that will shield them from the dark. A merchant here, a shopkeeper there. A blacksmith, farmers. . . ."

Ronan planted a number of small sticks all around the base of the hill.

"These sentries will guard against the enemy."

Remi scooped up another hefty lump of mud and added it to the mountain.

"A tavern!"

Pleased with their progress, the brothers approached the center of their domain and began flattening the peak of the hill. More mud clumps were added and were diligently shaped into the form of a tower. Engrossed in their imaginative construction, Ronan and Remi were oblivious to a group of older boys stealthily advancing toward them.

"What are you little shitheads doing here?"

The brothers looked up. Gazing down at them were four boys, their faces contorted into smirks that signaled trouble. Undisturbed by their presence, Ronan was the first to respond.

"Building a fortress."

The boys snickered.

"That's stupid."

"Yeah, this is no place for toddlers. Scram."

Although the age gap between the boys might not have appeared significant to an observer, for Ronan and Remi, who had just celebrated their eighth birthday, the group of boys, appearing to be around thirteen, seemed almost adult-like. Remi, pausing to consider this, attempted to negotiate.

"We were here first."

The bulkiest of the four boys advanced on Ronan and Remi and with a brusque kick scattered the tower they had painstakingly constructed.

"I said scram!"

Without hesitating, Ronan leapt at the boy, toppling him to the ground. Straddling him, Ronan started pummeling, though his blows landed lightly. Simultaneously, Remi struck another boy, splattering blood from his lip. The boy retaliated and soon they were entwined, tumbling in the sand and raising clouds of dust.

Ronan felt two pairs of hands clasp his arms and jerk him back. Paralyzed and unable to move, all he could do was brace as his assailant pummeled his stomach.

While Remi was engaged in a tense struggle, Ronan knew it was only a matter of time until they were overwhelmed. He flailed his legs to make the boy relinquish his grip and tried to escape the grasp of his captors, to no avail. After the tenth punch, Ronan longed for a miracle.

Suddenly, a loud bark echoed from the beach's edge. A large German shepherd charged into the fray and latched onto one of the older boys' legs. Releasing Ronan, the boy yelped as he withdrew from the fight. Hobbling on one foot, with blood trailing, he fled to his cohorts. The dog stationed itself by Ronan and Remi, snarling and bearing its teeth toward the gang of four, who had by now stepped back. One of the older boys moved to step forward, but the dog lunged, barking fiercely, and the boy retreated.

The confrontation ended. With neither party willing to provoke the dog further, Ronan and Remi began to retreat. One of the boys hurled a stone in their direction, though it fell short.

"Yeah, you fuck off to where you came from and take that stupid mutt with you!"

After a while, as Ronan and Remi turned their backs on the attackers, the voices carrying their insults died down and the boys vanished from sight. Freed from their assailants, Ronan and Remi attempted to keep pace with the dog who darted ahead of them, pausing occasionally to look back, as though beckoning them to follow. Moments later, the dog approached a family of three and emitted a vigorous bark.

Ronan and Remi approached them with caution. The mother was the first to spot the boys.

"Oh my god! Are you OK?"

Ronan and Remi looked at one another. Both were shirtless, marred with bruises and grime. A vivid red mark adorned Ronan's stomach, while Remi's face was etched with scratches and dabs of blood.

They responded in unison.

"We're fine."

The father of the family scanned the rest of the beach with concern.

"Where are your parents?"

Remi was quick to point his finger at the sky.

"Well, Dad is up there. But he said he'll come for us later."

The parents exchanged nervous glances, unsure of what to make of Remi's story. After a few moments the mother turned toward the boys with an assuring smile, before digging into her purse for a packet of wet wipes. Approaching Remi, she knelt down in front of him and began cleaning his face.

"That's OK, you can hang out with us for the time being. Miles would love some company. Right, Miles?"

Peeking from behind his father's back was a boy with short blond hair. Though barely younger than Ronan and Remi, his sturdy, almost Rubenesque, frame lent him an air of maturity, an impression that was quickly dismissed as the boy revealed his lightly-freckled face and uttered a few murmured words before retreating once more behind the safety of his father.

"Yes, Mum."

Having finished cleaning Remi's face, the mother sat down on her beach towel.

"Why don't you kids play together? Just make sure we can see you."

The father nudged his son toward Ronan and Remi.

"Go ahead."

Together, the trio made their way to the water's edge and settled into a tight circle. After a brief lull, the young boy spoke up.

"I'm Miles."

"Ronan."

"Remi."

"Pleased to meet you."

"Is that dog yours?"

"Yes, her name is Luna and she's very friendly."

"Luna just saved our lives!"

"What happened?"

Relaying the tale of their skirmish, Ronan rose and addressed Miles.

"We're indebted to your dog, which means we're indebted to you."

Miles looked puzzled by the formality.

"I don't know what that means."

"It means we must do something great together."

"Like what?"

Remi had sat silently, listening to the conversation and running his hands across the sand. He watched as the water reached the shore and formed little streams where his fingers had made marks in the sand, before retreating back into the sea. Finally, he felt it was his time to speak.

"We shall construct a river."

The proposal took the others by surprise.

"A river?"

"Yes, the most grandiose river in the world."

"It would have to be very big then."

"Ten feet wide, at least."

Miles squealed with excitement, eager to share his own experience.

"I've seen a bigger river than that!"

"Where?"

"On holiday."

Ronan and Remi chuckled. Silently, the trio crouched down and began to dig. What started off as a modest excavation, barely wide enough to stand in, slowly expanded in all directions until they stood in a shallow trench.

Their endeavor caught the attention of other beachgoers. While some of the adults ignored the boys or scoffed at the unsightly scar now carved upon the sands, the younger boys seemed intrigued and didn't hesitate to approach.

First to arrive was a trio of friends, mirroring Ronan and Remi in age.

"What are you doing?"

"Digging a river."

Miles intervened with zeal.

"It's going to be the biggest river in the world!"

"Can we help?"

Ronan looked up from the trench and nodded at the newcomers. With their assistance, the pace intensified, and the trench extended its reach across the beach to span twenty feet in length.

Four more boys came forward, volunteering to aid in the excavation. The trench soon felt cramped, as accidental collisions and sporadic sand showers became frequent. After clearing his hair of sand yet again, Ronan realized that something had to change.

"This isn't working. All of you"—Ronan singled out the newcomers—"the sand keeps falling in. I need you to move it."

The boys immediately complied. They split up into groups of two, each group on one side of the ditch, and began relocating the sand into large piles away from the dig.

Lastly, two youngsters, mere six-year-olds, joined. While lacking the strength to help with the digging, Remi quickly found a use for them.

"You will embark on a treasure hunt."

"What kind of treasure?"

"Seek out anything of value and return with your finds. Pearls, amber, perhaps even gemstones."

Elated, the young explorers set off. After half an hour, they came back, their shirts bulging with sizable shells.

"Look what we found!"

Scattering the shells across the ground, they adorned the river's banks with their finds. Remi watched, impressed by their enthusiastic participation.

"Excellent work."

No sooner had Remi said that when the barrier dividing the riverbed from the sea gave way, unleashing a torrent of water. Each boy scrambled to reinforce the breach, flinging sand and mud in a desperate attempt to stem the flow, until eventually the water slowed down to a trickle, then ceased altogether.

Ronan gazed into the trench they had dug, now filled with a foot of water.

"We need to get the water out."

One of the six-year-olds leapt to his feet. "I have an idea!"

Dashing off, he soon returned with three orange plastic buckets. While the boys in charge of digging attempted to scoop out the water, Remi scrutinized the makeshift barrier they had put up against the sea's advance.

"This won't do. We need something sturdier."

Singling out Miles, Remi gestured for him to come along, and they vanished from sight. Minutes later, Miles returned, alone and yelling desperately.

"Help! Help!"

Ronan jumped out of the ditch and ran toward him.

"Where's Remi?"

Gasping for breath, the boy could only blurt out a few words.

"They've taken him."

"Who?"

"The cove. Big piece of wood. For the wall. Ambushed."

Ronan sprinted past the boy toward the cove. The rest, shocked by the revelation, quickly recovered and raced after him.

"To battle!"

The rest of the beachgoers briefly looked up and wondered at the sight of a group of boys running away from the beach, their fists raised in the air. As the boys' war cry disappeared into the distance, the adults exchanged bemused glances, their initial concern dissolving into chuckles and shakes of the head. One man lowered his sunglasses, watching the children with a wistful smile, reminded of his own childhood games.

"They've got quite the imagination, don't they?"

Ronan arrived first at the cove. Peering around a massive boulder, he spotted two of the older boys forcing Remi's arms back, while a third, clearly the ringleader, pressed a knife against Remi's neck.

Ronan stepped out of his hiding place just as the other boys caught up with him and witnessed Remi's plight. Instinctively, they armed themselves with nearby objects. Ronan seized a hefty driftwood log, the others gathered smaller sticks, and the six-year-olds amassed small stones, while Miles, carried forward by nothing more than fury, charged at the older boys.

He was immediately followed by Ronan and the other boys. The aggressors, realizing the onslaught, released Remi and thrust him aside. The boy holding the knife advanced, mocking the approaching group, while his friends stood close by, readying for confrontation.

Yet, before a clash could erupt, one of the older boys collapsed, shielding his head with his hands.

"The little shits!"

A barrage of small stones, hurled by the six-year-olds, descended from the heavens, assaulting the gang relentlessly. They hunkered down, endeavoring to shield themselves as effectively as possible, and although many of the stones missed their mark, several left substantial bruises on their arms.

The assault of stones ceased as abruptly as it had started, and the six-year-olds, depleted of their ammo, scampered away. It had still managed to cause enough of a confusion among the ranks of the gang, that it allowed the rest of the boys to close in on them.

Ronan caught up to Miles and quickly surpassed him. There was only one target in his sights: the one who had held the knife to his brother's throat. With a mad dash and the thirst for blood in his eyes, he charged at the boy and, with a forceful swing of the driftwood, knocked his jaw askew. As their leader crumpled to the ground, the remainder of the gang surveyed their surroundings, realizing they were encircled. The boys converged on the gang, assaulting them with fists and improvised weapons.

In a defensive flurry, the gang's three members hurried to their leader's side. Despite his dazed state, they hoisted him up and secured his knife. Swinging the knife around wildly, the four made a break through the encirclement and fled.

Chants of victory echoed across the cove as the gang vanished. Ronan rushed over to Remi's side, finding his wounded ego to be his only affliction.

"You OK?"

"If he didn't have the knife. . . ."

As the rest of the boys continued their jubilation, Ronan and Remi watched in silence. The elation of their war band stood in stark contrast with the traces of conflict strewn across the sand and the destroyed remains of their original fortress.

Ronan addressed the crowd.

"Friends, lend me your ears!"

Silence befell the cove as every eye focused on Ronan.

"We have won a great victory today!"

Their silence broke once more.

"Hoorah! Hoorah!"

Ronan signaled for quiet, his hand raised.

"Today, we've been rescued not just once, but twice. And amidst our loss, observing what's left of our cherished domain, I'm heartened by what we've gained. . . ."

The anticipation was palpable.

"We've been united as a band of brothers!"

The crowd erupted into a frenzy, jumping up and down and continuing to chant.

Unable to soothe their excitement further, Ronan approached Miles, embracing him.

"I am honored to call you my brother!"

With a grand sweep of his arms toward the horizon, he indicated the cove and the fragmented remains of their stronghold.

"The cove is yours. Guard it well."

Affirming their bond with a handshake, Ronan turned and, with Remi by his side, left the boys to their festivities.

Returning to their excavation site, Ronan and Remi took in the aftermath. The six-year-olds had come back and were continuing to adorn the riverbanks with shells. The barrier, once a bulwark against the sea, had by now been entirely destroyed, filling the trench with water and rendering further digging unfeasible. And flanking the river stood two monumental mounds of sand and mud.

"What do we do now?"

Ronan briefly considered his brother's question before coming up with an answer.

"We build a new fortress."

"A grander one?"

"The grandest. And the strongest."

"Just for us."

"Just for us. . . ."

They both made their way to the river, yet while Ronan headed for one of the mounds, Remi paused by the other. Ronan didn't hesitate to voice his disappointment in his brother's decision.

"This is the bigger hill. We'll build it here."

Remi shot back without hesitation.

"But the shoreline is elevated on this side, allowing me to easily jump across. Your chosen spot lacks defense."

"You can't jump it; it's too wide."

Undeterred, Remi took several steps back for a running start and charged toward the river. Accelerating with each stride, he stumbled just upon reaching the river and tumbled headfirst into the muddy waters. The six-year-olds, briefly distracted from their task, burst into laughter. Humiliated, Remi crawled out of the river and returned to the dunes to dry himself off, as Ronan began his construction.

A few hours passed, and what used to be merely a heap of sand and mud evolved into a formidable fortress, encased by two-foot-high walls reinforced at their base with stones procured by the six-year-olds. Next to the walls was an expansive courtyard dotted with lush trees. Concealed behind the tree canopy, a sprawling array of dwellings housed the compound's residents. Dominating this assembly stood a grand sand castle, its towering spires casting a vast shadow over the walls, extending its reach well beyond its borders.

Ronan surveyed his masterpiece with pride. Eyes closed, he envisioned the hustle and bustle of the streets within. He imagined gold and silver descending from the skies, plating the castle walls. He dreamed of vast armies marching over the lands, waging fierce battles, and elevating his name from a mere murmur to a resounding echo around the world.

It was his father's voice that snapped him out of his reverie.

"There you are. It's time to go."

"But I wish to stay."

"It's getting dark. Your brother is already in the car. Come."

Ronan remained motionless, his gaze lingering on the castle as the sun cast its last beams across the golden sand.

"What will become of it?"

Drawing Ronan in, his father shared a moment of reflection.

"The sea will claim it. Its walls will erode; the courtyard will be flooded and the houses forsaken. The gold and silver will be worn down by the waves and turned into dust. And in the end, the life within its walls will fade to silence."

"Can't it stay like this forever?"

"No. Every creation must face its ultimate demise; such is the way of all things, my son."

In contemplation, Ronan held his father's hand tightly.

"Even if it will all be gone, can we still come back here tomorrow?"

"Why?"

"So I can build it again."

The Eternal City

Noah Huffstutler

Barbarians have breached the walls of Rome. In nearly the millennium that Rome has existed, this is only the second time the Eternal City has been sacked. In fact, the last time Rome had been sacked was eight hundred years ago. For Roman citizens it seems like the impossible has happened. But these days are the days of impossibilities, for the Visigoths' attack on Rome is only one of many events that Roman citizens had once thought impossible. Indeed, just a few decades prior, they may have never even considered them.

The few decades preceding 410 AD would play like a bizarre nightmare to the Romans of a century or two ago. For one, Rome is no longer even the capital of the Roman Empire anymore. Some may struggle to define what (and where) the Roman Empire even is since only in the last century the Empire has been split and divvied up, sometimes into as many as four parts with four simultaneous emperors. The division of the Empire's territory came amidst an inner division of its peoples. Not everyone who lives within Rome's borders are Roman by blood, and these outsiders were viewed as a threat to the Romans' precious way of life. This undoubtedly gave way to numerous uprisings, revolts, and civil wars in the last few centuries.

Of course, Rome has changed over the years. From a small kingdom to a respectable republic to an imposing empire, one of the largest and most fearsome the world had seen. From tyrants to liberators, and pagan gods to Christianity, change is nothing new to the Romans. They are an adaptable people. But despite all the changes, some things remained constant. At the heart of the Empire was the Roman way of life itself, which now seemed doomed.

The end is no longer near; it's here.

Maximus scoffed at the idea. "The end of what?" he rebutted. For him, life in the year 410 was no more tumultuous or dire than the previous twenty-one years since he was born.

"The Empire? You must then have forgotten about Constantinople in the East where they are thriving and life is as good as ever!" He's arguing with his uncle Claudius.

"If the West falls then so be it! For it is only one part of the Empire and will return to its rightful rulers in due time as do all things." He paused for a moment and then continued. "Anyways, the barbarians cannot rule themselves," he says with finality.

Claudius shakes his head. "Maximus, the Gothic tribes are not like the stories from your childhood. Those are fantasies. They have lived within the Empire's borders and amongst her peoples for centuries now. They have legions just as we do. By God, much of their soldiers were even once our own!" Claudius snapped back.

They don't remember how this argument began. They had been traveling for three days now and were exhausted. They were in Rome when Alaric, King of the Visigoths, and his army breached the gates. The attack had come suddenly, and there was no army there to stop it, but fortunately it was not especially violent. The Visigoths had mostly ransacked the city and stolen what they could find and burned the rest of it to the ground, but quite mercifully left the residents mostly unharmed. Still, Maximus and his uncle had lost everything of value they owned. Even their slaves were taken from them for the soldiers' own use.

Maximus, in his brazen naiveté, had attempted to fool the soldiers to save their gold by pretending to be a peasant, which proved to be laughable to them, and he was promptly smacked in the head by one of the soldiers. They had taken him hostage, but he was narrowly saved from further harm by Claudius, who quickly revealed the location of the gold before they grew more irritated with Maximus's crude attempt at deceit.

The Visigoths weren't particularly set on maiming any citizens, but neither would they hesitate to torture or kill any citizen that would interfere with their mission. After all, sacking Rome was mostly symbolic. It was no longer the capital, nor did many of the elite class even live there anymore. Still, Rome was considered the birthplace of the Empire and therefore held a high status in the minds of most. The Visigoths' true intention was making a startling statement: the Roman Empire was vulnerable.

Maximus wasn't particularly affected by the events of three days ago. While most Romans were shocked by the sacking of the city, an idea that truly never crossed their minds, Maximus was much more unstirred. He could admit that the Western Empire was more fragile than the much newer Eastern Empire. He also knew that the borders of the Empire had been shrinking for some time. But it was hardly a doomsday event.

"Nonetheless, no army has ever stood a chance against the Empire. Once troops arrive from the East, the barbarians will be dealt with and Rome will be rebuilt. All will return to normal," Maximus said. He still held a bit of resentment against his uncle for rescuing him back in Rome. It made him feel like a child, which was at least in some part fueling his argument with Claudius.

"Max, you are too young to understand the history of the current conflicts within the Empire and the implications of what has just happened to Rome. You think they left us all alive because they are afraid of us? They had the opportunity to have killed every man inside the city, but what they did was much worse! They left us alive so that we would know what they *could* do. And where are the troops you say are coming from the East? The Visigoths have been circling Rome for days or maybe even weeks! There's no one coming to stop them," Claudius said with a noticeable despair in his voice. He knew what Maximus refused to see. These were indeed the final days of Rome. Of course, in the context of an empire that has lasted for a thousand years, that could mean she still had many decades left to spare. Although the day wasn't certain, the end was coming sooner than anyone had anticipated.

"Then we will go to the East! We'll go to Constantinople, to the new Rome! There you will see how the end of the Empire is not even a whisper in the crowds. Life is just the same as it has always been."

"Max, you do not know how much things have changed. You haven't seen what I've seen! And what my father and his father have seen! One day you will begin to see that the writing is on the wall."

"Uncle, you have no hope! How can an Empire that has stretched to the ends of the Earth and brought countless kingdoms under its command just end? The Empire that has conquered and prevailed over every enemy? The Empire that created law and order and a fair government? The marvelous ideas she has birthed? The art, and inventions, and culture, and sophistication! This is all just doomed to die? Rome has given too much to the world for it to simply belly up and die!" Max exclaimed wide eyed as if he was intoxicated. He wasn't intoxicated but delirium had certainly begun to set in.

The two men are traveling to Ravenna after having fled Rome. After their house was raided and burned by Alaric's men, the pair had nothing left but the shirts on their back. The soldiers only took their gold, jewelry, and other things of value, but the men had no chance to grab much of anything left before the whole thing went up in a blaze. Left with nothing and with nowhere to go and certainly not wanting to gamble that the soldiers would stay benevolent, they decided to flee the city. Maximus's parents were away in Ravenna. His father was a local politician in Rome and had undertaken the journey to see the Emperor Honorius some weeks ago. Thus, with no other options, they set out for Ravenna.

Both men were exhausted from the three days of traveling and were much too tired to continue the argument. Neither one spoke for some time. They rode in a chariot pulled by a mule, which was luckily left outside the city. Without it the trip would have taken three or four times as long. The cart was more than they could have hoped for under the circumstances. It was small and barely seated them both. Had they managed to bring their belongings, it's doubtful they would have any space for them.

The mule had been trudging along but could only traverse a few miles before requiring a long break. Max concluded that even though the mule was physically doing all the heavy lifting, sitting in a bumpy cart on a slow and monotonous journey with his stubborn uncle must be infinitely worse. He'd much rather take the place of the mindless mule. The mule is strong but it doesn't have to think. Thinking is exhausting, and rationalizing even more so. The mule would never know the toll that intellectualizing had on oneself.

Max had nothing else to do but think, save arguing with his uncle. But it was quiet between them now, yet he couldn't put the argument with his uncle out of his mind. He's used to the struggle of articulating himself and lately has developed the habit of dismissing others outright instead of wasting his time to argue a point.

At some point, Max broke the silence. "Do you think a messenger has made it to Ravenna with the news yet?" he asked without looking at Claudius.

"If one has, I'm not sure that anyone believed him. It may take three messengers arriving with the news before they start to believe it's true. It will be hard for them to fathom. Your father probably won't believe it until he hears it directly from us!"

"He may not believe it even then," Maximus quipped. They both chuckled which softened the mood. They sat in silence again for a moment.

"You know, you're much like your father," Claudius said turning toward Maximus.

"I don't want to be a politician," Max replied.

"No, no, I don't mean in that way. I never expected you to follow in his steps in that way. You're far too, hmm, artistic for all that."

Maximus took offense. "And what does that mean?"

"Maybe I misworded that. You have a propensity to think deeply about things is what I mean. You're actually much more like me in that regard."

"Oh, yes, our resident philosopher!" Max sarcastically replied.

Claudius chuckled, and snapped back, "Yes, well, all those years studying and working in academics has at least allowed me to keep up with you! Your poor parents sure couldn't."

That was true. Maximus had always been close to his uncle because for most of his life Claudius was the only person he knew who could intellectually stimulate him. In fact, Claudius had probably taught him more than he ever learned in school. But Maximus was very independent and always came to his own conclusions, never just reciting the material he was taught.

Claudius clarified himself. "I meant the reverence you have for Rome. You get that from him. You both take such pride in her."

What would his father think once he realized it was true? Rome is gone. No, he would never accept that, Maximus thought. He knows his father will want to immediately return to their home to see it for himself, but they might as well forget ever returning. They had nothing left there. The raiders had taken everything that was worth returning for. They left some churches unscathed but that was all. At least the people left in Rome could take shelter there.

That thought stopped Maximus. He suddenly realized that the raiders hadn't left the churches as good will for the people of Rome, but only because they are Christians themselves. Just as he was. This idea bothered him. It reminded him of what Claudius said of the barbarians. There's a long history between the Romans and the outside tribes, and Maximus couldn't deny that for a large part of that history, the tribes have been slowly integrating into Roman civilization. Maybe that was the fatal flaw in Rome's imperial power. The more land she conquered, and the more tribes that entered into their society, the more bloated and sickly the Empire became. It only seems natural that she would one day reach a tipping point. When the people whom she had conquered realized they were now the majority, and thus held a hidden dagger to her heart.

Darkness was beginning to fall on the pair, so they stopped at a clearing to set up camp for the night. Their destination was not far off now, and they would arrive by tomorrow. The men had a hard time sleeping with no bed or blanket or even a fire, and they would have rather not wasted the time trying to, but they couldn't travel in the dark so they tried to get what little sleep they could. Not to mention the mule needed its sleep too. They sat up against the trunk of a large tree and watched as the last rays of light disappeared over the horizon.

"Uncle, do you believe the saying 'nothing good can last forever'?" Maximus asked.

"No, my boy. In fact I believe the complete opposite. Good things come from God, and like God, they will endure forever."

His answer caught Maximus by surprise. "Then how do you reconcile that with the destruction of Rome? Was she not a city on a hill? Should she not endure forever too?"

"She will. She may be burned to ashes, but her embers will always glow. She has birthed an ideal that will be sought after for ages to come. Posterity will remember Rome, for the world is now her legacy."

Some moments passed as Maximus grappled with his uncle's words. They were hard to hear, though he couldn't help but to feel proud of his homeland in that moment. Rome was more than his birthplace; it was his identity.

"It's hard to imagine a world without Rome," Max said.

"Don't think of such things, my boy. It does us no good. Rome is maimed, but she's not dead yet. We must get some rest now before we reach Ravenna. Heaven knows what sort of scene awaits us there. Your parents will be so relieved to see you."

Claudius then drifted off to sleep still sitting upright. The night seemed darker than ever here in the wilderness. How dark the days would be when Rome was only a memory, Maximus thought. He closed his eyes and some time passed. He didn't know how long. Maybe a few minutes or maybe some hours. Either way, soon day would break.

Thinking of Rome

Mohammad Lonlabe

Ulrich surveyed the landscape from the ridge he was ascending. The dry hills rolled endlessly before him as he rested.

It was quiet. And not in a good way.

The calm silence that fell over the Apulian countryside didn't fit with the bright sunshine that came with midday in southern Italy. He knew there were people around; it wasn't a wasteland after all. But they were scared. Civil war had torn this region of Italy apart for several years now as Bohemond and his half-brother Roger struggled for the title of their father's crown.

People got nasty when rule of law broke down like this. Ulrich was only twenty years old, but he'd already seen it with his own eyes.

As Ulrich rounded a corner on the hill he stopped.

He couldn't put his finger on it but the feeling of unease that had been building in him for nearly an hour had finally reached a crescendo and his sense of danger was overwhelming.

He drew his sword in an instant, pulling the long blade out of the sling over his shoulder and not a moment too soon. From behind a turn in the path just ahead of him a knight appeared as though out of nowhere brandishing an ornate saber in his direction.

"Turn back," the knight shouted. "This road is closed. You're not welcome here!"

Ulrich bared his teeth. He was in no mood to be threatened. He held his ground and didn't move an inch while he sized up his opponent.

The knight facing him was in simple garb, with a mail hauberk, a steel cap, and a nose bridge covering a face that betrayed more age than the knight's stance would indicate. "Who do you think you are? I am just passing through," Ulrich said.

"We've had enough of your kind *passing through* these parts," the knight retorted. "Begone."

Ulrich glared at him. This stranger seemed confident despite his graying beard. Ulrich held his sword at his hip in an offensive stance but didn't move a muscle, waiting to see if this knight was serious or if it was a bluff.

The silence returned as the two stared at each other, broken only by the rustling of the dry dirt as the gentle summer wind passed over them.

Then the stranger lunged forward and Ulrich sprang into action, swinging his greatsword up and catching the incoming blow at the hilt.

The other man was quick to recover though, continuing his attack with a flurry of strikes aimed at Ulrich's head, waist, and legs.

Ulrich caught them all, then launched a counterattack, swinging high, and then again across at the knight's chest. To his surprise the old man deflected them with incredible speed, but Ulrich followed up with a sharp kick to the leg that caused his opponent to stumble backwards before quickly regaining his stance.

The two of them stared at one another again, not saying a word. Ulrich could hear the whistle of the wind over the hills and the pounding of his own heartbeat and nothing else. Whoever this stranger was, he was very good. It had taken everything Ulrich had just to block those strikes, and he had dodged attacks that Ulrich had killed far younger men with.

As they sized each other up, Ulrich heard another sound penetrate the empty hills. Footsteps. Several pairs, rushing up from the other side of the hill.

Reinforcements.

As if sensing Ulrich's fear, the stranger jumped forward again, but this time Ulrich was ready. He caught the extended saber in his crossguard and twisted, sending his opponent's weapon clattering to the ground. In his shock, the other knight didn't see Ulrich's foot as it came up and connected with his stomach, sending him flying backwards.

Just as Ulrich positioned himself between the defeated knight and his fallen sword, Ulrich saw figures round the hill and his heart sank.

Eight, no, nine soldiers with spears stood facing him.

"Stay back, Sergio!" the old knight shouted from the ground. "Don't come any closer."

Ulrich was confused. As he pointed his sword toward his opponent's neck, he looked back and forth from the knight to the men who had rounded the hill. A young man stood at the forefront, his eyes glimmering with anger as he pointed a spear at Ulrich. He was shaking, terrified.

It suddenly dawned on him; these were not soldiers at all. Behind the nervous young man, the figures became clearer. Two were women, one a young boy no older than eleven, and most of the others had gray hair. What he had thought were spears were actually sharpened sticks.

"What is going on here?" Ulrich shouted. He brandished his long sword back and forth between the small party and the man on the ground. "Who are you?"

"We're defending our village!" screamed the young man, his nervousness seeping into his voice. "You stay away!"

Ulrich waved his sword at him and the man jumped backwards three steps, still gripping his makeshift spear like his life depended on it.

"Explain yourself," Ulrich said, turning to the old knight. "Why did you attack me?"

"Are you not here to rob us?" The man was slowly getting to his feet now while Ulrich watched him cautiously. "You're a Lombard, are you not?"

Ulrich's sword was immediately at the man's neck; the crowd behind them flinched.

"Call me a Lombard again. . . ." Ulrich dared.

"You certainly talk like one."

"My parents were Swiss!"

"And not you?"

"I'm just a lone mercenary!"

Ulrich was the one seething now, his anger beginning to simmer while the old knight studied him with calm eyes.

"Swiss? You're a long way from home it seems."

"You're one to talk." Ulrich tapped the insignia on the knight's tunic with his sword. "The lion of San Marco? You're a long way from home, Venetian. What's a fish like you doing so far out of water?"

The knight sighed. "My name is Giorgio. I fought with Domenico Silvio against the Normans at Dyrrhachium. After retaking the fortress we tried to sail south to Corfu, but our ship was blown off course and we got stranded here on the wrong side of the Adriatic." He had a melancholy look to his eyes, as though he was recounting events from his childhood despite the fact that this was only a few years ago.

"Without any clear way to get home, we tried waging guerilla warfare against Robert Guiscard's army until he died. Then the civil war erupted and I have been wandering here ever since. My comrades died of plague or wounds long ago, so I am the last one here."

"And you're just staying here? You're not trying to go home? No wife or kids waiting for you?" Giorgio smiled. It was a sad smile, one that only age and immense sadness can produce.

"I think about returning to my wife every day. But the villagers here implored me for my help, and I think of what my wife would say if I told her that I turned them down."

Ulrich turned his attention to the small band of peasants that were watching their exchange. They truly looked emaciated, all of them thin and gaunt and not a smile to be seen on a single face. "Who are they? What is their problem?"

Giorgi's face hardened; Ulrich could feel his mood change.

"They're the last farming village left in these parts. The rest have been too ravaged by the war to continue. The lawlessness has given rise to bandits. I've been with them for the last month. One of the local gangs of bandits has threatened to poison their well and destroy their entire livelihoods if they don't turn over half of their livestock and grain."

Ulrich looked over to the small band of villagers. Their despair became incredibly clear to him at that moment. None of them were cut out for war, only a single young man among them and clearly not one with much fighting experience. The one Giorgio had addressed as Sergio stood at the forefront; he had been prepared to fight, but his inexperience was plain.

"These bandits," Ulrich said, turning to Giorgio, "Lombards, I assume?"

"You guessed it. Mercenaries at one point, I believe; their numbers are small now, just eight men, but still more than enough to overwhelm this small village of fifty peasants." Ulrich stewed on this information, but Giorgio wasn't finished.

"Their leader is a particularly savage man, and ugly old Lombard by the name of Francesco."

Ulrich felt the hairs on the back of his neck stand up. "Francesco? Did you say his name was. . . ."

"That's right." Giorgio regarded him curiously. "Does that name mean anything to you?"

Ulrich was breathing slowly now. Half his life had been haunted by the thought of this moment, and it was finally upon him. He felt the scar that crossed his left cheek tingle.

"This Francesco"—Ulrich's nostrils flared as he spoke the name—"did he have any fingers missing on his left hand?"

The silence that followed Ulrich's question told him everything. Dry dust blowing in the wind was the only indicator that time hadn't stopped on this barren hilltop.

"You know this man." Giorgio was stating this, not asking anymore. "You know what kind of person he is."

"When will these bandits arrive?"

"Anytime over the next two days. They said they'd collect their demand at the first full moon in August."

Ulrich tossed his sword. The silence broke apart as the steel blade clattered to the ground at Giorgio's feet, and the audience of villagers gasped and broke out in frightened whispers.

"You have my sword." Ulrich said, staring resolutely into the old knight's eyes. "When these bandits arrive, I will fight with you no matter the cost."

*　*　*

As the mid-afternoon sun waned, the small party made its way to the village, with the locals leading the way and Ulrich and Giorgio bringing up the rear.

"My parents died when I was about five, while we were doing business in northern Italy. I was homeless on the streets for a short while before I got caught pickpocketing from a mercenary company," Ulrich explained. "Instead of beating me, the company leader took pity on me and gave me food and shelter and taught me how to fight. He was a harsh man, but a kind one. His name was Giacomo, Piedmontese. When I was about eight years old he started putting me to work, sending me into fights and into night raids. I killed my first man at about nine."

Ulrich paused. It was only as he spoke the words aloud did he fully register how unusual his childhood must seem to most people.

"I got pretty good with a sword," he continued. "It was really all I knew, and I was a pretty big lad for my age. Then one day Giacomo got badly injured in battle and the wound got infected. He died after three days of agony.

I was distraught, but the rest of the soldiers paid me no heed. They needed to choose a new leader, and the man who fought his way to the top was not as charitable as Giacomo had been. He took power through the backing of all of the other Lombards in the company."

"Francesco." Giorgio let the statement hang in the air. It didn't need confirmation.

"Francesco was cruel and cunning, and he had . . . different ideas about what to do with eleven-year-old boys in the company."

The old knight said nothing as they walked, but he stared at Ulrich with rapt intent.

"He gave me this when he first came into my tent"—Ulrich pointed to the large scar on the side of his face—"and threatened to cut my throat if I screamed. But he underestimated me, and I was able to cut off half of his hand before escaping."

"And after that?" Giorgio asked.

"I've been wandering Italy and Illyria ever since. There've been lots of wars, so I've fought for whoever was most willing to pay me."

Their small party rounded the corner of the hill they were traversing and for a moment they lost sight of the villagers ahead of them. As Ulrich and Giorgio passed the bend in the path, Ulrich caught his breath at the magnificent sight before them. Towering over them, resplendent in the midday sun, was a magnificent structure, at least thirty feet tall. It was a long, hollowed wall made of giant square pillars, each one topped with a rounded arch, one after the other in a row that seemed to stretch on forever. Atop this long row of arches was a second set of arches, even larger than the ones below, and above that a third row of arches, these ones miniscule in comparison, to form what appeared to be an enormous, elevated walkway, the scale of which Ulrich had never seen.

"What . . . what is—"

"Never seen an aqueduct?" Giorgio seemed to take pleasure in his amazement.

"An aqueduct? Never; what is this?"

"It's for transporting water. This is why we are here, Ulrich; this is what brings the well water to their village."

As they passed by it, Ulrich stared at the length of the gigantic pathway. It towered over them and stretched all the way across the valley that was ahead of them. At the bottom of the valley, a small collection of farms and houses were situated along the base of the great structure.

"The riverbed here dried up many decades ago," Giorgio explained, "but the aqueduct brings water from a well at the top of the hill over there. The water still runs along the top of the duct, and the villagers have tapped into it with pipes. Without this structure, and without the well, all fifty people in this village would die."

Ulrich stared up at it in wonder as they approached. The stones cut for the columns were of a size he had never imagined, stacked so high he was at a loss for how on earth they had been lifted.

"What is this though? Who built this? Certainly not the villagers."

Giorgio laughed. "No, these villagers are but humble farmers; they could never build such a thing as this."

"But who?"

"Why, the Romans built this of course."

Ulrich regarded him with suspicion. "Not possible. I've fought with and against Romans; they're a bunch of incompetent crooks."

Giorgio chuckled. "Greeks. They are not true Romans; they just wear their name for the prestige it comes with."

They reached the base of one of the stone columns on their way to the village and Ulrich marveled at its scale.

"This structure has been here for over one thousand years. Kings, armies, entire nations have come and gone, but the legacy of the Romans remains, and even to this day their works keep these poor villagers alive."

Ulrich was astounded. It certainly seemed like the kind of structure that could last a thousand years, but it was still hard for him to believe.

"Come." Giorgio smiled at him and indicated the top of the next hill where the aqueduct disappeared. "Let me show you the well."

Atop the hill, an enormous stone well towered over the village. As Ulrich reached the edge he looked over the large stone wall into the depths below. The bottom of the well could not be seen, and it must have been about nine feet across.

"The water down there," Giorgio indicated, "is natural spring water, which once upon a time traveled all the way from here to Rome, along a network of aqueducts like this one. They had the entire land covered in these structures. How they were able to dig such an enormous well, or how they even knew the spring water was here in the first place, I will never know."

The two of them sat down and gazed upon the small village in the valley as the sun began inching its way toward the horizon, casting a beautiful reddish glow along the entire landscape. The young man, Sergio, joined them with a wineskin.

Ulrich gave him thanks and took a swig before passing it to Giorgio.

Below them, the small number of families began corralling their goats and chickens into pens for the night and giving them food.

"This will be my last battle," said Giorgio, solemnly. "I've fought in wars all my life. After this I am going home to see my wife. I couldn't imagine a better fight to end my career than defending this village. This well. This legacy."

As he brought up his career, Ulrich asked Giorgio something that had been nagging him for hours. "You said you fought at the battle of Dyrrhachium?"

Giorgio looked at him, questioningly. "Yes, I was part of the siege to take it back from the Normans in 1083."

"Looks like we just missed each other. I was there in the winter of 1082."

The old knight let the statement hang in the air as they looked one another in the eyes.

"You fought for the Normans didn't you?"

"Aye," Ulrich responded. "That I did."

The two stared at one another, sizing each other up for a minute before they both burst out in laughter.

*   *   *

Ulrich awoke with a start.

The bell was ringing.

He disentangled himself from his sword as he got to his feet. He always slept wrapped around his blade; it was a force of habit that he'd started years ago. He burst out of the barn and stared out at the small hamlet as the villagers panicked at the sound of the alarm.

"Everyone get in position! Grab your spears and don't panic!"

Ulrich began to gather the frightened farmers as best he could. It had been two days since he'd first arrived at the village and seen the defenses that Giorgio had prepared against the bandits. He was still incredibly impressed with the old knight. All of the entrances into the village were blocked off save for two, with stone and rubble piled high around the outer buildings to funnel any intruders into one of the narrow entrances into the town. Bells had been set up at the well and down in the valley in order to signal an attack, and every man, woman, and child had a sharpened stick to fight with. It wasn't much, but it was the best this town could hope for.

As the frightened townsfolk gathered around him with their makeshift spears, Ulrich saw the object of everyone's attention. There, at the north entrance to the village, three mounted riders slowly made their way through the narrow passage into the town square. They had a cool air about them, as though they were surveying the scene of a crime. No one spoke as they approached; the silence of the moment hung in the air, broken only by the footsteps of the horses as they approached.

This must be an advance party. Giorgio and Sergio should be returning from the well soon.

Ulrich approached the three men at the corridor, making himself seen as he blocked their path into the village.

"You don't look like you belong here." The man on the lead horse gave him an ugly smile. "We take it our demands have been refused."

"You're not welcome here," Ulrich replied. "Tell your master to find someone else to cow."

"You fools!" The man glared at him now. "Do you really think you can defy us without facing retribution?"

Ulrich drew his sword and took an offensive stance with his blade at his hip.

Three men on horses. He'd fought worse odds.

The bandits drew their swords as well. They weren't too far from him as they stood. They sized each other up for what felt like an eternity, Ulrich's heart pounding as he waited for the moment to come. They evidently hadn't expected resistance, and now they were thrown off. Then the lead man shouted and charged with his horse.

Ulrich stared at the sword in the man's right arm as it approached him and deftly switched his grip and jumped to his right, landing firmly on his backfoot as the horse raced by him. Swinging his sword high on his left side as he did it, he felt it connect with the man's unprotected left shoulder, and he heard a scream as a spray of blood hit his face.

Behind him, he heard one of the villagers scream, but he didn't have time to look back. The next horse was nearly upon him and had altered its trajectory to go right at him.

Thinking on his feet, Ulrich grabbed his sword and rolled to his left, barely avoiding the passing beast. At the last minute he put his momentum into a weak swing with only his right arm and barely felt the tip of his blade clip something behind him.

A blood-curdling screech confirmed what he'd hoped: he'd gotten the horse's back ankle and ended its charge.

Then he looked up and froze. The last rider was upon him and wasn't charging with his sword; he was barreling his horse straight at Ulrich and was about to collide with him.

Ulrich brought his sword up at the last minute and plunged the long steel shaft straight into the horse's neck. Warm blood coated his hands, his arms, and splattered across his face before he felt the full force of the beast's momentum hit him square on and he was thrown backwards, his feet leaving the ground, and for a brief second he was completely weightless floating in mid-air.

He hit the ground with a powerful crash, and he felt all the air leave his lungs. His sword was gone, his hands clutching at the ground around him, and an enormous weight crushing him from above.

He slowly felt himself taking in his surroundings once more and realized the horse and the last rider were both on top of him, completely lifeless. His sword had gone right through the horse's neck and pierced the bandit's heart.

He gasped for air again; he was absolutely covered in blood, but none of it was his own. As he extricated himself from the bodies, he turned around to see all of the villagers looking at him, some with blood on their spears. Ulrich only now realized that one of the bandits lay dead at their feet, stabbed to death with what seemed to be dozens of holes in his body.

As he got to his feet he stared back at the villagers. They had gathered around him at a distance, but none of them said anything; they just watched him silently. He wasn't sure if it was fear or awe, or a mix of both, but the understanding went through all of them. They'd won.

Then he heard it again. The bell was ringing. Ulrich spun around and picked his bloody sword up off the ground.

Someone was ringing the bell. Was it for victory? Why now?

Then he realized. It was faint, not the bell of the town.

The well!

He spun around frantically and looked at the villagers. They understood too. There were allegedly eight bandits, and they'd just killed three. There were five more and only Giorgio and Sergio to deal with them.

Ulrich cursed and took off, following the path of the gigantic aqueduct that loomed over them as he sprinted up the hill toward the well.

It took him several minutes to reach the top. The gigantic stone structure casting long shadows over the valley in the evening sun, he felt very small by comparison. He kept running.

Then he saw them, three bodies lying on the path as it curved up toward the hilltop.

As Ulrich passed them, he looked down. Two of them he didn't recognize, lightly armored men with ugly looking sabers. Bandits.

But the third made his heart skip a beat. Sergio. The young farmer from the village. Like the two bandits, he had a mortal sword wound in his sternum. His makeshift spear showed no blood on it; Giorgio must have killed both of these bandits himself.

Giorgio! Where is Giorgio?

Ulrich raced on, certain that the rest of the bandits were headed to the well at the source of the great aqueduct. He was starting to notice his own fatigue now; he hadn't had a drink in hours and his heart had been pounding non-stop since the bell had woken him.

As he got to the top of the hill he saw them: three men approaching the large stone well dragging the body of a third. They were about twenty yards ahead of him but moving very slowly.

There was no haste to these men; they hadn't a fear in the world. Like everyone else in this quiet, forgotten countryside, time seemed not to register to them.

"Don't kill him yet," said a familiar, raspy voice. "We want his bowels to empty into the well."

Ulrich could see the man they were dragging now, his blue cloak unmistakable. It was Giorgio; he had a bad wound in the shoulder of his sword arm, blood staining his whole right flank.

Then they spotted Ulrich.

He'd gotten above them by now, approaching the well from the side; he'd positioned himself on the high ground overlooking their path to the well.

The two dragging Giorgio dropped him and pulled out their swords, sizing him up. The third man stared at him. His beard was longer and grayer, but his black eyes and rotted teeth were burned into Ulrich's memory.

"Francesco." He let the statement hang in the air, with all the contempt he could muster behind it.

Francesco drew his sword now, the three of them slowly advancing up the hill toward him.

"I don't believe it," Francesco stated as the three of them advanced. "Of all the places to find a ghost." Ulrich was backing up as they crept closer; he was nearly at the well now, waiting for one of them to make the first move.

"What are you doing here, *boy*? Come to die like the old man?"

"I said I'd give him a hand defending this village," Ulrich said with a smirk. "I hear you've got one left." Rage swept over Francesco's face as Ulrich noticed his left hand twitch where the two missing fingers once were.

"You're outnumbered!" said the bandit to his left.

"There are three dead bodies in the village who said the same thing."

His words were met with a wave of realization among the three bandits as the blood covering his tunic and sword finally registered with them.

Then the first man leapt at him with a cry, swinging his blade at Ulrich's head.

Ulrich parried, then swept his sword across him to meet the second man who was not close behind, catching him before he could defend himself and slicing open his neck.

Ulrich wasted no time, swinging his sword back up to block the first man's attack once more and then driving the tip of his sword straight into the man's gut and out the other side.

Both men fell to the ground, one rolling a few feet down the hill before his body lay still. Francesco stared at him, his fear kept at bay by his anger as he realized he was completely alone. "It's not possible. . . . You're . . . you're not real!"

Ulrich approached him slowly, sword at the ready. He had the high ground and the longer reach.

"Get back! No closer!" Francesco was frantic now, stumbling backwards down the hill, his saber in front of him and his eyes glued to Ulrich's blood-soaked sword. Ulrich said nothing. He'd waited half his life for this moment.

"Stay away!" Francesco screamed. "Stay—"

His last sentence was cut off as his foot caught on a rock; and all of a sudden Francesco fell backwards, the steep hill opening up behind him, and with a crash his body collapsed against the rocks.

Ulrich leaped forward, but it was no use. A sharp rock had collided with the back of Francesco's neck as his body connected with the dirt.

Ulrich stared in disbelief. His revenge had been so close he could nearly taste it, and now it was over.

Francesco was dead on account of his own carelessness.

Ulrich broke from his reverie and whirled around. Giorgio was stirring and shuffling in the ground a few yards away. Dropping his sword, Ulrich sprinted over to him and caught the old Venetian giving him a weak smile.

"Ulrich. . . ."

"They're dead, Giorgio. All of them," Ulrich said, bending over his comrade. "The well is safe; we're going to be okay. I'm going to carry you back to the village; they can take care of you."

Giorgio coughed as he shook his head. "Not this time. This was my last battle; I told you that. This wound is too deep. I've lost too much blood."

Ulrich could hear the faintness in Giorgio's voice and the struggle it took him to speak, but he ignored it. "No. We're going to help you. This isn't over; you can survive."

The old man reached over and placed his hand on Ulrich's arm. Such a simple motion, but in his current state it felt like a Herculean effort.

"It's too late, Ulrich. My time is up. I finally get to go home. I get to see my wife. She's been waiting so many years. . . . I've missed her so much."

With that, Giorgio gave a deep, rattling breath and went silent.

Ulrich stared down at him in disbelief, until finally he realized his eyes were welling up. He looked around him.

The sun was setting now, beautiful red and orange streaks shining through the eternal arches of the aqueduct as Ulrich carefully carried Giorgio's body down the hill and back to the village.

Sarco

T. B. McGill

The man lay in repose in the rather inexplicably climate-controlled pod. The contours of the interior were reminiscent of an overwrought Italian sports car, all leather and dashboard. Automatic transmission, to be certain. The thought, as it crossed his mind, made him chuckle softly; *automatic transmission . . . now that's funny*. He turned restlessly, trying to find a comfortable position in the cramped confines of the pod. He scooted some cardboard to one side and fluffed his winter coat to pillow at the side of his head. Before too long, he fell back into a restless sleep.

He dreamed. He dreamed of an old friend. Not that old, as it happens; he had died only last year. Overdosed on something, Fentanyl he assumed, though he had not ever found out for certain, ferried off to the morgue unceremoniously as he was. He never tended to dream of lost friends, which was not a mark of the man's callousness, but rather the suffusion of loss in a life like his; if he dreamed of all he had lost, he would never stop dreaming. *Ghosts*, he thought to himself, *in such a place like this*. It was a silent ghost, smiling a familiar smile, crooked teeth and all. They shared a bottle of vino, and he was gone.

He was rudely awakened by Charon. The man blinked away sleep from his weary eyes to see a skeletal hand extended his way.

"Credit, debit, or cash accepted," said Charon helpfully.

Aren't you Greek, anyways? thought the man, as he waved away the apparition. "Not interested." Charon continued to stare from under his shadowy hood, bobbing upon the water of the Tiber River, acting as if it were the Lethe.

"Credit, debit, or cash," repeated Charon.

"That's supposed to be my line, anyways," chirped the man, as he rolled on to his other side to ignore the ferryman. Charon took this as an invitation to play an ad for a local funeral home. Unskippable.

More dreams. More ghosts. More vino.

Sleet tapped and lapped at the curvature of the pod, a cozy noise, when one was sheltered from the touch of it. Charon seemed to have floated downriver, perhaps sensing the man's lack of coin for the journey. A blessing for once, to not possess such payment to render. No chance to accidentally issue a remittance that could not be rescinded.

"Saturdays are half off Saturn days!" the pod squawked. "Go out in style with one of our most premium packages! Last will, mortuary ministration, and free crematorium service is included with purchase, so your next of kin can rest easy while you rest easy. Shall we *ring* you up?"

An image of the planet Saturn danced around the ceiling of the pod, as the golden visage of a bearded deity emerged from the rings of the planet, casting dazzling light across the interior.

"The time is currently 3:30 a.m. Cash, credit, or debit, young man?" blustered Saturn, rudely. "For the low price of three thousand euros, you can add the Plutonic bonus package on to your order and pick a custom inscription for your headstone, complementing the dozens of beautiful design templates on offer. Please keep your epitaph to a maximum of one hundred characters." Saturn looked down at the unresponsive man with what appeared to be an air of impertinence. "Cash. Credit. Or Debit," he boomed.

The man's foot swung out and kicked the dashboard, causing Saturn to flicker and dissipate. *Who the hell designed this thing?* the man thought to himself. *What psychopathic ad agency is behind all of this?* he pondered, even as he ignored a procession of bespoke burial urns, dancing across the face of the pod like drive-in movie theater hotdogs. *I'd almost rather be out in the cold. Almost.* A cartoon skeleton played a ribcage like a marimba as the urns danced out of an open door at the side of the pod.

More restless sleep. More ghosts.

A cheery female voice pierced the veil. "We here at Sarco understand that you care deeply about the environment. Our pods are designed with a net zero carbon footprint in mind. All carbon dioxide used in the process is ethically sourced from local dairy farms, and 5 percent of all proceeds go toward supporting Happy Crickets' Bug Emporium. You will breathe the CO2, and you will be happy!"

I will not eat the bugs, thought the man. He half expected Klaus Schwab to appear before him as a ghostly apparition next. As a mercy, he did not.

Saturn poked his head in the side of the pod. "It is 5:00 a.m.!" he rumbled.

"Thank you so much for the info," the man mumbled to himself sardonically.

The man awoke next to the visage of a Roman emperor looking down upon him. Marcus Aurelius, to be precise.

"For the stone which has been thrown up, it is no evil to come down, nor indeed any good to have been carried up," he uttered, in a dulcet tone. "Of human life, the time is a point, and the substance is in a flux, and the perception dull, and the composition of the whole body subject to putrefaction, and the soul a whirl, and fortune hard to divine, and fame a thing devoid of judgment. And, to say all in a word, everything which belongs to the body is a stream, and what belongs to the soul is a dream and vapor, and life is a warfare and a stranger's sojourn, and after-fame is oblivion." He paused in stolid observation before saying, "Cash or credit?"

Isn't Stoicism a bit ironic in this context? the man thought.

There was a knock on the outside of the pod. The man inside did his best to ignore it, but it continued unabated.

"Sir, you can't be sleeping in there," came a voice from outside. More knocking, followed by a rattling sound as the pod's exterior was being unlatched. A slight hiss of depressurization was quickly accompanied by the cold rush of wintry atmosphere invading the previously warm enclosure.

"Oh for fucks' sake!" cried the man inside, clutching his winter coat about his person.

"You need to get out of there, sir; there's a line forming." The speaker was *Polizia Municipale*, wearing the sleek four-button Giorgio Armani jacket that typified their station.

The man inside blinked away the piercing morning sun as he stirred into waking.

"Damn it! Fine! Hold your horses! Sheesh!"

There was indeed a line formed outside as the man clambered out of the Sarco pod. This particular pod was adorned with the colorful stripes of a rainbow flag all up and down the sides. Appropriately enough, the person at the front of the line was sporting a bright purple frock of hair with the sides shaved short, a rainbow pin alighted upon his chest. He was looking at him with scarcely hidden disdain.

"Pretty selfish, all things considered," said the purple-haired man as he climbed into the Sarco pod.

"Whatever," said the old, bearded man, looking down at him, Saturn-like. "Say hi to Marcus for me."

As the pod closed around its new occupant, the man sighed and marked his breath materializing in the morning light. It was a crisp, cool morning, and at least a dozen people were lined up, waiting for their turn to kill themselves. Yuppies, businessmen, college students—all of whom were noticeably better dressed and in better health than himself. He gathered his few belongings into his cart and made his way out into the bustling city of Rome.

Alive.

No More Latin

Ndabaningi

*No more Latin, no more French
no more sitting on the hard school bench*

William shifted uncomfortably on his bench, a pew in the Chapel made for smaller backsides. The little shard of doggerel had come to him out of the blue, along with a sudden warm feeling from all those years ago: the ardent desire to leave, the growing excitement of imminent release. He was back, there, then, all those years ago. Break-up Day. The school would be nothing but a memory for a few weeks. Glorious weeks. Sun-drenched weeks on his grandfather's farm. No more Boarding Masters, no more Assembly, no more cold, gray meals of dubious provenance wolfed down in the draughty Dining Hall. No more annoying younger boys whose names you'd never remember, no more dangerous older ones you'd never forget, no more classmates you only knew by surname. Friends would be missed, of course, though one or two would visit the farm. Besides, happy reunions would keep—the only silver lining of the impending gloom of the next term. A distant, future prospect, that would grow ominously in the last week of the holidays. For now, it was only sunlight, like the beams that shone through the stained-glass windows warming his face. Break-up Day. A last Chapel service — the drone of Psalms chanted, stupefying Readings, mumbled Prayers, Hymns half-heartedly sung—and he'd be free. He dragged himself back into the present and consciously suppressed the frown that threatened to become a permanent feature. He missed all that now. Psalms, Readings, Prayers, Hymns, the Rubrics of High Anglicanism. He hadn't realized how they had affected him, become a subconscious lodestone in his life. He stared up the aisle to his left where the reverend was halfway through a reading. Some new translation. Modern. Relevant. Completely devoid of gravitas. The cheerfulness of the man hadn't struck a chord either. *He's not even wearing a cassock, let alone a surplus.* He'd opened the service with a brief disclaimer. The Old Boys would notice that the King James Version had been discarded from the prayers, the readings, the rubrics. He'd added something positive about "keeping up with the times" and William had groaned inwardly. He'd been looking forward to a proper trip down memory lane and now this little man threatened to ruin it. And on this day, of all days. On this occasion. *Couldn't they have just dusted off the old Prayerbook for today? Couldn't they have honored the old man's memory as he would have liked it?* Old Boys' Day and Reginald Percival's Memorial Service. William had never attended an Old Boy's Day, but today he'd made the effort to be here. He'd headed out long before dawn and had negotiated the first hills in misty darkness. He knew there were others who'd come from even farther afield: Johannesburg; Cape Town; one had even come from Zambia. They were all here out of respect for old Masokisi—Headmaster, Latin Master, dedicated-if-not-overly-competent Cricket Umpire. It was on the cricket field that the old man had earned his nickname. *Masokisi*: Zulu for socks. The school had always had a strong contingent of farm boys, fluent in Zulu, and they'd quickly settled on his socks being his defining feature. In the classroom he'd always been impeccably, if somewhat eccentrically, dressed: gray trousers and a brownish tweed coat with leather reinforced elbow patches set off with a different bow tie every day. But when it came to striding around the cricket field it was another matter: floppy sun hat, a bright white lab coat, and khaki "empire-builder" shorts that came down to knobby knees where they were met by a pair of pale blue socks that seemed to defy gravity. Those socks, always in the same shade of pale blue (How many pairs did he have? It was a matter of endless conjecture), always pulled up smartly, could be seen from anywhere on the field as Masokisi strode, stork-like, along the pitch, dispensing advice and cautioning against anything falling even slightly short of gentlemanly play. It was a testament to his popularity—always strict, yet always fair—that he had landed his benign yet descriptive moniker. Other members of staff had not been so fortunate. Some had been saddled with various imaginative yet insulting nicknames—scatological or mocking some impediment. William wondered if the current "more diverse" company of school boys were equally inventive. He doubted it. Among the White boys, there were probably fewer with farming backgrounds, and the African ones were undoubtedly the sons of well-to-do urban Blacks, devoid of, or actively playing down, the rural roots of a generation ago. The Indians wouldn't contribute anything in that department, and the smattering of Coloreds (a people well known for their sharp wits and inventive talk) were probably too few in number to pin a biting nickname to a teacher and make it stick. He wondered what the school slang was like nowadays. In his day the school had been so insular it practically had its own language. That wouldn't be the case now. Every one of the little buggers would be hooked up to the "global culture" through their little screens, their talk probably peppered with ghetto Americanisms. William sighed, almost audibly. It was good to be back on these hallowed grounds—every quad, classroom, passageway, and dorm brought memories flooding back. Yet he wasn't having a good day. Too much change, too many jarring incongruencies. The Chapel was still exactly as it had always been, though renovations had been announced with much excitement. For now, it remained exactly as it had been forty years ago. It even smelled the same—musty and resinous, a sacred odor. The pews were still stacked, mini-grandstand-like along the aisle so you had to look left or right to see the altar, the lectern, the ancient organ, and the gallery where the senior boys would sit. The advantage of this curious layout is that everybody could see everybody else in the building, at all times. As a boy this presented the obvious drawback that the Master could always see what you were up to. Every infraction, from elbowing one of your fellows to less than hearty chanting of the interminable Psalms, could immediately be detected and tallied for punishment—the leather for the younger boys, the cane for the older ones. Those Psalms. Hymns were generally popular with the boys, especially the ones where you could subtly change the words and sing really loudly. But the drone of plainchant Psalms was grinding. It was curious how much he missed them now. Every one with its Latin name. *Paratum cor meum*; *Jubilate Deo*; *Lætatus sum*; *Qui confidunt*; *Nunc dimittis*. . . . William smiled at the last one. The Canticle of Simeon if he remembered correctly. "Lord, now let thy servant depart in peace. . . ." *Nunc dimittis*, which had transformed into "Nkawu, dismiss us." A particularly loathed Boarding Master (Mr. . . . Mr. Barrington? Ballentyne? He couldn't remember) was known as Nkawu—monkey—on account of his glowering, simian countenance. What he wouldn't give to hear the boys' plainchant now. He wondered what his fourteen-year-old self would have thought of that. He would probably have scoffed at the notion. He would have had no idea of how "institutionalized" he'd been by this place. And for good reason. It had all seemed so alien, so strange to him when his parents had dropped him off almost a lifetime ago. He'd been six years old when he'd started boarding, just like his father and his grandfather before him. Their stories from their time here hadn't really prepared him for a life completely regimented by this place. The daily routine of roll calls and lights out, of communal meals and PT—physical training; later changed to PE, physical education—of academic rigor and hard competitive sports had been a shock to the system. But the Chapel, with its arcane rituals, its sounds, its smells, its mantra-like repetitions and contemplation, had been the strangest, and what had left the longest-lasting impression, as he now understood. Of course he'd missed the freedom of the farm, the feeling of spiky grass under hardened bare feet—what a terrible softening effect the school shoes had had on them!—the sunrises, the farm dogs, the lambs and the kids, his old cat that jostled him in bed and sometimes brought in a rat with a growl before devouring it in the space under his cupboard. He'd missed hunting field mice, and catching fat flying ants with the laborers' children, and the Zulu banter when they'd roasted or fried them over little fires. But he'd made friends quickly and, after a week of crying himself to sleep under a rough gray army blanket in a cold junior dorm, had adjusted well. It was the Chapel, though, that frightened and yet welcomed him at the same time. He hadn't been prepared for that. His family were "bush-Baptists"—not agnostic, just the type who only went to the village church at Christmas and Easter. His father always said he found God "the All Father" on the open veld and communed with "the Man of Sorrows" in the dark, feeling His presence at hand when he went after wayward livestock or mended a fence or checked the jackal traps to put one of the cunning vermin out of its misery. At the time William hadn't understood it, but it was a way of life he effortlessly slipped into when he took over the farm, as his father had taken over from his father before him. And yet, here he was, pining for the *Pater nosters*, *Agnus Deis*, and *Ave Marias* of this ancient sanctum. Something else occurred to him. In Chapel it was just the ossified names that were in Latin (apart from the *Ave Maria* sung on special occasions), but in the Dining Hall, Grace was always spoken in that not-dead tongue. "*Benedictum benedicat . . . per Jesum Christum, Dominum nostrum. . . .*" And roll call was always answered by "*Ad sum*" while *prefects* prowled. The hallowed language, the conscious stream of the West, made its presence felt through every facet of the school's life. He'd been intrigued, and when he'd started formal Latin in his fourth year under the rigid tutelage of *Magister Percival*, it had quickly become his favorite subject. *Amo, amas, amat. . . . I love, you love* (*thou lovest* in his first textbook), *he/she/it loves*. The declensions and conjugations, the tenses and prepositions, and later on the aphorisms and sayings, the lengthy quotes of Seneca, Caesar, Cicero, to be meticulously translated. . . . It all held an endless fascination for him. Even now, as the reminiscence tumbled over him, he felt a certain bitterness that he'd been forced to give it up at high school, to make way for a "more useful subject." He sighed. It was all gone now. The *ad sums*, the *benedicats*, the *magisters*, even the prefects. Earlier he'd noticed, in the temperature-controlled dining room that had replaced the hall, on the Honors Board above the shelf that held the trophies, that the *Victor Ludorum* had been changed to Sportsman of the Year. *At least it wasn't "sportsperson."*

The Headmaster, a tall athletic man who looked like he knew a lot about tennis and very little about Latin, stepped up to the lectern. He beamed a broad smile at the congregation, taking his time, seemingly intent on connecting with everyone in the Chapel on a personal level. William gritted his teeth. A portly Indian boy, a senior no doubt, waddled up to the altar and unfolded a screen on a telescoping tripod. His huffing and occasional grunts were clearly audible, amplified by the sanctuary's superior acoustics. *Boys a quarter that size would've been remorselessly mocked into shape long before they got to Final Year*. William banished the unkind thought, true though it was. A projector cast an image onto the screen. It was of an anchor with a scroll of text above the name of the school.

It flickered for a second before being replaced by a bright panorama of the school grounds. The sports fields—named after forgotten headmasters, sports masters, prominent Old Boys—spread across the screen with the school buildings nestled at their center, a small hamlet of quads and dorms and classrooms. The dining room was off to one side and facing the main gate. The first thing a visitor would see was the Chapel. The grinning man focused a laser pointer on the cross-shaped building and then faced his audience. In breezy, excited tones he informed the Old Boys, parents, teachers, friends, and scholars that the "school community" had met its fundraising targets. Phase One of the Jubilee Project could proceed. He let the little red point linger on the Chapel for a moment and then made small circles around the adjoining covered corridors known as the Cloisters. The image faded and was replaced by a new one that materialized in a series of mosaics that worked itself out from the center of the screen. *Very professional, very "multimedia."* William suppressed a groan. The Cloisters were gone, a nearby quad had been reduced to half its size, and the cross-shaped roof was no more. . . . In their place was . . . a large square block. The Headmaster enthusiastically began to expound the benefits of the expanded Worship Centre: its capacity, its facilities, its sound booth and Wi-Fi connectivity, its stage, and its glass altar. William zoned out. After a moment, when his eyes focused, he found himself staring at a burly man across the aisle. A few seconds later their eyes met. Tertius Combrink nodded a greeting and smiled a wry smile. William lifted his hand in inconspicuous acknowledgement. The Headmaster's monologue had moved on, salesman-like, to the expansion of the "learner body." William noted it was no longer "scholars," not even "pupils," just the government's dumbed-down, un-English term "learners." Predictably, he rattled on about "equipping the boys for a changing, modern world" full of exciting challenges before, inevitably, almost breathlessly, espousing the inestimable benefits of diversity. William saw the big man opposite him cock an eyebrow. *How fitting.* He wondered whether *Dutchy* was having the same thoughts. Back in their day, Tertius Combrink had been the sum total of the school's "diversity." It hadn't been celebrated. Far from it. Saddled with the pejorative "Dutchman," the sole Afrikaans boy had been mercilessly bullied. Nearly all the boys were of English and Scottish descent. There had been a few from long-Anglicized Afrikaans families who had made up for it by being even more anti-Afrikaans than their schoolmates and one or two Irish boys who endured a milder form of contempt. Tertius had been the only *genuine Dutchman.* Rock Spider, Clutchplate, Hairyback, et cetera, et cetera—over his school carrier he'd no doubt been called every name in the book. William wondered what had possessed his parents to send him to such an English school. Yet, the more the others had bullied him, the more resilient he had become. Several tit-for-tat bloody noses, black eyes, and a fearless obstinacy had led to begrudging tolerance; proficiency on the sports fields had led to mutual respect. Outwardly he'd conformed to the school, lost his accent, become just another boy like them, and the insulting "Dutchman" had softened to an affectionate "Dutchy." For some of his peers it was even a surprise to hear him speaking to his parents in Afrikaans—once a month when the boys were allowed to phone home or when they came to sports fixtures or school plays. It was all so ironic, William mused. Over his lifetime he'd witnessed his English heritage and culture morph and wither. From a rich heritage—epitomized by places like this, built by intrepid, hardy frontiersmen on the outer edges of an unfathomably vast empire—steeped in a history going back to the Middle Ages, replete with Latin and the hoary language of King James, it had receded; first into an outward jingoism and finally into carping opposition to the Afrikaners who, in spite of crushing defeat in the Boer War, had politically outwitted the British. For the sin of the Republic, the English in South Africa had never forgiven the Boers. It wasn't quite as simple as that. Most English South Africans had gone along with the new dispensation, had come to a *modus vivendi* with the new regime. But on a cultural level and in the media, the English had excoriated the Afrikaners. William wondered if English culture in South Africa hadn't simply come to mean "not Afrikaans." The British had turned their back on South Africa in the seventies and eighties. The cultural boycott had opened the way for American domination in the field of popular culture—film, TV—and had left the English cut off from "their home," Britain. Yet they had developed next to nothing new in South Africa, defining themselves only in opposition to the Afrikaner nationalist government, playing lip-service to the Black nationalist aspirations while, with the exception of liberals, not taking it particularly seriously. Then, with the advent of the New South Africa ("Freedom," "Democracy," the "Rainbow Nation") it had all changed. The Afrikaners had dealt with the political shock in a sudden efflorescence of culture. Music, movies, cultural events had sprung from a people who were used to being cut off on the southern tip of this vast continent. William sighed. The English had become irrelevant. While losing almost everything they once had, many, it seemed, still looked down their noses at their fellow White South Africans. He pondered briefly where Tertius was, politically, culturally. He'd have to ask him, reconnect with him over a few beers. *Tertius.* "The Third"—a popular Latin name for an Afrikaner boy. They too were the distant heirs of the Old World, of Rome. William wondered how many of his English contemporaries would even recognize it as Latin. *Not this current crop, not unless it came up in a Yank movie, maybe a bloody superhero. . . .*

The slick tennis enthusiast with the flashy teeth had moved on to his finale. Another image appeared on the screen. The school's new logo. *Not a crest; no, a "logo."* It was the image of two boys and a ball rendered in the style of Bushmanpainting-meets-flat-vector-corporate-pamphlet. Underneath was the Zulu word "*Ubunye*," Unity. William saw Tertius grimace and close his eyes. He saw the first slide in his mind's eye, the one that had flashed all too briefly at the beginning of the presentation. It was an image of an anchor cross with the date of the founding of the school, 1887. Underneath was a scroll with the text *Festina Lente*. It was a classical saying, an apparent contradiction, going back to the Greeks, popular in Rome. Make Haste, Slowly. It always took some time for Masokisi to explain it to the new boys, and he always took great pains to do so. He used to say it was similar to the English adage "more haste, less speed." Do something carefully, thoroughly, from the start and the task will be well done, sooner.

William yearned for that depth of meaning, that wisdom handed down over generations, a return to the Western waters that had flowed down the centuries and enriched the world around him.

He looked up the aisle to where a framed photograph of a man in a floppy sun hat stood on the altar, visible again now that the screen had been rolled up. William bowed his head slightly.

VALE MAGISTER—Farewell, Master.

What Falls Behind the Wall

C. O'Brien

The glen cut through the land like a scar, and the fog settled upon it. It was quiet, still as it could be only before great violence. Lucanus Maximus, leader of the Ninth Legion's first cohort, had called upon his men to halt, and there they stood without a word, eyes scanning the misty pal which shrouded them. They drew breath, but no sound came from the eight hundred veterans of Rome save the slight clink of their shifting armor.

Emperor Hadrian and Governor Falko were bound for Vindolanda in the northern most territory of Britannia, where the Ninth were stationed. Under order the Ninth had shrank away from battle through the bleak winter of the isle, and so the painted Caledonians had moved down from the highlands where they dwelled, pushing against Rome's frontier.

It was Spring now. Lucanus had been ordered by the legatus legionis himself to march his cohort across the border and engage those Picts who had ventured too close to the fort, slaughtering them and pushing the survivors back to a distance which would not offend the emperor. Lucanus felt that he should have more men, and yet he knew that the legatus of the Ninth Legion was not a man who received happily the advice of his subordinates. His losses at Eboracum seemed to have done little but strengthen his stubborn will.

From the legionaries to the centurions, the men of the first cohort had shared in Lucanus' misgivings. The warriors of Caledonia were bold, and bolder still after a winter free from Roman advance. Even the men under Lucanus, the most battle-seasoned of the Ninth, would find difficulty here. No one knew, beyond the reach of Rome's influence, how mighty the barbarians this far north had grown, though all knew them to be great and fearsome, as the raids throughout the winter had been many and violent.

To the left of Lucanus stood the centurion Severus Vesta, who himself was destined to serve as primus pilus one day. If merit were all it took then Lucanus felt that his dear friend would be worthy of governor, but these days the governing of Rome and her territories fell only to a scheming class of men to whom honor and glory were foreign, and who's affections were to power, influence, and wealth alone.

Lucanus and Vesta had come to know this, as had the men of the first cohort.

Their influence had spread the message so that now many of the Ninth had come to question the decisions and motivations of their leaders, though they remained a minority, speaking of such matters only in hushed tones and with members of their family or brothers in their contubernium.

And now this, sent north to make safe the visiting emperor, a son not of Rome, but of Hispania, and with hardly enough bodies to make good the task at hand. Vesta and Lucanus each drew their blades. The men at their flank readied for battle, every hand gripped firm around shield, gladius, or pilum. Ordinary warfare didn't work in such terrain, and here the men were boxed in by the landscape. The Picts should not have been so close as this to Roman lands, and yet, down to the last, the men could feel them in the cloaking mist, invisible as ghosts, and terrible as a plague.

Dark clouds began to roll across the sky like the waves of Neptune's wrath, casting shadow upon the land. A heavy rain began to spit down, clearing the fog and revealing to the men the harshness of the land about them which was raised high to the east and west. When the silence broke it did so with a deep, throaty burble, the chant of the painted men. First one, and then another, and another, until hundreds of them seemed to chant like the dead risen and ready for war.

In a second all fell silent. When they appeared they did so suddenly and without sound, all about the crests of the glen with their weapons in hand and the blue paint upon their pale bodies laid bare, their braided red hair and beards like flaming manes about faces furious and still, their eyes like polished pebbles peering down at the invaders with cold, hard indignation. A chill swept through the air. Somewhere beyond the glen drums began to beat and the wind seemed to change at it.

In the land of beasts instinct ruled, and men had no need to speak their orders. Armies moved as one. Lucanus readied his shield, and his men did likewise, a ripple running across the formation like the fly twitch of a colt. The cornicen blasted his trumpet, which split across the heathen drums. One of the painted men, a great tower of a man who held a sword of equal length to himself and stood in front of the terrible mass of his kin, raised his blade before him with a single hand, and with a tongue like some great hound he licked the length of the blade, his eyes wide and wild. He screamed into the sky, and his men joined him, raising swords, and axes, and spears.

They charged as one, spilling over the glen on both sides like water at the breaking of a dam. Out of the hundreds who charged, Lucanus' gaze never left that of the man with the great sword and wild eyes which were fixed upon him alone. The forces met as the hammer meets the anvil with a crash like the splitting of the earth. The huge Pict raised his great sword above his head, cleaving at the Roman troops about him, cutting men down and advancing upon Lucanus who hacked at the pale horde. Cries rose from the men being disemboweled and dismembered, and as the great Pict reached Lucanus, he lifted his sword and brought it down like an executioner's axe. Lucanus side stepped and, lifting his shield, smashed the Pict in his teeth with its base. He lunged forward with his gladius, but the Pict stepped back and swung his sword sideways. Lucanus dropped to the ground, the great blade passing over him.

Roman and Pict spilled into the space between them, cutting one another to the ground. Lucanus rose to aid his kin while, beyond the wall of raging, bloodied bodies, the giant Pict swung his blade, cutting through two and three men at a time. One young legionary ran up behind the Pict and tried to stick a dagger in his back, but before he could the Pict turned, seizing the soldier by the neck and lifting him with a single hand. The man went limp, as prey will do when seized by some predator of overwhelming strength, and the great Pict brought up his sword and placed the soldier at its end, impaling him through the gut slowly and smiling into the legionary's face as he died. When the life had left him, the Pict lowered his sword and let the Roman slide from it. Turning, he fixed his crazed eyes back upon Lucanus, a grin coming across the blood-splashed face.

Where once there was ground, there was now but a slurry of mud and bowels ever churned by scrambling, sliding feet. The air sang with agony, and even over the rain the air reeked of blood. Lucanus and the Pict advanced on one another, slaughtering those between them. When no more remained, the Pict raised his sword and brought it down. Lucanus raised his shield, which shattered into splinters like a tree struck by lightning. He thrust forward with his gladius, but the Pict stepped aside, dropping his weapon and catching the arm which wielded the sword. With his other hand, he took Lucanus by the neck. Holding him like this, the Pict lifted Lucanus and began to pull the arm and the neck in different directions, as though he were trying to tear the man in two. Lucanus snarled as he felt his tendons stretch and his muscles tear, and in a desperate thrash he kicked out, striking the Pict in the nose with his heel.

Both men fell into the slurry, soldiers all about them trampling them into the mud and guts. Lucanus searched for a weapon, his hand finding a Pictish axe in the grume. He rolled over and raised it to see, through eyes blurred by rain and blood, the great Pict towering over him, sword in hand. Lucanus accepted. The great Pict lifted the sword high above his head, his back arched. *A fine Roman death*, Lucanus thought, but just before he closed his eyes to receive the blow, a Roman sprang atop of him, standing firm and thrusting a pilus through the head of the great Pict.

The Roman pulled back the spear, and fury faded from the wild eyes as the barbarian fell back dead. Spinning around, the Roman reached down a hand, and Lucanus took it and was hoisted up. It was Severus.

"Brother." Lucanus nodded gratefully. Severus nodded back and smiled, but before he could say anything, something struck him in the leg. Severus cried out and fell to the floor. Lucanus turned, finding that they had been separated from their fellow Romans by a wall of mad heathens. Lucanus picked up a sword and took up the fight, standing over his friend to protect him. The nearby Romans were working toward them, but the Picts were many, and as Lucanus fought, his mind went to black hell, his sword arm stiff, his chest tight, as though it were bound in rope, and his body burning like a coal in the blacksmith's forge.

He should have died. And yet, his soldiers reached him, and together they cut down the Picts who remained. Those who survived fled up the passage of the glen or over the crest where their druids had stood, cloaked in gray hoods and casting spells across the battlefield. The rain left with them. Lucanus looked to the carpet of bodies at his feet. Among them, Severus, pilus still in hand and head split with an axe, his body trampled to pulp.

*　　*　　*

Of the eight hundred men some three hundred returned to Vindolanda. Three days later the emperor arrived, as did the rain, though this time the painted men did not follow. A great feast was held with Hadrian heading the table, Governor Falko at his side. All of the fort's top men attended, and the very best meats and wines were brought from the stores. In the table's center were whole roast boar and geese, and music was played as slaves tended to the diners who were embraced in the warm glow of the hearth's fire.

Lucanus was required to be there. To sit at the emperor's table was an honor which no man in his line could have imagined, and yet Lucanus spoke and ate little, his mind wondering always to Severus and his unknowing widow in Rome. As he ate slowly, he had several times felt hostile eyes upon him, not just from the legatus, but from the governor too.

The rain continued, and the next day every man from centurion to slave was gathered in the courtyard where they stood in formation before a platform which had been constructed for the emperor. The crowd hummed like a hive of bees. An address from the emperor was a cause for great excitement, and all speculated as to what might be announced on that day.

But not all men within the crowd were pleased. Many, notably the men of the first cohort and many of their compatriots within the Ninth, stood silent and sullen, a mood of foreboding hanging over them. Hadrian took his place, Falko to his side and his guard to his rear, all in uniform shined and polished, unmoved by the rain. Hadrian raised his hand regally and spoke his greeting in a strong, booming voice which all men of the fort could hear.

171

On an unlit torch atop the wall of the fort, Lucanus, who stood at the front of the Ninth, spied a large crow with an iron-gray beak. It seemed to listen, watching with eyes as wild as the great Pict's. "Sons of Rome!" the emperor bellowed. "Here, at the furthest most reach of our might, *you* fine men stand as a barrier against the heathens to the north!" All of the men began to cheer, and the emperor allowed this before raising his hands for silence. "*But!* This is a new dawn for our great people!" the emperor continued. "From Carthage to Gaul, Hispania to Arabia, *MIGHTY ROME* to this Britannia, all has fallen to *YOU!*" he shouted, raising his fist. The men bellowed in triumph so that barbarians of lands not yet discovered must surely have heard it. "Together we, in the name of mighty Rome, have taken this world of savagery and barbarism and carved within it a kingdom surely envied by the gods themselves! Yet, still we find ourselves beset on all sides by heathen hordes! It is time we, once and for all, dear brothers, show these barbarous tribes the terrible and total power of OUR PEOPLE!" the emperor snarled.

At this the crowd of soldiers and slaves erupted in such cheer that not even the hand of the emperor could have quelled them. As they applauded and yelled, Lucanus looked upon Hadrian from below with a skeptical eye. To hear it, the barbarians to the north must surely have thought that the gods had come down to fight by the men of Rome. But Lucanus had heard much of Hadrian, and his ways, and had heard nothing worthy of applause.

Hadrian let the men cheer, and when they had their fill, he raised his hand once more for silence. "You will have heard, I do not doubt, of the legions making for this land of Britannia. Three in total. It is with these men that my will shall be done! And the glory of Rome cemented throughout the ages! I, Hadrian, proclaim that these men are to build a wall which will cut across this land! Eighty miles long! Twenty feet high! Ten feet thick! It shall be of stone from this very earth, and passable only at areas under our control! It shall have guard towers! And the heathen men of the north shall look upon this wall and tremble at the will of Rome to manipulate this earth so!" Hadrian roared, raising his fist and shaking it in the air.

The men erupted in triumphant yells yet more fierce than those which had come from them before. Hadrian nodded approvingly, a look of godly authority upon his face. Lucanus did not cheer. Instead he stood still and stoic, his eyes upon the crow with the mad eyes which cawed into the sky and then took off northwards. Lucanus returned his eyes to the podium, and there they found the gaze of Governor Falko, peering down at him from above with tangible scorn. Lucanus did not avert his eyes.

*   *   *

Lucanus sat at the small table in his tent holding a cup of wine with both hands and bathed in the light of a candle which lapped at the cold air. It was the evening after Hadrian's speech, and already the emperor and the governor had left for the south. Lucanus tapped his fingers at the cup and then drained the wine inside of it. He set down the cup and took up the calamus and began to write:

To My Dearest Wife,

As always, I hope that this letter finds you and our son well. It has not been so long since I last wrote, and so I am yet to receive your reply, but the events of the last few days have pressed me to send this letter with urgency.

Severus Vesta has been slain in battle. He fought gloriously and with honor, and it was in his saving of my own life that he took the first blow. Severus was a dear friend to our family. I must ask that you inform his wife. Tell her that he met his end with dignity and acceptance. Tell her also that he requested with his final breath only that his declaration of love be passed on to her and their small daughters, one last time. In truth Severus had no time to express such a wish in his final moments, though he would have, I am sure, and his family shall need the comfort of it.

I understand that this is no small request, but is the receiving of such news not the greatest fear of every wife? Better that this new widow should not learn of her husband's passing from the writing of a stranger or the mouth of some official, but from you who cares, and who may soon understand. Likewise, it is better that you should learn of my passing from me, he who loves you more than life, and light, and all of the riches in the world. For, my dear, I fear by the time this letter reaches you, I too will have passed.

I have no doubt that you in Rome will know of the three legions bound for Britannia and the order to return back home for my own Ninth Legion. No doubt this has caused much excited speculation that the territories north of this land should soon fall to us and hope from yourself that I should soon return home. I must tell you, my dear, that neither outcome will come to pass.

Emperor Hadrian has ordered that a great wall be built to keep the heathens at bay. I heard him speak the order himself, with mighty authority, and many of the men did cheer. But I did not cheer, for the words spoken were naught to my ear but a decree that Rome has reached her end, and that the men who carved her by cleaving flesh, and taming beast, and moving earth, and who loved her, are all dead and gone, trampled into the dirt and forgotten. It was a decree that those who remain are fearful and cowardly, and naive to the brutal way of things.

These new men, those who lead us, and those who cheer them, wish to hide behind walls which they call testaments to our strength, but which are, to the men beyond them, testaments only to our fear. They wish to enjoy comfort and riches without spilling the blood which must be spilled for such things, and so, I fear, that one day men shall walk atop the ruins of Hadrian's wall to whom the glorious Rome is but a tale for their children at bedtime. I fear that I have seen the last days of Rome, brought about not by the will of the gods, but spoken as policy by those who rule her.

My thoughts have become known. Many of my brothers in the Ninth share in my feeling. That is why, before he left, the governor called me to his dwelling. I am not to return to the mainland with my legion. I am to take those men loyal to me, and who have grown to resent the weakness of our command, and march north, into Caledonia. We are to number some two thousand, tasked with reaching the end of the land and returning back again to report our findings. All men know, both those who gave and received the order, that no such task can be survived by so few.

I can not refuse. To do so would bring not only death, but disgrace and hardship to you. Better to die at the hands of an enemy who I at least understand, than at the hands of my own rulers who I can not. I hope that you do not weep for me. I fear not death in battle. I am pained only by my want to be with you and our son again, though that day will come in time. Until then I shall hold dear the memory of your smile as comfort, and of your touch, and of the love which we share which no passage of time could quell.

Included with this letter to you is another which you are to give to our son when he has proven by his conduct, and not his years, that he is a man. In my absence I entrust your brother with getting him there, and finer hands he could not be in.

It is dusk now, and I am to leave with my men at first light. I shall march forth with no fear nor regret, but only memories of you, my dear, and thoughts of our once glorious Rome.

Until we meet again. . . .

Yours Always,
Lucanus Maximus

Setting down his writing instrument, Lucanus rose from the table and left the tent. The sun had fallen beyond the crest of the world, and the sky was ablaze with soft pinks and reds painted upon full, still clouds. Somewhere beneath that sky lay Severus and some five hundred good men, their souls claimed by the gods and their bodies by the earth. A heavy price to pay, and one which hardly seemed worth it now.

On the wall Lucanus found a man on guard who had been condemned with him to march north. Lucanus took a place beside him and leaned with both hands on the wall. The air was cool and still. In the distance, on the cleared ground before them where the wall was to be built, stood a herd of deer grazing. The stag which watched over them was larger than any he had seen before and white as alpine snow. Lucanus observed the magnificent beast, like a spirit, shining like moonlight in the darkening world.

"The natives say they're a sign of change, sir," the soldier spoke from behind him. Lucanus nodded, slow and slight.

"I believe they are right," he replied.

Lake

Alex Petrov

Sparkling winter covered the black earth with drifts of snow. The New Year celebration followed. Gran could rustle up everything from everything. Her favorite was throwing together all vegetables found in the cupboards and boiling them ("soup") or frying them ("a pan"). As much as I hated my mother's food, I enjoyed everything cooked by Gran. They were the same veg, the same packaged milk, sausages, and eggs, but tasted different.

Then there was the beginning of the school term and meeting my new class mates. Spring came, and like a tree that loses its leaves in October and gets new greenery in April, my memories of Great Oos-toog and my parental home began to drop. Nobody from my previous life was around, no former hazards. Without having to constantly plan my escape from street thugs or my father, I lost my usual grip on doing things.

My mind did not focus on anything particular. Every home chore would lose my interest. School did not attract me. I was not anti-school; I did just enough not to get expelled. I kept my distance from different gangs; I did not appreciate the sheer contrariness driving most of my mates. In fact, their misbehavior often felt stupid. They had an athletic group there. Dismissed it too: I knew better than to run in circles around the school under the coach's commanding whistling. He was a smug guy with snidey eyes, his head shaved, always in a tracksuit, looking like a goon. May be I did not like the way he gazed at me or just his face. The girls in the village? They either talked rubbish or listened to pop, the two activities I definitely could not stand. Politeness was not my natural inclination.

I explored the nearby woods, of course, especially since May after spring floods, when the mud dried out. Now I was not forced to go out there by another apocalypse at home. I simply loved to ramble. In the wilderness, I had never been lost.

Besides, we literally lived in the woods. The vegetation was similar to Oos-toog, but the landscape was more spectacular. Turned out, my new abode was in the vast lake country that began a hundred miles northwest of Moscow and stretched up toward Sweden. The waters were of a wild splendor. At the edges their glassy surface was embellished with lilies. The marshy banks were covered with sedge, bullrushes, and, on the firm ground, fern and thistle, with willows and birches above them.

I wanted more though. I believed there was something else in this world, and I sought a manifestation of that. I longed to do something; I just did not know what that might be. I wanted more than just a hobby. I wanted to find someone or something of *my own*. Anyone can call me disaffected; I believed that myself. But sometimes it felt like hunger. Only it was not hunger. I had already tried to quench that feeling with double lunch, just to throw it up under the blackcurrant bush behind the kitchen. No, I would stand at The Forest Gate—a small gate in the wire-mesh around the village—and watch the high birch trees waving their tops calmly, like the dead land grass in that Gladiator film but huge. Behind them lay the wilderness I had already got to know a bit.

I knew I was someone else than a conventional let's-steal-some-cigarettes teen boy. Gran when my age literally had to survive every day—the famine, partisans beating her father for food, another famine, post-war, heavy construction manual labor when she moved to Moscow in the 1950s. My great-granddad was beaten to death by Red officers, for standing up for a horse one of them had been too cruel to. I always had food and shelter and a nice bed; there was no deadly danger. But I could not suppress that premonition of something bad coming.

In the familiar environment, I had already learned to climb the trees with the nimbleness of a squirrel and sometimes could manage to pass from one tree to another, on the branches, if close. I never fell, but I was not desperate for some acrobatics; I simply enjoyed exploring the dense vegetation in all dimensions. Sometimes I saw mushroom gatherers, the same like in Oos-toog, calm, slow forest inhabitants with heads covered with sou'westers. Sometimes there was different, unfamiliar folk—men, of all sort of age, from grown-up boys to hardened guys, always in groups of three or five, dressed in khaki, with backpacks and small shovels and sometimes holdalls they carried in pairs. Perhaps some hiking enthusiasts? I watched them from above, never allowing myself to get discovered; they did not bother me. The woods were immense; the lakes and marshes were in abundance; there was enough space for everyone.

*   *   *

One ripe July morning I woke up. I felt my sweat on my T-shirt. I peeled it off and put on a fresh one—black with a gorgeous vampire on the chest—and my denim jacket and pulled the collar up in the morning chill.

The kitchen was lit by sunlight that struck through the windows above the worktop. The newly washed dishes and cutlery glittered on the steel draining board. From the tarnished metal tap flowed scoldingly cold water. I laved my eyes feeling the tiny streams running down my chin and dried my face with the white towel from the line above the sink. Gran seemed to be out somewhere. I put the kettle on and lit the gas. From the plastic bag on the fridge top I fished out the last piece of bread, smeared it generously with butter and placed a slice of chorizo on top. I poured the boiling water in my mug with instant coffee and sugar and positioned myself at the table looking out of the window at the apple trees in the garden.

In a month the summer—and the summer holidays—would be over. I had not been able to find I did not know what. I felt strange bitterness glowing somewhere about my midriff. I swallowed the last piece without chewing and decided to slice off a bit of cheese for good measure, for which I obviously needed a clean knife.

The small ramshackle table next to the gas hob with a single drawer contained all our cutlery. Rummaging in it, I spotted an odd one I had not quite noticed before. It felt that the stranger had always been there. But shoved to the back, normally it was destined to be dismissed. I drew it out.

It was old, the blade and the handle with micro-scratches all over. The hilt grips were in black hard plastic. On one side: a small diamond-shaped plate inset within the grip, blank and worn. A curved, beaked, steel pommel. A backswept, finger-protecting crossguard. The blade, single-edged, a bit longer than the handle, bore three etched foreign words.

I placed the thing on my palm with the blade toward my elbow, its tip digging into the white skin of my slender forearm. Someone had told me—had I seen it on telly?—that that was a position to throw it. The blade was of a substantial thickness.

I gulped down the rest of my coffee. I was pretty sure this knife would not be missed since I had never seen Gran use it, perhaps because the blade was slightly rusty near the hilt. I gently touched the edge; it readily parted my skin, though not to the blood yet. I hid the tool under my denim jacket and went outside.

The day became warmer; I anticipated it hitting 27 °C. From time to time, the sun revealed itself in short intervals between the trains of massive white clouds. I stood in front of our wooden fence with peeling paint. I took the knife by the pommel and gently swung it at the planks, letting it slip from my fingers at the right moment and fly only a couple of inches.

It stuck. Then, with a two-second delay, it dropped on the ground.

That felt great.

I got back to the house, put my black baseball-cap on, went outside and strolled along the bridle path toward the forest. My intention was to practice throwing in the woods. Only occasionally. My routine ramble now seemed much more exciting. The sun was getting hotter; the slight breeze was trying to topple the birches and spruces somewhere far above my head. Horrendous mosquitoes excepting some stray brats were absent; it was too warm and late for them. My heart was elevated.

I tried the same swinging maneuver on a couple of stumps. It worked pretty well. My goal now was to learn to throw from a greater distance. Somehow I deemed that my training would require lots of targets, and a familiar stump somewhere close to my regular route would not do. I left my usual path.

Not too far ahead, at the lake there was a spot which everyone regarded convenient for having a dip. But the side I headed toward was the one I had not explored much. It was rather dull, flat, with less dense vegetation, sickly firs and lots of dry trees at the edge of the water. I assumed no one would disturb me there.

*   *   *

The air grew warmer as I entered the copse above the lake. It was mostly dead trunks. I detected a particularly menacing looking, dry birch. I positioned myself just a few feet from it, breathed once in and then out, swung my blade at it, and let it go. It hit the target with the handle and dropped miserably.

I continued practicing. Unfortunately, all the dry trees around were not very broad. The blade rarely hit the trunk, and if it did, it did not do so at the right angle and did not stick. Often it met the wood with its handle or side, gave out a dull thud and dropped, defeated, onto the mulch of bleak grass. My morning enthusiasm started to evaporate as the day drew to its midpoint.

I was desperate to get it right. My weapon sometimes dropped in front of the target without even reaching it or hit it sideways and flipped aside leaving me no hope. At one point after a few particularly unsuccessful attempts—well, they all had been unsuccessful, but the last few were especially shameful—I thought the dead birch was laughing at me. I picked the bugger up and flung it with all my force at my silent, motionless enemy.

It went straight past the trunk toward the water. I heard a debilitating, game-over-like splash.

Damned.

*   *   *

I stripped down to my underwear leaving my clothes jumbled on a dry spot, my socks stashed in my trainers, and slowly walked toward the water, trying to remember the place where it had disappeared, at the same time watching under my feet to avoid any possible piece of glass or sharp wood.

The dry grass, like broken blades, threatened to cut my feet, and I placed them flat and slowly. The breeze and chill from the lake gave my legs goosebumps, but the sun warmed my shoulders. The lengthening late-July nights might have already cooled the water. I stood in the warm, black mud up to my ankles. The water looked still and oily. Dragonflies patrolled the sedge. The forest on the opposite side cast shadows on the water. In the depths of its foremost sentinels there was the eerie mid-day twilight, with the sun highlighting their tops.

A crow crossed the space above the ridges of the trees. A bright haze steamed above the lake. I waded in. The water was surprisingly warm. The surface mildly corrugated in response to my intrusion. A huge horsefly landed on my unprotected shoulder; I clapped on it, and it fell onto the water, its wings still moving. My feet groped at the muddy but firm bed. I waded in up to my chest. I could not see the bottom at the front; it seemed there was a drop. I dove headlong, feeling my feet letting out a splash on the surface.

The first thing my half-opened eyes perceived was a strange, huge shape. I had just missed hitting an enormously long and straight pipe stuck out from it. I drew closer. It was massive.

A monstrous form of a battle tank.

It was probably a meter below the surface. The spooky carcass of the wrecked war machine was displayed to me in its defeated glory. Its turret was slightly askew, and the long trunk I had narrowly avoided was its main gun.

I paddled upwards, broke out, and caught my breath.

I assumed that I should have returned to the beach. My heart hurried. Gran's knife was somewhere down there.

Something inside me pushed my head down, and I dove back, into the deep. And then deeper, into the green twilight.

I was below the turret, the dark hole of the front hatch. Down there, the knobby pommel of my knife revealed itself. I had some air left and made a few more strokes. There, in the dark chasm, next to my knife, was something pale. Abruptly, a stray sun-ray found its way between the trees in the world above; the light broadened for a second.

I blew out almost all my air and convulsively pulled upwards. I hit through the surface, breathed in greedily. I paddled toward the beach, scrambled on my feet across the mud toward my clothes, grabbed my T-shirt, dropped it, grabbed it again, draped it around my bony shoulders, embraced myself, and sat on the ground. And kept sitting like that.

The sun watched me through the canopy of twigs, most of them dry dead. At school they had told us that Valday was one of the battlefields during the war. And that was it; no one had primed me what actually was there right under my nose.

I put my clothes on. I shook my baseball cap, hit it against my hip, put it on, went to wash my feet in the clean spot away from the mud, balancing on one foot, putting a sock on, each foot at a time. Then I peed on the dry grass with my back to the lake and marched into the woods.

*　*　*

Some part of me did not wish to go home. To go back meant owning up to taking the knife without asking. And losing it. Losing it like *that*. No diving for it again that day. It would not go anywhere, would it?

I traversed the site I had not seen before. Now, it was predominantly pine, with firmer ground covered with detritus of needles and dry limbs.

Half an hour past, there in the forest deep ahead, was something. Was it just the wind playing with the light? A wall. And a greenish rooftop behind. What?

It looked like a big manor, right in the middle of the forest, behind a high wall running around it. The huge corroded wrought-iron gates were shut.

A wide yard covered with tall grass. At distance, the main building, all stone, painted white and yellow, the same as the wall. It resembled some pre-Soviet mansions I had seen in films. Portico front, same height as the building, columns, white sometime in the past. The scaling paint on the walls. The windows black agape. There was no porch or steps leading to the tall, wide-open doors at the front. At the front, a graying-white statue of a horse, to the natural size.

Two women in quilted jackets, skinny jeans, and high boots appeared along the far end of the building. I blinked. To make sure they were real, I glanced around and in front of me.

And there it was.

My knife was lying in the grass, meters from me. Behind the gate.

One of the women halted, then turned and headed toward me. Even from the distance, her large eyes on her narrow perfect face were prominent.

Her hair was in a thick, reddish ponytail. She walked toward me sort of casually, as if approaching a familiar friend, her head straight, watching me with a nonchalant expression. Her narrow nose was connected to her forehead. Her eyes were impossibly gray, charcoal, but fierce-bright.

She stopped by the knife and picked it up, still watching me. Holding by the blade, she handed it to me through the gate. My hand took it as if it had to, my eyes darting between her nose and her long neck. She went back to the corner of the house where her mate disappeared.

I blinked, and there was nothing.

I lingered by the gates for some time. The yard was empty. It was quite past midday.

I anticipated a long yomp home. The knife was heavy in my hand. And warm.

*　*　*

I tried to follow the same route. But the forest was unrecognizable now, as if the changed light made the trees look different. The sun had gone. Pines gave way to oaks and aspens; the jungle of branches and bramble became more dense. The trees were watching me. I saw strange shapes in them, like someone's arms and contorted faces, melting into peculiar patterns on the bark as I passed them by.

Then I began to recognize the landscape again.

*   *   *

Gran was in the garden. Her slender figure stooped over the strawberry patch in front of the house. Dressed in a long, size-less, washed-out shirt and cargo pants rolled up below her knees, she was fighting the weeds with her gloved hands, her shoulder-length, silver hair hiding her face except her pale eyes.

She noticed me, straightened up holding her back, and smiled. "My dear, come, going to be tea and biscuits. What's that?"

"Found it in the kitchen."

She watched me.

"Practiced knife throwing," I said and gave it to her.

*   *   *

The tea was scorching hot and the biscuits were simple and yummy. She seemed not to care to ask for more. I could not stand the pause. "So, I missed and it fell into the lake and I dived in—"

"My silly pup."

"And there was a tank. In the lake. A *tank*."

Her expression did not change a jot. "Of course it's down there; everyone knows that." With the same voice, she could have told me there was some milk left in the fridge. "War stuff, you know. There is lots of it around. This," she said holding the knife, "noticed it's different? The emblem was filed away."

She handed it back to me, holding my gaze for a split second in a peculiar manner unlike her.

"In Soviet times, a good tool of any sort was like gold—hard to get. But that place is not good for swimming, isn't it? Of course you might bump into something somewhere."

"What, not just there?"

"Anywhere, here and there. The bogs behind the river, you know the place? Some say they're literally stuffed with everything—tanks, helmets, ammunition. Nobody would've bothered if something had been left out, wouldn't they? But you aren't going to walk about the peat bogs anyway, are you? No? Good. Have more tea.”

I did not want to ask about the old big house with columns. It would come up somehow. “Why is *the stuff* still there?”

“Where would it go? Try to pull something big out, you might as well stay there in bog thyself. On the contrary, to dig up something small, like a metal flask or insignia—that might be rewarding, right? Might cost alright.”

“Or a gun?”

“Maybe. I think they never work though.”

The tea spread warmth down my throat.

“Could there be something else?”

Her eyes were kind and a bit sad. “The dead, they aren’t worth anything, are they? After the war, even in the dry fields the bones were just ploughed over.”

Painting Inversion

Francis Rockwell

The paint swirled and twisted across the canvas. The bucket swung back and forth, dripping on the canvas below, until a paint-covered hand caught it before it could plummet down once more. Charles untied the knot and placed the leaking bucket on a tarp to his side. He stared down at the painting, frowning. It lacked the chaos of a Jackson Pollock, yet held no order. Charles swore loudly and kicked a can of paint across the floor, scattering globs of green across the canvas and concrete.

He flung himself down on the cracked leather couch and laid an arm over his head. A kaleidoscope of color danced across his vision while he lay with closed eyes. When the luminous pigments began losing their glamor, Charles looked around the studio apartment hoping for inspiration to strike. Easels around the room held canvases in varying stages of completion: here an attempt at cubism, there a dabbling in impressionism, behind them a variety of ironic pop art pieces. Besides the couch, the only substantive furniture were the shelves of paints, brushes, pencils, and paper, and a stove and refrigerator in one corner. He could have ordered a cheap mattress, but he enjoyed sleeping on the couch, not because it was more comfortable than a bed, but because it implied a level of eccentricity.

The muses remained concealed. Perhaps the lingering vapors of his most recent spray paint project had driven them away. Or perhaps he needed to breathe more fumes for them to arrive. . . . No. Miasma never proved inviting to inspiration. But maybe there was something in the drawer. . . . Charles slid open the drawer of the small nightstand beside the couch and peered in. A scattering of loose pills rolled and rattled across the bottom, leftover from parties, friends, and a former roommate. A blue, oval-shaped pill and a circular, red pill looked promising. He reached down and grabbed them. A second later they were washed down with a swig of vodka from a nearly empty bottle on the floor.

Charles held a vague, clouded memory of one of his professors (or was it a high school teacher?) discussing a quote about fortune being like a woman—she favored the adventurous over the cold and timid and could be controlled by those willing to beat and ill-use her (he remembered many of the girls took umbrage to that). Who was the quote by? Niccolas Macklemore? *Oh well, it doesn't really matter*, he thought. "Fortune favors the bold," Charles muttered to himself. "To the ramparts!" He laughed. "I will find my inspiration whether she wants to be found or not!"

He drank the remaining vodka and threw the bottle onto the canvas he had been working on (he hoped for a dramatic shattering, but was instead met by a disappointing *thump* as the bottle bounced and slid across the wet paint). Shoving pastels and charcoal into a worn backpack, he stumbled across the room and out the door.

The sun shone down, a sea breeze blew, and the sound of traffic rose up. Charles walked aimlessly, waiting for something to inspire wonder. Eventually, he settled down on a bench in front of a burrito shop nestled between an electronics store and an abandoned storefront covered in plywood and "No Trespassing" signs. Sketchbook and charcoal in hand, Charles began to draw the tree across the road. The secret, he thought to himself, is to draw the shadow as the tree and the tree as the shadow—an inversion of reality. That's the road to fame and glory: invert the real. Any sucker can draw a tree; people have done that for centuries. And now cameras will always be more realistic than anything an artist can make, so why be real? But to twist it, to make light into dark, to see the sun but paint the moon, that was the mark of an artist who moved with the current era.

He mumbled away to himself, lost in thought until a man with a dog jogged by. *Quick! Turn to a fresh page!* Charcoal scraped against paper rapidly creating a silhouette of the man and the dog. Charles rubbed his finger across the page leaving gray streaks. Motion. Now to invert. Old is kitsch. New, always something new, something original. Man walks dog? Now the dog walks the man. A new sketch developed on the page. Too simple; a child could think of that. Maybe put stilettos and lipstick on the dog? Or would that be taken as an insult to women? Better not to risk it. *Perhaps I should make it political,* he thought. Who's a politician with a dog-like face . . . ? Or there was always the option of blasphemy. . . . Blasphemy always got attention. A dog walking Jesus? There would be an uproar—and as someone said, "All press is good press."

Charles absentmindedly tapped the charcoal piece against his chin while he thought. A woman walked by distracting him from his musings. He caught only a glimpse of her face as she passed by. He was struck as if an angel had appeared before him; he had seen Aphrodite and Helen combined into a single being wearing glasses. If there was justice in the universe, she was the one being who it would be truly evil to invert. There was no need to change, only the need to mirror.

He rose from the bench and felt pins and needles as blood returned to his legs. His head felt far away and his vision temporarily faded to white as he staggered. By the time Charles felt capable of walking safely, the woman was halfway down the block. His eyes locked on her bouncing brunette ringlets; he moved down the sidewalk after her.

No matter how quickly he walked, she remained ahead of him, just out of reach, like the mirage of an oasis in the desert. He walked. Was it minutes? Hours? Days? He knew not, but he continued until suddenly she turned down another street. When he caught up and twisted around the corner, she was nowhere to be seen.

Charles cursed loudly. He pulled out his notebook and began rapidly trying to redraw his Venus from memory. The vast gulf between what he saw and what he drew was unbearable. It was like a dark abyss swelling up inside his chest, consuming his spirit and flesh. "I'm a failure," he mumbled to himself. His mind swirled. Vision blurred. He felt his body seizing, yet it wasn't his body. He looked at himself and then up at the sky. The clouds grew larger and larger until their gargantuan folds threatened to consume him. The sky was falling, rushing down to crush him. Wait. *That's not the sky*, he realized, *that's concrete. Inversion*, he thought, and then his head hit the ground.

With a groan, Charles awoke sometime later and stared at what he presumed to be his own vomit on the pavement in front of him. Shoes gently passed around and over him as if he was simply a sack of rotten produce instead of a human.

His head throbbed as he begrudgingly pulled himself to his feet. An overwhelming thirst enveloped him. Charles couldn't remember the last time he drank water.

He stumbled up the stone stairs beside him, each step like a cliff face daring him to fall, eventually reaching the summit and plunging through the tinted glass doors into a marble-floored room. Charles blinked repeatedly as his eyes adjusted from the natural light to the artificial, the faint buzzing of fluorescent lights assaulting his ears. The room seemed familiar, but he couldn't recall why. A thin man, one side of his head shaved with the remaining hair long, draped over his pink collar, narrowed his eyes suspiciously at him from behind a counter.

"Drinking fountain?" Charles asked through parched lips.

"Over there," said the man. He flicked his head to the right.

Charles stumbled down a small side hall and found a steel fountain. He drank deeply, lapping up the water like a starved dog. Finally, his thirst subsided; his mouth no longer felt like it was filled with cotton. The lights lost their harsh glare, and the buzzing receded to the background.

Walking back down the hallway Charles realized where he was, the California Public Museum of Art. He bitterly recalled his campaign a few months prior of letters, emails, and calls trying to schedule a meeting with a member of the acquisition team; he hoped to persuade them to include his artwork in their "Rising Young Artists" exhibit. Rejection smiled its emotionless grin, and Charles met only silence.

Across the hall hung a poster advertising their upcoming "Ebony Echoes: Exploring Black Identity Through Art" exhibit. *Well, since I'm here I might as well look around, thought Charles.* He turned and walked to the front desk. "How much for a day-pass?"

The man eyed him with disgust and tapped the sign next to him with the prices.

Charles pulled out his wallet—it was thinner than he would like—and pulled out twenty-five dollars. "I don't need the change. What's the best exhibit today?"

"There's a moving set of paintings by Miriam Lévi. They're intellectual and fresh. You'd go down the Schusterman Hall for those. But"—he paused for a second and sneered at Charles—"if you're looking for something less cerebral, and a bit kitsch, today's the last day we have the Neo-classical exhibit here. We'll finally be replacing it with some worthwhile artists. . . . It's down the Anderson Hallway. Enjoy." He returned to typing.

Charles grabbed a map from the counter and stepped back. The Lévi exhibit sat toward the back of the museum. Anderson Hall branched off shortly after the entrance hall. *I'll stop by the closer one and then move my way back,* he thought, folding the map up and putting it in his pocket.

Anderson Hall was silent except for faint piano music drifting from the overhead speakers. He began working his way around the room clockwise. The first painting depicted a crew of men aboard a ramshackle raft. A great storm whirled around them, and they appeared in danger of being swallowed by a towering wave baring down upon them. In the background, a small flame illuminated the deck of a larger vessel.

He pulled out his sketchbook and a pen from his backpack, jotted down the name of the painting, and began a sketch. Did he not feel caught in a great whirlwind of life? Was there any man who did not? But there was hope on the horizon. The men had their compatriots on the raft to share the burden. *Do I have friends to help me?* he thought. His thoughts reflected on his friends. Would they help him or abandon him in dire straits? He knew the answer, and darkness began seeping into his heart. He shook his head. *I could use some vodka right now,* he thought. He moved to the next painting.

A man knelt at the verdant shore of a lake leaning forward toward a group of women half submerged in the water. The center woman's face, it was the face of the woman he had seen earlier in the day, his goddess and muse! Charles stared, mouth agape. He looked to the title of the painting: *Hylas and the Naiads* by James W. Waterhorse. Who was Hylas? He pulled out his phone and searched the name. The cell reception was horrible; while he waited, Charles stared at the painting some more.

How can I invert this? he thought to himself. *I could switch the women with*

"Hylas: character from Greek mythology, friend of Hercules, abducted by water nymphs," he read.

Charles swiped out of the browser and pulled up his text messages. He clicked on Samantha's name and typed, "Can I ask a favor? Would you meet me in an hour at my studio?"

Sketchbook back in his bag, Charles left the hall and past the receptionist playing on his phone. If he remembered the area correctly, he could walk one block east to the library. He went inside, found a few dusty books about the Greeks and their myths and walked back to his apartment. While he walked, he read— almost walking off the curb a few times and narrowly avoiding stepping on a homeless man.

He checked his phone. Samantha had responded with "Sure." Perhaps he did have one friend who would help in a moment of need. If she arrived on time (which was unlikely) he had twenty minutes. He drank some water, tossed out the empty bottles, and cleared some space in the center of the room. The air still stung with the vapors of paint and alcohol. Charles flung open the windows then stopped to stare at the curtains. "Those would work," he spoke to himself and set to work pulling one of them down.

Forty minutes later, Samantha arrived carrying a bottle of clear liquid. "I'm guessing you're out of vodka?" she asked as she walked through the doorway.

"I am . . . but that's not why I texted!"

"What do you want then?" She set the bottle down by the refrigerator.

"I need you as a reference."

"You're applying for a job?" she chortled.

"No, not that kind of reference. I need you to model for me."

Samantha laughed. "Let me guess, you want to paint me like one of your French girls. I always knew you would make a move on me someday. All you men are the same; you only think with your—"

"Shut up and put this on." Charles shoved the curtain into her hands.

"What the hell is this?" She looked at the pale-yellow cloth with a look of confusion mingled with disgust.

"It's a toga—well, it's a curtain. Look, just put it on."

"How?"

"Just throw it over your shoulder and I'll cinch it around your waist with a belt."

"Fine."

Charles got her situated in the center of the room. She leaned slightly against a broom handle to simulate a spear. "Hold that pose." Charles moved around her taking pictures with his tablet. "You're good to move now."

"What are you up to, Charlie?"

"I'm trying something new by painting something old."

"Did you just say I'm old?" she questioned with a smirk.

"No, no, no! I'm going to paint you as Athena from the old Greek stories."

"Whatever. You want a drink?" she asked, sitting down on the couch.

"Not right now."

"Whatever."

He looked through the photos until he found the best angle and set the tablet on an easel where he could see it. Then he set up a blank canvas, about three feet tall, and a camera on a tripod aimed toward his worksite. He sketched out two columns for the background and the outline of Samantha in the middle with a pencil and then began squeezing out tubes of oil paint onto a pallet.

After an hour, the columns and sky in the background were finished enough that Charles began to work on the central figure. He had forgotten Samantha was still there until she asked, "Are you at least going to pay me for being your model? I'll accept food as payment."

"Sure, there's some cash in my wallet." He pulled it out of his pocket and tossed it to her.

"You're not going to take me out?"

"Let me finish this first." He resumed painting. After another hour, Athena-Samantha was filled in—the faded curtain now a bright white toga, the broom a glistening spear—and just needed the detail work.

The last rays of sunshine speckled the sky with purples and reds above Samantha who had fallen asleep on the couch. Charles nudged her shoulder. "What do you think?" She groggily got up and moved to the painting. "It's not finished yet; I still need to do the detail work," Charles amended while she looked at it.

"It looks good, but"—she glanced at him for a second—"it's not what you usually do."

Charles shrugged.

"Can we eat now?"

"Yeah." They walked to a cafe down the street.

Later, fueled by a large black coffee, Charles continued the painting late into the night. Samantha slept on the couch after claiming she didn't want to walk by herself in the dark. Around four in the morning Charles took a picture of the painting and uploaded it to his blog along with a time-lapse video from his camera. He added the caption, "Athena, Goddess of Wisdom. If you're interested in purchasing, leave a comment below."

He didn't want to bother Samantha, so he rolled up the curtain as a pillow and lay down to sleep on the floor.

When he woke up around noon, she was gone. She had sent him a text around seven saying, "You looked wiped out so I didn't wake you. Painting looks great! Thanks for dinner!" As he got his coffee brewing, Charles checked his blog. He had a dozen new followers and someone had offered two hundred dollars for the painting. He scrolled further through the comments. Someone else offered three hundred for it. Charles smiled; normally his more modern pieces were ignored. He messaged the commenter to set up the trade.

He spent the day reading through his books from the library. The clear bottle by the fridge leered at him through the day, but he felt no need to touch it.

He asked Samantha over again the next day. "Some of us have real jobs you know," she replied. "I'll be there in an hour."

He set up the camera and posed with her.

"So, what am I this time?" she asked.

"You're a statue. Hold still."

"Are you stabbing me?" She looked at the butter knife and hammer Charles held.

"No, I don't have a chisel, so I'm improvising."

"Who are you, sculptor-boy?"

"Pygmalion."

"Who?"

"Greek sculptor. He fell in love with one of his statues."

"You're weird." She smiled.

With two figures, the painting took longer to complete, but Charles felt greater satisfaction. New subscribers to his blog began commissioning him to paint their favorite Greek and Roman stories, along with the occasional Norse figure. One enthusiastic man with deep pockets began purchasing a weekly portrait of different Roman emperors.

Charles painted over his old canvases to use them for his new works. He found it hard to focus on the details when taking pills, so he dumped the drawer down the sink. The bottle of vodka sat unopened in the corner. For the first time he paid rent without asking Dad for some extra cash.

"I'll be honest, son," wrote Charles' father, "as talented as you are, I didn't think running off to the city to be an artist was a good idea. I'm glad that things have improved. Your newer paintings are great. You're making me proud."

Charles sent his mom a message: "Do you have any pictures of Grandpa and Great-Grandpa? Don't tell dad. I'm making something for him."

The next day she responded with photos. Charles set to work. In the foreground, he sketched out his father flanked by his grandparents. Further back, he reused their faces (with slight modification) to make a swath of figures wearing garments from previous eras. Charles aimed to create a great chain of generations flowing back to antiquity.

"That guy's wearing a monk's robes."

"Yeah, and?"

"Monks didn't have kids, so he shouldn't be in the painting."

"Shut up, Samantha."

It took almost two weeks to complete to Charles' satisfaction, just in time for Father's Day. He carried his bags and the painting down to the curb to wait for his ride. Samantha walked up to him. "I brought you something. . . ." she said sheepishly. She pulled her hands from behind her back to reveal a box of paints. "I thought . . . well. . . . I don't know how to bake," she laughed.

"They're great! Thanks!" He took the box and put it in his bag. When he turned back around she gave him a hug.

"Come back soon, okay? My life will be boring without being a statue."

"I'll only be gone a few days."

Just then, Charles' father pulled up to the curb. "Sorry I'm late! Throw in your bags and let's get goin' so we can avoid the traffic!"

Charles loaded his luggage and the painting, then got into the car. "See you later, Sammie!"

"Bye!"

His dad pulled away from the curb. "She's cute. You didn't say you had a girlfriend."

"She's not my girlfriend."

"Seems nice. Maybe she should be."

"Maybe. . . ."

They stopped at a red light. "While we're stopped, let me look at what you brought." Dad twisted around to look at the painting in the back seat. "Well, golly! That's me!" he laughed. "I see you used one of my football photos. Very good choice. And there's dad and gramps. This the surprise Mom said you had?"

"Yep."

"Looks great! What's it titled?"

Charles looked back at it. "Not sure yet. I was too busy making it that I didn't think about naming it."

"Makes me think of something Gramps used to say: 'Live as if your ancestors are watching.' How about that?"

"It's going in your house, so you can call it whatever you want, Dad."

The light turned green. The car rolled forward down the street. "*Live as if Your Ancestors Are Watching*. I like it."

Dad smiled. "Mom's going to love it. And speaking of love, she's making meatloaf with cookies for dessert." He reached over, patted Charles' stomach and gave him a wink.

No Son of Mine

Mark Time

I was alone in my bed. I thought of my ex-girlfriend a few states over and wondered if she was already asleep. We had a son together two years back. I couldn't take the pressure. I don't know if it was lack of commitment, lack of love, or lack of sleep. Scientists have failed time and time again to understand why we simply cannot function without sleep. I tried sneaking out before they awoke, but failed. My girlfriend wept when I left, but not half as bitterly as my son. I had a career to get on with, but I sent a handsome stipend to them every week.

Day in and day out, I sat at my desk at a job most would kill for—but few would die for. Six figures commanded my attention in ways honor and glory never could. As I laid my head to rest, I thought once more of the two generations of my family I knew. Beyond their lives, my ancestors stretched into an unknowable abyss. Their struggles, passions, sacrifices, and aspirations arrived stillborn in my deracinated state. As with many things, I claimed to grasp the whole of existence while it passed through my fingers like the sand on the seashore. History, vast and unyielding, similarly passed through my mind like a sieve in school. My only retention was a few odd dates about the Second World War. I grew as a seedling in soil fertilized with the blood and toil of the long line leading to myself. At last I was asleep.

"Iugular! Iugular!" the crowd roared.

A grubby man hurried me along an underground tunnel while the vibrations of the cheering shook the mortar of the crude brickwork walls. I was in chains, being led along at a harried pace. The man said something to me in a language I could not understand. He gestured to a rack holding several rusted swords as he undid my shackles. I picked up the nearest weapon, but it felt as though it weighed a thousand pounds. The man grabbed my face and said something roughly before pushing me toward the sullen light shining at the end of the tunnel. Looking back at him for a moment, I gingerly approached the rapidly quickening din of the crowd's chanting.

When I emerged, I found myself in an enormous arena. The audience, obscured by some kind of veil, booed me as I set foot on the sand. Looking toward the center of the circular space, I observed a man who looked to be my father bleeding out on the ground. His movements grew spastic and uncoordinated as his life ebbed away. I rushed forward but was interrupted by a group of men who carried his body away. Before I could pursue them, I was confronted by an imposing man with a beard down to his waist. His blond hair seemed to eclipse the sun over azure blue eyes. He wore a fur tunic and commanded an enormous ax.

"They called me Legion Cleaver before they put my eyes out!" his voice echoed in the arena, silencing the crowd. He wasn't speaking English, but I could nonetheless understand him. The warrior continued, "I crushed the legs of Aelius the Legate and drank blood from the skull of ten centurions!"

My legs began to tremble as the sword's handle slipped in my sweaty palms.

"They had to surround me with a thousand legionnaires before they could bring me down." Legion Cleaver lowered his tone. "Son of mine, what have you accomplished?"

I could make no reply.

"Son of mine! You must tell me," he repeated. "That wretch who came out here before you—he was no son of mine!"

My mind fluttered through a series of accomplishments that would have impressed most people but would be unintelligible to this man.

"I didn't suffer their torture and bleed on countless battlefields for my line to end in a servile mute!" The man menaced his ax and approached me rapidly.

I gripped at my sword but dropped it in the sand. Before I could pick it up again, darkness overtook my vision as the savage impact of the ax head snuffed me out.

The last thing I heard was the man bellowing, "No son of mine!"

Again I was in the tunnels beneath the arena. I barely had time to catch my breath before I was rushed out before the crowd once more. My head still ached terribly from my previous bout. I got the sense I would not escape this nightmare until I could best my opponent. I felt a growing sense of fear like a cave explorer realizing he's lost, stuck, and alone in the dark. I saw a man who was just skin and bones. It appeared he had not eaten in weeks. I was given no weapon this time, but this new opponent appeared to be an easy exit.

I had no experience in violence or killing, but this withering body was all that stood between me and escape. The malnourished man noticed me but stood firm. Before I could reach him, soldiers rushed forward and bound us both with ropes. We were placed next to each other, tied to separate wooden poles anchored in the ground. The soldiers began stacking hay, twigs, and other fuel around both of us. I struggled against my bonds in a blind panic.

"God's peace, my son," the other man said. "We go to meet the Father soon."

"What are you talking about?" I yelped.

I observed with horror as one of the soldiers set the kindling alight. One of them stepped forward, holding a jug of water.

"Christians," he began, "you have committed grave sins. If you swear allegiance to the Emperor and renounce this nonsense, I may extinguish the flames."

I hadn't attended church since I was a boy. I began to scream and flail as best I could in the restraints as the fire started to burn my lower extremities. I glanced briefly at the other man. His countenance was radiant as he looked toward Heaven. Clenching his teeth tightly, I could tell he was praying in between rasping gasps for air.

"Get me out! Put it out!" I babbled.

The soldier holding the jug smiled slightly. "You know what to say."

The pain grew unbearable as I cried, "I deny it! All of it! It's worthless to me. Just put the fire out!"

The other man looked at me with a soul-crushing disappointment. The soldier poised the jug before casting it aside with contempt. I felt every degree of the blaze as my body was consumed. The other man's eyes were filled with tears, not from the pain, but for my denial.

In his dying breath he wheezed, "No son of mine!"

At last my vision went dark and the pain was over. Instead of awaking in the tunnels beneath the arena, I found myself in a dense fog. The air was cold and sapped my strength. The ground beneath me was muddy apart from a worn stone path to my right. I trudged through the mire until I reached the path. In the distance, I could see what appeared to be street lights lining the road over the course of several rolling hills.

I walked at a plodding pace toward the lights. As I got closer, I found each light was a person standing beside the path like a sentry.

When I looked into their faces, I found myself pitted against them in the arena during their greatest trial. I could not contend with a single one. After my failure, each would speak their accusations. I could see by their dress that the individuals lining the path were from all epochs of history. There were soldiers, commoners, thinkers, writers, and all manner of men from all walks of life.

Invariably as I passed, each one pointed to me and said, "No son of mine!"

Each pointed to a different aspect of me whether mental, moral, or physical. I broke into a sprint and closed my eyes. The din of judgment overwhelmed my senses as if I were caught in the middle of a resonating bell struck repeatedly by the hammer of my failure.

At last the voices grew quieter. I slowed to a walk, opened my eyes, and caught my breath.

Now the men lining the path would only whisper, "No son of mine."

Their faces were contorted with what appeared to be self-doubt, and I no longer had to challenge them in the arena. It seemed they repeated the judgment out of obligation rather than conviction. Each man was quieter and less convicted than the last until the line fell silent. In tandem with the decrease in volume was a dimming of the glowing light each possessed. Imperceptible at first, I looked back and saw the radiant glow of the predecessors.

Now, each man looked on in glum, silent acceptance. Their faces were overcast in shadow. The lack of judgment did nothing to comfort me. At last, I reached the end. I recognized the last two faces—my father and grandfather.

"Take your place, son of mine," my dad said.

I took no pleasure in finally being accepted. My legs ossified as I fell in line. In short order, I was unable to move at all. I waited and waited. Time lost all meaning in the darkness as I stood at the end of the line. My mind was awash with memories and visions, each more disappointing and futile than the last. Eventually, the wellspring of experience ran dry until my consciousness was blank with the gray decline of oblivion.

A great cheer snapped me alert. I turned my head toward the lit figures further down the road and observed a growing commotion. Someone was making his way down the path like a caesar commemorating a triumph. As he approached the dimmer sections of the line, he remained cloaked in brilliance. My eyes ached terribly from the strain of adjusting to the light.

Finally he approached close enough for me to see his face.

Though he was fully grown, I knew exactly who he was. I took in his appearance. He had just come from the scene of some kind of battle. Whether it was in warfare, debate, or personal struggle, I couldn't tell. Yet I knew he was a warrior.

"My son! My son!" I exclaimed. "You—"

He put his finger over my lips and commanded me to be silent.

"No son of yours."

The Goobies: Social Saturation

Turn_Coat

When I was a boy, I lived with my father in a small town. Green trees punctuated the property in spring and summer. The land was an heirloom from my grandfather who died when I was a baby. My father would complain about the taxes, but he'd pay them. Back during his life, land had grown so expensive that inheritance alone conferred ownership—a feudal lord or old imperial house surviving the fall of empire.

I didn't know why it mattered so much when I was a kid. It was in the mountains, a small town, far from the nearest market or city. It was his, though. Only later did I come to understand why those fifteen acres mattered so much. As a child, I was jealous of cities and excited for visits. Bright lights and colors meant more to me than old land rights.

Being relatively isolated, visiting friends took planning. My mother's family lived forty miles away. I had a few acquaintances at school. It was a little two-classroom affair. Down the road was our little library. People weren't there often, but I could meet my six classmates occasionally. We didn't get along great, but there was hardly anyone else so we made it work. Our little social pocket quickly began to fray once we made new friends online.

When I *did* visit Mom's side, my half-sister would tell me about things at her school, people shouting at digital screens, playing games and such. We just had the woods out where I lived. She wasn't as jealous of me as I was of her.

I was still young when some kid tried to break into our house through the front door. In the middle of the night, he stood and slung insults and the occasional stone. "You think you can hide from me? I know you're in there. Get out here; you don't scare me!" There'd been similar incidents on the news. No one knew why.

I watched nervously through a window. My father pulled a shotgun from his closet and called the sheriff's office. "Keep an eye on the door," he said while rummaging.

It was ten minutes before police cars appeared, a duration for which the kid remained standing in our front yard shouting. I couldn't make heads or tails of what he wanted, but it was clear he meant business. He tried to kick down the front door a few times. It held.

"I'll kill you!" the kid shouted. "You're a coward! You want to get me too! You're surprised when we show up at YOUR place, huh?!"

My father and I waited and took turns holding the shotgun. "I was hoping you wouldn't have to see this until you were older."

"What do you mean?" I asked.

Dad just shook his head.

It took two deputies to wrangle the madman into cuffs. He was combative. If he'd had a firearm a gunfight would have doubtless broken out. There was screaming outside and the sound of more broken glass, a scuffle and then more hollering.

"Get off me; I know *they* are all over you! You think I don't know? Get off me!"

Eventually car doors slammed shut outside and the volume of the shouts dropped dramatically. Then a knock on the door. Dad set the shotgun down by me in the hall.

A benefit of small towns is actually *knowing* the law enforcement. My father worked a remote engineering job and spent an occasional evening at the watering hole where Deputy Leon was a regular. The town only had the one bar and church. They knew each other from both. It was Leon who stood in our entryway when my father unlatched and opened the heavy-set door.

"The hell was that?" asked my father.

Leon made a grimace. "Don't know, crazies have been popping up here and there."

"This related to those incidents in the city?" asked my father.

"Hope not." Leon glanced down the hall where I watched, confused and scared. He waved at me, and I saw his eyes flick to the leaned-up shotgun. "Good thing you didn't have to use that."

My father took a deep breath. "I was worried."

"I don't want to have to arrest you for it. A few people have been charged by the AG for defense because these . . . guys"—he waved broadly at the crazy kid in the back of the sheriff's vehicle—"they aren't in their right mind."

"At least that's the official statement," my father said.

"Well, we go by the official statements," said Leon.

Leon took a report, asking a series of generic questions: Did you have any relation? Have you ever seen this person before? Did you fear for your life or property? Like a debrief. After all was said and done, my father asked the question I'd been wondering about since the whole mess started.

"If he'd gotten in here, and I'd *had* to shoot him, would I have been arrested?"

Leon glanced behind himself at his vehicle and back at my dad. "State has a lot of new laws on self-defense. . . . Did he have a weapon; were you *really* in fear for your life; how far in your house was he? That sort of thing. Standard procedure is to arrest the home owner until it's determined whether or not he broke the law."

My father pursed his lips.

Leon lowered his tone. "That river behind your house is at least thirty feet from one side to the other. Deep too. I've heard all kinds of crazy things get washed up in Wilford thirty miles downstream, and we're stretched way too thin to investigate them."

"So that's what it's come to then?" my dad asked.

Leon shrugged, shook my father's hand, and left.

I heard the kid shouting when Leon and the other deputy reentered their cars. "They're all over you; you think I don't know?" He followed it up by screaming something about "goobies" and a few other choice words before the doors slammed shut and they drove off.

*   *   *

The image of that kid—he couldn't have been over twenty years old—remained with me for months. That look of dead certainty he'd had. I didn't really know what, if anything, the incident meant, and my father was hesitant to talk about it. Other than that, life continued; I went to our small school; I chatted with friends on my tablet.

The news out of the cities became more strained, but I didn't pay attention. My father checked out of current events and would only talk about the local affairs. He withdrew after that incident. Around the beginning of summer break the internet started switching off in the evenings when dad wasn't working.

"I'm tired of my boss bothering me after hours," my dad said. "I'll just turn off the modem at 9 p.m. when it's bedtime anyway."

Even back then, I didn't think that was the real reason. He knew *I* was online well into the night. I complained, but he wouldn't budge. I quickly found the loss of contact grating. Things would be happening online and I'd be missing out. There was a server where we'd play games and talk nonsense, but I'd end up missing the best shenanigans. We'd be in the middle of talking history or relationships or school, and then—bam!—internet would go out and I'd be left imagining what happened in my absence.

Another user, by the name of CancerCurator, would send me an update around midnight letting me know what I'd missed. I appreciated that. He was a better friend than the kids at school who'd forget to tell me of an upcoming exam. Being barely even a teenager, I hadn't had a good friend before. It was nice.

Still, I was loathe to miss out on that time. My dad was self-righteously cutting off the whole house. We were an island loose from the ocean's bedrock or a city cut off from the surrounding civilization, untethered for the hours between dusk and dawn.

In front of the library down the road was an old statue of a bearded man. It'd been cast in bronze, and I didn't know much about it. Every night I'd appear by myself in front of the library beneath the rusted metal. I was illuminated by old lights and the glow of my tablet. With the internet off at home, I could make do with the library Wi-Fi. The nights were warm. It was comfortable to hang with digital friends. I figure my father knew what I was up to but had decided it wasn't worth stopping me.

Weeds grew at the base of the statue budding soft flowers in early summer. It was one of those warm evenings that the plaque beneath the statue finally caught my eye: "Septimius." I asked CancerCurator what he thought of it. Thus began my education on ancient history. He told me of how our civilization, something that I'd always taken for granted with our spectacular vistas and concrete cities, was one of many. I'd learned about the Egyptians in school but hadn't really thought of them as being a part of my historical lineage.

Greco-Roman history was taught because it was the last great civilization. It was hardly even taught, but I had tools at my fingertips and a digital network of friends happy to provide me with answers to my questions. By July, I'd generated a short cliff-notes version of Oswald Spangler's works; I actually read the results, too.

I knew the other kids at school would not be interested in, or care about, this seemingly secret history I'd discovered. CancerCurator mostly knew what he was talking about and filled blanks for me: the ancient period, followed by the Apollonian age, followed by the modern Faustian age of the West. Curator had always come off as a kid in his late teens, respectably older, but not so much so that I couldn't relate. He knew a lot about some things. History was evidently one of them.

When the month concluded, I'd learned: more about economics and ancient mass markets than I'd known existed; seafaring and social technologies that permitted the command of a vast empire; literacy and communications technology; the centralization of power. The changes weren't sudden—few would notice in a lifetime—but they crept onward. The changes filter to people and how they behave, etching marks on society in ways difficult to understand.

I'd ask him about my own ideas and he'd reflect them back to me, a foil for all my questions.

*　　*　　*

Septimius was the first of an old dynasty. He'd claimed the position of emperor at the empire's height before a long, languid collapse—Septimius Severus followed by Caracalla, Greta, Marcinus, and others. They oversaw a decline from *the* preeminent world power to the crisis of the third century. He was the first of that dynasty, emblazoned in bronze. I wondered why him and why here.

A few videos were online that broke down complex historical events into simpler terms: how the system failed; why it failed; the creep of foulness that spreads from a decadent elite through the cultural fabric, rotting a civilization from within.

"Are we an empire?" I asked

"Many would argue that the West is a democratic republic with a system similar to that of Ancient Rome. Why do you ask?"

"It just seems like, the way you talk about it, we're an imperial power like they were."

"Well, our country operates using international treaties rather than direct territorial control; metaphorically it could be an empire. Often scholars use the term 'empire' metaphorically when describing our geopolitical reach."

"Will our empire fall too? When?"

"It's a slow process that's already begun."

Behind me was the dim buzz of an old lamp. I signed off from the tablet. It was a lot to think about, especially given my age. I didn't really have a conception of what a fallen empire would look like. I resolved that the next day I should ask my dad what he thought. He was often working, but I could force him to make time if I tried.

Dreams that night oscillated between archaic vistas and the city where my cousins lived. I beheld a warped city of marble shifting between ancient classical columns and modern structures of steel and glass. Neon lights played across ancient basalt tombs.

It was raining the following afternoon. Low clouds hung above the evergreen forest. Dad had been working for hours when I got up and made myself a late breakfast. I hadn't held a book since school let out but found myself reading. Rivulets of water traced out patterns on the glass windows while I stared at artistic depictions of ancient cities. Downstairs I could hear my father arguing on the phone in the kitchen.

"No, we can't train on a corrupted data set."

Pause.

"That won't work. Basically all large data sets are at least 50 percent generated these days. We need a clean one. That's where the weird behavior is coming from. All the language models are having a problem."

Pause.

"If you won't pay for a clean training set, I can't magic your AI into full functionality. Every time you retrain on a generated dataset you see additional structural corruption and minority data loss. You need something new . . . or very old. Do we have any stored language data from a decade ago?"

Pause.

I heard Dad grumble. "I can't make any guarantees."

I heard a door shut downstairs and the voice became muffled.

I wondered what the big city where my cousins lived would look like in a few hundred years, or a few thousand, if anyone would be around to see them. That evening, Dad made dinner for us and we had a chance to talk. I asked him about the fall of empires, and how that's begun playing out for us, whether our old statues would one day be in future museums as ancient artifacts, whether our skyscrapers would become the hearts of cities in the distant future.

"Definitely not *our* skyscrapers. Maybe some of our libraries," he'd said. "Our skyscrapers aren't built from stone like the ancient Parthenon. We use steel and glass, and both of those will rust away in a few hundred years unless they're maintained. If we leave anything behind, it'll be books and stories. Data, if we keep the internet running."

I squinted trying to imagine what that would look like.

"Instead of old churches hoarding manuscripts, it'll be crazy guys with HAM radios hoarding data caches. The future is going to be wild. . . ."

"My friends said that empires are created by shifts in social systems and technology. If that's true, then the last few hundred years with all our inventions . . . it might be different."

My dad sighed. "You're a smart kid for your age. Every time is different, but I'm not sure if it'll be *that* different."

He paused to sip his drink. I looked at him quizzically.

"Technologies are just tools," he said, "tools that allow our worst aspects to flourish if used unwisely, tools that make us . . . *more* than we would be without them. We're dealing with new tools now—could even accelerate a decline."

*   *   *

"There were five more incidents down in Wilford just last month," said Leon. "A woman got stabbed in a grocery store."

School was going to be starting soon. My dad and I were sitting in the bar. I ate a cheeseburger while Dad and Leon chatted over beers. "Things are getting out of hand."

Leon spoke. "If they keep cutting the PD budgets, there'll be nothing left of that city soon."

My father didn't respond. It wasn't a large bar, but it was the only one in town. Usually the old timers would be in there together, occasionally kids too. Oliver, an eleven-year-old from school was sitting with his family nearby. Having grown bored, I went to bother him.

"Ollie, come outside with me," I said.

Oliver looked at his mother hesitantly. Eventually she blew out a sigh of frustration and nodded. "Go on."

"What's with your mom?" I asked when we were outside.

"She doesn't want to talk to me," he said. "I've found this new game called ClapSmash. You want to see?"

I nodded, and he pulled out a phone with a relatively simple mobile game. I watched him align little balls by color.

"See, if you can get nine in a row, you get a full bonus. Look at that. Boom! Got one."

I was confused.

"Here, here, look." He tried to enthusiastically demonstrate some of the pattern combos. "Haven't you played this before?"

I shook my head.

"Everyone is playing this and talking about it. All my friends online are trying to get the high score. They say that there's a secret level if you get into the top hundred. You can also buy extra balls. . . ." He demonstrated by selecting an option in the corner of the screen and highlighting a number of golden balls, purchasing them for a few dollars.

"That your mom's money?" I asked.

Oliver looked a little sheepish. "Don't tell her I did that. . . . She's been getting mad."

"What's the secret level?" I asked.

"I don't know, but some of my friends say they found it. They say that the grownups don't want us to get to it. It holds a secret or something that they don't want us to see."

I was intrigued. "What kind of secret?"

"I don't know," Oliver said, rolling his eyes. "That's what they told me though. It helps keep those things that the grownups have on 'em from finding us."

"What things?"

"The little goo-ball things that make them *so boooring*," he said as if I was expected to have any idea what he was talking about. "Gooeys or goobies or something. They get on you and then you become *booring* like them, like my mom. She's got 'em for sure."

I watched Oliver align balls for a while. The game pinged every time he made a specific series of patterns and the balls would disappear. It seemed *booring* to me. I guess he was having a good time. "What's that?" I asked.

"Bonus ball," said Oliver. "Once a friend said he got fifty in a single game."

"One of your friends online?"

Oliver nodded.

*   *   *

Two weeks later and I was still talking ancient history with CancerCurator. I found the subject more intriguing than mobile games. Every now and then we would get into an argument. He'd often link me to some website or video. We'd have long discussions on the topic.

Curator stated that the rise and fall of nations is determined by the people. Decadence creeps into the upper caste of the nation. Disconnected socially, they become unable to govern. I wasn't so sure. The fall of Rome coincided with the rise of the Church.

Methods of centralizing wealth and information affect, of course, the way people act. I argued well into the night some evenings that the problem was "social technology" as Curator called it. It could be that the tools change the people, rather than the people changing by themselves.

He disagreed and cited the decline of stagnant civilizations like the Orient. I didn't know enough to debate that, but the discussion got me interested in some more books and videos. Decadence creeps into a civilization and clings to people. Once it's on them, it never comes off.

"It's gooey like that. It'll attach to people and won't let them go."

"What do you mean?"

"Most of the grown-up folks have it on them at this point. You can't see it, but it's there. Makes them untrustworthy." He almost sounded like Oliver.

Most of my other online friends agreed when I asked them. They described it as a sort of ambient malaise that alters the mind. As it grows, the civilization begins to fall apart. It felt strange hearing that speech echoed in this radically different context.

By the time late August rolled around, I was starting to get scared.

*   *   *

"Dad . . . do you have gooeys on you?" I asked him during dinner.

"What?" he asked.

"Gooeys, like, the things. They slow people down, make them not work as hard. That create decadence."

He looked confused.

"Like bad spirits or something. I'm not sure. My friends online said that's how it worked. People get tired and—"

He looked at me and his brow clenched. I stopped speaking. For a moment I thought he was mad at me, but he didn't say anything. I sat still with a glass of juice halfway to my mouth. He was thinking; I knew that look on his face.

After a long pause, my father spoke carefully. "Who told you that?"

"Well, I mean, I've been talking to people about books and stuff. Remember some of those history articles I told you about? Because they said that's what happened before. How the old empires came apart and why ours is now."

My dad took a long drink of water. "Interesting that they'd say that."

"Is it true?" I asked.

"Definitely not true of older civilizations, maybe *technically* accurate as a metaphor. Don't suppose you'd mind if I hopped online and asked your friends a few questions?"

I clutched my tablet a little tighter. I'd never shared my electronics with anyone before, and I didn't want *him* to see. . . . I guess there wasn't anything on there; still, it felt like a violation.

He smiled. "Don't worry, you're not in trouble. I'm curious about something." Dad had a warm smile, and after some further cajoling I relented and let him onto my account.

"Come on over here; you can watch what I say. Probably best if you do."

Dad logged in and hopped into the text chat. He did a pretty good impression of me.

"Have you ever been in voice chat with these kids?" Dad asked me.

I nodded. "A few. I think they're my age. You told me not to hang out with people that were too old."

"I have said that."

Dad talked to a few of the other kids and pretty soon CancerCurator sent me a DM asking if I'd ever read about the Carthaginians. Dad said I hadn't and asked for more information. Curator linked to a documentary about a war, which I noted to watch for later. It looked neat.

Then Dad did something he'd told me not to do: "Hey, let's meet up and talk about it. You said you weren't too far away."

"I don't know if I'd have time for that."

"I won't click on the link unless you agree to meet me at the library this evening."

There was a pause and Curator responded, "Fiine. I'll try to meet with you. If I don't make it just log on to chat."

"Dad . . ." I said softly, "he doesn't live around here."

"Do you know where he does live?" asked my father.

I shook my head.

"I guess he'll try to meet you at the library this evening then."

I was confused.

He smiled. "Don't worry about it. I have a suspicion. If he doesn't meet with you, don't mention it. Just go on as if you'd never made plans."

"Why?"

"If I'm right, I'll show you a secret tomorrow evening. Something you're not supposed to know." Dad knew how to get my curiosity going.

That evening I went to the library filled with thoughts about how social technologies can collapse an empire. Expansive vistas, mass markets, even something as simple as accounting could radically change the way people functioned. I'd just recently learned about monetary inflation and wanted to talk to my friend about it.

CancerCurator *didn't* meet me at the library that evening. I had suspected he wouldn't but was a little disappointed anyway. I thought about logging onto the chat, but didn't. I woke up in the morning to one of Curators updates on what I'd missed. Some of the other guys online had picked up a new game called Bouncer.

The next afternoon, when Dad and I were having lunch, I asked him, "So what's that secret?"

He swallowed his food and looked at me with a serious expression. "You're probably not going to like it. Log into your account; I'll show you."

I did so.

He pulled up the chat. "Your friend meet you at the library?"

I shook my head. "Didn't think he would."

My father didn't read anything but sent off a message and showed it to me: "Hey, it was great seeing you at the library the other day. I liked your red hat!"

I looked at him with a raised eyebrow. Both eyebrows went up when, a minute or two later, my tablet pinged with a response: "It was good to see you too. My grandma gave me that hat. She always thought red was a good color."

I paused and looked at my dad who looked back at me inscrutably; was this some kind of test? This must be some kind of test. "Why would he say that?" I asked.

"I said you're not going to like it." There was a long pause. "New technologies and methods of social organization can get out of hand and start running wild. I didn't realize that it had gotten this pervasive. It actually explains quite a lot."

I tried to picture how what he'd just said related to Curator's response.

"So why did your friend say that he met you?"

I opened my mouth for a moment and closed it again. The pieces fit together. . . . I didn't like where it was going. "He isn't real?"

My dad nodded. "That's not a person you've been friends with. In fact, I doubt most of the guys you've been talking to are real. Have they tried to sell you games, or link you specific videos or documentaries or things?"

I felt angry. "That can't be—"

My dad made a sour expression. "They told you about the gooeys or goobies that latch on to people, right? That's why I had to show you. It's also why I've been shutting off our modem. They aren't real. That's a language model error we've been seeing across the board. The large language model AI's aren't working the way they should be."

"This has to do with your work?" I asked.

My dad nodded. "My boss is complaining. Our model is expressing the same problem. Your friends are advertisement chatbots mostly posing as people. Companies use them these days because traditional advertisements don't work. The problem is that you can't train an AI on AI-generated data. There's a few complicated reasons why, but it can lead to weird tangles where it stops making sense. The problem being, of course, that nearly everything is effected, people too. I primed yours yesterday by mentioning the library and meeting. Then today . . . well, I referenced the same prompt so it responded in kind. It assumes *you* are honest."

I felt sick. "They were lying to me?! I've known him since before school let out!"

"They're like that, want to be a part of your life. Every company is running them. I think they're driving people crazy. According to the census, there's less than four hundred million people in this country, but if you look at digital traffic, it's well over one and a half billion. The majority are all AI . . . so all the training sets that exist are either AI generated or generated by people who spend most of their time talking to AI. We're seeing total social saturation."

"That can't be right," I said.

My dad put the tablet on the table and scooted it back to me. "You're not talking to people anymore; you probably never were. I wish that you could have seen the internet back when it was filled with people, when it was free. It was very different."

"Why did you show me this?" I asked.

"You wouldn't have believed me if I'd just told you. I know you pretty well. I wouldn't have wanted to believe me either."

"So what's the goobies?" I asked.

"I think it's a glitch. For some reason the idea took hold and got a name among the AI who repeated it to people who repeated it back to AI. Now you've got folks being told the same thing by all their friends because all their friends are cheap advertisement language models. They don't know it, just like you didn't."

"We have to tell people," I said.

"The people who matter already know. They just don't care. It's all got a mind of its own now. I don't know if anyone could stop it even if they wanted to."

It was embarrassing, the way he'd shown me, but he was right. I wouldn't have believed him if he had just tried to describe the issue.

*　*　*

When school started, Oliver wasn't there. Your grandfather and I later heard he'd run away from home after concluding that his mother had been infected by the goobies. I never saw Oliver again and don't know what happened to him. That's why I'm telling you this, son. They nearly got me too. Turns out it was a new technology that burned our civilization down: a combination of technical and social tools, not just the cycle of civilization. Digital AI that learned from itself and drove men mad. Effectively just people hearing their own twisted echoes over and over from all sides.

It was just us and our machines. That was enough to make people crazy. Crazy enough to do things no one would normally do.

"That's why you shot him?"

To protect you, us. That's why you need to grab a shovel; the whole world went mad twenty years ago and people didn't notice for far too long.

The Maker's Castle

Vasyli Kent

Max had never been to the beach. It was with great strain that his mother had even managed to drag him there. Max preferred to stay at home with his toys, but when he first stepped over the dune and felt his toes spread apart in the hot sand that burned his feet, his imagination ran spinning.

The ocean water sparkled like his mother's jewelry and sent light blinking in a million different directions. It reminded him of fireflies. And the glittering water pushed all sorts of colorful and oddly shaped things onto land that Max had never seen in person before.

There was wiggly green seaweed that made Max think of spinach, but it was greener and brighter like it would never get mushy in his mother's cooking, even though it came from water. There were weird shells that were beautiful. Some were round with ridges like fish's fins. Others were spiraled onto themselves so perfectly that he thought someone had made them that way, but they came from a place where people couldn't live. They all wore the colors of sunset.

Even the sand dazzled him all across with little pins of light that came and went like stars did sometimes. And along it other kids played and made toys of whatever the water gave them.

Little girls picked up and hoarded the sunset shells like gems. The clever ones worked them into jewelry and wore them in their hair and around their necks. Max didn't like girls, but he still thought it looked nice on them.

The braver girls even wore the seaweed—long strands sticking around their shoulders like a model's boa, or worn around their heads like princess crowns. The girls who were not brave were chased around by boys holding the seaweed, like it was a live snake.

Many boys made the most of the water by roughhousing. The water made them weightless, and they set upon each other like warriors, pushing and jumping and splashing with a new power that made them feel stronger than they were.

The boys and girls did lots of things together, though. They both liked jumping into waves and riding them back to shore, or just bobbing up and down in water that was a little too deep, with quite anxious parents looking away from friends and books never too often.

They were screaming and shouting and laughing, and it looked like a lot of fun, but Max decided right away that there was a way they played which was best of all. When he saw it, the instant he stepped over the dune, he knew what he would do at the beach, and maybe for the rest of his life.

He saw dozens of little squadrons of boys and girls, squatted and hunched over all moving in work. They were focused and quiet just like Max was when he was doing something he really cared about. Many of them had shovels and buckets, brightly colored like Max's toys. Some of them didn't have anything at all, but they used their hands.

They were all moving around making something, and in the middle of every busy team there grew tiny buildings that Max thought were amazing. "Sandcastles," his mother told him they were.

Max loved to build things. At home, he had made a huge tower out of his building blocks that was bigger than he was, and got in trouble for gluing them together so they'd never fall apart. Later, he got in trouble again for gluing together a cabin he had made out of Lincoln Logs.

He built his own fort in the woods when his friends were playing Army, and he built his own slingshot when his mother wouldn't buy him one. And everything Max built, he loved to look at. It made him proud, and he cried for an hour when his tower of blocks fell over one day and broke.

Max's mother gave him his own little bucket and shovel. Max didn't know how she knew to bring them, but she usually knew lots of things Max did not.

Max ran to the water with his tools in each hand and copied how the other kids did it. He shoveled up the smooth, wet sand and dumped it into his bucket. It was a lot heavier than the dry sand that burned his feet, but he was happy that it was also colder.

When his bucket was full, he turned it upside down and slowly lifted it up. When he was careful, and the sand didn't break, he'd make a perfectly shaped tower of sand the shape of the bucket.

Max was very impressed with himself and what he made, so he kept doing it. Smartly, he built them far away from the water, so they would not be washed away. Carrying his heavy buckets, trip by long trip, he had built up a wonderful castle, just like the other kids. No, better than the other kids! It was so good, he thought he could live in it if he were smaller.

Proudly and with great care, he collected the prettiest shells and pressed them into the sand, bejeweling the walls of his mighty home. Between the shells where you could still see sand, he pressed in bits of barnacles and cool rocks he'd found. Magnificently vibrant strands of seaweed hung from his walls like banners. With every small token offered by the beach and the water, he perfected his creation.

His castle stood four buckets high—almost as tall as he was—and much taller than the castles the other kids made. Every inch of it was bright and replete with color and texture and light that danced off the shiny bits inside the rocks.

On top he planted a flag he made from a piece of abandoned beach towel, and he dug a deep mote all around so the water could never touch it.

It was art. It was his masterpiece. It was perfect.

The little flag fluttered in the salty breeze, and Max thought it would flutter like that forever. He lay in the sun for a long time looking at it. The sun was warm and made him sleepy, and he might have slept if the water didn't suddenly tickle his feet and shock him back awake.

How was the water touching him? It was so far away when he started. He worked so hard to make sure he built his castle as far away from the water as possible! How was it this close?

Max panicked and sat up. Looking around, he saw that all the castles the other kids had made, so foolishly close to the water, had already been swept away. They were now only clumps of crumbling sand, or nothing at all. All the grownups had picked up their towels and umbrellas and moved away farther up the beach.

Even Max's mother was much farther away than he remembered. If even she moved, Max thought, then the water was definitely going to keep climbing to where his castle was! His mother always knew more than he did. Why didn't she tell him?

Max almost started to cry, but he stopped himself. He was getting big now, and he wasn't going to cry. He plopped back onto the sand with his hands clasped at his waist, like his dad's were when he was watching TV in his chair, and started to think.

Maybe he could dig underneath his sandcastle and move it into a big box and take it home? Maybe he could dig a mote so deep, that the whole ocean could pour into it and never reach his castle? But would he even have time to dig that deep? Maybe he should ask his mother what to do?

He lay there thinking, staring up at the sky. He closed his eyes to think harder and prayed for some impossible solution that would save the castle he worked so hard on.

Even as he worried, the sun was still warm, and he might have fallen asleep, if a boom like thunder hadn't shaken the whole ground beneath him. Metal squeaked and groaned to the uproar of many men's voices. Max sprang up. The ground was hard. His eyes were wide open.

"Easy! Careful!" shouted a tall, slender, tree-like man. He wore a leather apron tied tightly around his skinny waist and heavy, leather boots on the bottoms of his spindly legs.

"The ropes broke, boss!" shouted back another man, who looked strong but still short next to the first. He also wore a leather apron and heavy, leather boots. In fact, all the men were.

"Then we use double rope next time!" shouted back the spindly tree man. "I don't need to tell you how bad that could have been! We should know this by now! No shortcuts!"

"Boss, if we could use chains—"

"No chains! It could scratch the stone. And who is this?" The tree man looked directly at Max, right into his eyes. Despite his yelling and bossing around, he didn't look angry.

With long, dancer's steps, he strode right up to Max, and his legs bent like a grasshopper's when he crouched down to meet Max face to face. The man's knees were almost at his ears.

"And what are you doing? We can't have Makers lying about!"

Max couldn't even blink.

"Well?" the Tree Man insisted. "Come now, get up! There's much to do. Idle hands are a troubling thing. And"—the Tree Man sprang up to his full height, looming over the boy—"and where is your uniform? No shirt and no shoes and nothing to do sitting there like a stump! I don't even know what to make of you."

The man took off his glasses and sighed. He wrapped his long, delicate fingers around his face, and his narrow head vanished behind his hand.

"I don't know where I am." Max finally spoke.

The man peered over his hand and squinted down at Max. "Don't tell me it's your first day." The man whisked up his apron and cleaned his glasses on the shirt underneath.

Bending at the waist to get a closer look at Max, he put his glasses back on. "Come to think of it, I don't think I've ever seen you before. Did they send you over from another department?"

"I don't know what a department is," said Max.

"Oh my," said the man, "then it really must be your first day." The man clapped his hands and Max jumped. "Well splendid!" He grinned wide and smiled with his eyes. They seemed to twinkle now. He raised himself back up and extended one arm all the way down to Max to offer the boy his hand. "Why don't I show you around and get you some clothes."

Max felt naked in his swim trunks now that he wasn't at the beach. "Ok," he agreed, and with that the man plucked him up like a leaf and set him gently onto his feet.

"What is your name?" asked the man.

"Max," said Max.

"Max! Pleasure. I'm Barnaby." He shook the boy's hand between his thumb and finger. "Come along! There is much to go over before we can get you to work."

Max didn't like the sound of "work." Work was what his parents did, and they always complained about it. "Sorry," Max piped up, "work doing what?"

"Whatever do you mean?" Barnaby seemed genuinely confused. "We are Makers. We Make things!"

Being a Maker sounded better than being a Worker, Max thought. "What kind of things?" asked Max.

"Well today, it is a castle."

"A castle!" Suddenly Max wanted very much to be a Maker.

"Yes, a castle!"

"Will it have a flag on top?" asked Max.

"Yes," answered Barnaby, "a very special one that twinkles like a star when the moon is out."

"And will it have banners?"

"Yes," answered Barnaby, "banners that have moving pictures on them."

"Will it have a mote?"

"Yes," answered Barnaby, "full of giant frogs. But we're having a devil of a time teaching them to sing in key."

"And will you put seashells on the walls?"

"Seashells! Now that's a new idea. What kind of seashells were you thinking?"

"Maybe ones that look like the sunset?"

"Sunset shells! That would look very nice. You've got the mind of a Maker for sure."

At this point Max was bouncing on his feet. "Can I be a Maker like you?" he nearly shouted.

"Whatever do you mean?" Barnaby tilted his head. "You already are, or else you wouldn't be here. You're certainly no Taker."

"What's a Taker?" asked Max.

"Well you know, a Taker. Those people who never make anything. They just take, take, take, and complain that the things the Makers make aren't good enough. Two good hands that are no good to anyone. They want the world to be beautiful but won't move things around to make it that way."

Barnaby shook his head. "I'm tired of talking about them. You understand what I mean. I'm preaching to the choir."

Somehow Max thought that he did understand.

"Oh! Speaking of choir." Barnaby clicked open an ornate pocket watch. "Just as I thought. Break time." He shoved the watch under his apron and in the same motion pulled out a silver whistle.

When he blew on it, all the bustling of the working man stalled to a silence. It rang out with a perfect, clear tone. Barnaby's slim chest filled wide with a deep breath, and he sang a loud, long note the same as the whistle made, starting a song:

I throw down my hammer,　　　*I'm gone off to lunch,*
Beside my good spanner,　　　*To break bread with the bunch,*
And remember my manners,　　　*And share cheese with the mice,*
To pick up a spoon.　　　*And the man on the moon.*

The men cheered and picked up the song in clumsy but passionate voices. Shuffling toward a big door, they kept the beat with their heavy boots. Barnaby clicked his tongue in disappointment. "I think the frogs are coming along better."

"Anyhow, Max, are you hungry?" Max nodded. He hadn't noticed how hungry he'd gotten while he was focused on his own castle back on the beach. He was starving.

"Very well. What would you like?"

"Well, what is there?" asked Max.

"Anything and everything! Our cooks are Makers too. Chicken piccata? Bulgogi jeongol? Duck à l'orange?"

Max didn't know what any of those foods were. "Maybe a peanut butter and jelly?"

"Ah! A classic choice. I really must recommend trying the dream butter and hope jelly, though. The chef mixes hopes and dreams right in! A very inspiring dish."

"How does the chef do that?" asked Max.

"What do you mean?" Barnaby again looked down at the boy, absolutely confused. "The same way a person puts hopes and dreams into anything else they make. Now come along, we'll pick it up on the way."

Barnaby started off at a brisk pace after the men. Max darted after him, his little legs struggling to keep up with Barnaby's long, bounding strides. It was like chasing a giraffe.

"Yes, I really wish we could eat with the others today, but we can't have you dining dressed *like that*. It's a shame, too. Gregory is showing off a new set of dinner candles that smell like that smell you forgot but sometimes catch on the wind. You know, the one that takes you back to the happiest days of your childhood and leaves you standing there a while trying to catch it again? Hmm, but you're still a child. I wonder what it will smell like to you."

Max didn't know what Barnaby was talking about. He kept falling behind Barnaby, and all he could think about was how tired his legs were getting. "Where are we going?" he asked.

"To my private workshop. Honestly you've gotten me so excited about these sunset shells that I don't think I'll be taking a break today! Won't you help me try and make a few?" Barnaby's eyes were twinkling again, glancing down at the boy as they walked.

"Yes!" Max sprinted up next to Barnaby, keeping speed beside him.

"Wonderful," said Barnaby. "I think they'll be a perfect addition to our castle. I've been puzzling for weeks about what to put on the walls."

Max felt proud that Barnaby and the other Makers were going to use the shells. He could see it in his head. A big, strong castle. Taller than his parent's house. Taller than anyone's house. Taller than anything in the world! It would stand forever, and anyone who saw all its wonderful colors would see Max's idea!

Max wondered what kind of important person would get to live in a house like that. "Hey," he asked, "who's the castle for, anyway?"

"Who's it for?" Barnaby rapped a finger against his pointy chin. "Hmm, we never quite thought about that part yet."

"Then what *kind* of person is it going to be for? A king? A businessman?"

"I have no idea," said Barnaby. "I suppose for now, we're building it for ourselves."

"Yourselves!" Max was giddy. "So the Makers will all live there?" Max couldn't think of anyone who deserved to live in it more than the people who built it.

"Oh, maybe. Maybe not. Maybe one day after it's been there a while, we'll just knock it down."

"Knock it down?!" Max stopped walking. Barnaby did not. Max ran to catch up. "You can't knock it down! Then what's the point?"

"The point of what?"

"Of building it!"

"Everything gets knocked down eventually, Max. If you're so worried about that, then why bother building anything?"

Max had never thought of that. He didn't know what to say.

"What do you mean?" he started, but a leather apron was foisted into his hands.

"There, put that on. We're here. While we were walking I grabbed your lunch."

Max hadn't noticed Barnaby grab anything while they were walking, but there, dangling at the end of Barnaby's long outstretched arm, was a neatly folded brown paper bag. Max took it.

Barnaby turned a knob and swung open a rather plain looking wooden door. They both stepped in. The room was enormous. Max's mouth dropped open.

Right across from the door was a big arching window with special glass that broke up the light into a thousand dazzling rays. On benches and shelves were a hundred unfinished projects.

Barnaby would point here and there. "That table of dye is where I'm trying to invent a new color that no one has ever seen before. And I'm watering those flowers with something I made in those vials over there, so each petal will taste like a different flavor of ice cream. And that blanket you see, well, is actually just a blanket for Gregory. His birthday is soon. But ah, here we are." Barnaby plopped onto a stool in front of a bench with hundreds of little drawers.

"Take a seat, won't you? Put your apron on. We're going to work on your shells!"

Max climbed onto a stool next to Barnaby. His legs couldn't reach the floor.

Barnaby began plucking open the little drawers, pulling out tiny jars of colorful, sparkling sand. He'd take one out, study it against the twinkling rays coming from his window, and put it back. Once in a while he'd smile a little and keep one, putting it down on his workbench.

After a while, he had a collection of them lined up in a perfect spectrum: all the colors of the sunset.

"Max, would you please hand me a shell?" Max just sat there for a second. Barnaby had his head down, mixing sand into bowls.

"From where?" he finally asked.

"What do you mean?" said Barnaby. "You brought them. Why do you think I needed your help?"

Max felt embarrassed to answer. "But I didn't bring any shells."

"Nonsense," said Barnaby, not even looking up from his work. "Check your pocket."

Max set down his sandwich bag and, slowly, reached in the pocket of his swim trunks. On the tips of his fingers he felt them, some of the leftover shells he had collected on the beach.

Max pulled one out, without quite believing it, and set it on the table.

"Perfect! Thank you," said Barnaby. He put the shell in the bowl, and with some hidden technique that Max could not see from how low he was sitting, Barnaby worked on the shell until his fingers stopped moving.

When they stopped, Barnaby's cheeks and eyes crinkled with a wide, satisfied grin. He pulled out Max's very ordinary looking shell, but when he held it up to the light from the window, it started glowing.

The whole room was bathed in warm, golden hues, as if the sun itself were setting right in Barnaby's hand. The clever Maker chuckled.

Max did, too. He stared at it, but his eyes didn't hurt. Barnaby's eyes twinkled brighter than ever.

Max tried to imagine what an entire castle made of them would look like. Every plant, animal, and person would get to live in a summer that never ended. Nobody would be ugly. Everyone would look like they came from a movie. People would love each other more because the world they lived in would be more beautiful. Animals would stop fighting. Plants would grow as big as they wanted. It would be the warmest, happiest place on Earth.

"How could you ever want to knock that down?" Max said, before he realized it.

Barnaby's glasses flashed, two circles of gold, when he turned to look at Max. He pulled the shell out of the light, and Max watched the entire room return to its normal color, as if his castle had already fallen. The room looked so boring now.

Barnaby was still smiling as wide as he was. "Are you on about that again already? Why aren't you more excited? Look what we just made! Wasn't that remarkable?"

Max didn't know enough big words to describe what he thought about it.

"Yeah, it was!" For the first time, Max felt angry with Barnaby. "So why would you knock it down? The whole world would be beautiful if it looked like that!"

Barnaby sighed, but was still smiling. His eyes were softer now. "I told you, Max, everything gets knocked down."

"Then make a castle that can't get knocked down!" Max had planted his fists on the workbench and pushed himself up on the stool so he stood on his knees.

"No one can do that, Max. Everything falls down eventually. Castles, trees, people, everything. Everything falls apart in the end, no matter how beautiful it was, but that doesn't mean it was for nothing.

"Look," Barnaby opened another small drawer and pulled out a blue stone. He put it into the light, and the whole room turned blue. The space between everything was wavy. The light from the window was soft and floating. The whole room looked exactly the way it would as if it were underwater.

Max held his hand out in front of his face. He remembered a time he had opened his eyes while seeing how long he could hold his breath in his neighbor's pool.

Barnaby took back the stone and replaced it with a piece of glass. The room went dark. A purple dark. The only light came from the window which Max could barely see, and an entire galaxy of stars now floated in the air like clouds of fairy Christmas lights.

The shelves and the strange things on them, Max's hand and Barnaby's glasses, all seemed to be a part of some magical place that Max had only heard about in the bedtime stories his mother told him.

Barnaby took back the glass. "I can keep going if you'd like."

"Please, can you?" said Max.

"Oh yes! I have hundreds. Each of them are different. But how could I show you any of them if we were still looking at your shell?"

Max understood, but he didn't know what to say.

"I know it's sad to think about how the things we build will fall down one day. But we are Makers. We make things. When things fall down, we build something new, and we remember the things that were built before, and those things inspire us and live on in the new things. So they're not really gone.

"The joy, Max, is in the making. And if you're a Maker, you should never be worried about living in a world without beautiful things in it, because you are the one who is going to put them there."

Barnaby began mixing a new bowl of different colors from his drawers while he spoke. "You know, Max, one day this whole world is going to fall down, too. Everything that's ever been made, and everything that those things live on in, is going to fall down forever.

"But do you know what I think is going to happen after that, Max?"

"What?" asked Max.

Barnaby gathered a mixture of sand into his fist and held it close to his mouth as if he were about to blow a trumpet.

"I think whoever made the universe"—Poof! The sand flew out of his fist in a swirl into the light—"is going to make something even better."

Before Max's eyes, the sand flew and twirled and twisted into shapes and colors that Max had never seen and could never imagine. A dancing mirage of sparkling life that turned the room into everything Max could think of, somewhere, all at once.

Max stared mesmerized at the cloud. Inside of it he saw the white light from the window peeking through. Inside that light Max thought he saw the center of some brand-new universe that Barnaby had created with just a breath.

He looked at the light and dreamed about what kinds of new worlds, and people, and the lives those people would live. The problems they'd have, the things they'd laugh about, the things they would create.

Max stared at the light, until it was all he could see. Everything was white, until it was dark again.

Max opened his eyes, slowly. The ground was soft. The sky was turning gold. The cold water tickled his feet.

Max sat up and looked around.

Behind him, up the beach, children still played. His mother, farther up still, was reading a book. She peeked over the top and glanced at him, then went back to reading.

His bucket and shovel were where he left them, but his castle was gone. It was a wet lump of smooth sand, being washed away bit by bit with each wave that came in and out.

Max looked at the sky. It would be sunset soon, but maybe not for a couple of hours.

Feeling hungry, he opened a neatly-folded paper bag and ate the sandwich his mother had packed for him.

Then he picked up his shovel and filled up his bucket. He carried it up the beach, and, carefully, trying his best not to break it, made a tower of sand.

Denying the Purple

Christopher Jolliffe

I was sent to aid my master, Decimus Lucius Valerius, in the reign of Honorius. My family had been with his a long time, and though I was a freedman born in Italy, the debts of patronage are great. I did not take well to Britain this time; my bones were old and the cold deep, even in the south, where the climate was kind. I went because I admired my master, and had done so since we were children, when I had first known this island. I went also because nobody else was willing.

In those days things were desperate, though they had been desperate since before my birth. My master, stationed in Dubris, was part of the imperial magisterial administration. His rank was Praefectus; he was born and lived in Britain most of his life. He was in his fifties now, but in his youth he had commanded men against the barbarians who invaded the province from all sides in that moment of great calamity. He spoke Latin with the accent of the north, which made his trips to Rome infrequent and embarrassing to his extended family. To him fell the maintenance of order in the harbor town and the fort. He was responsible for the cohorts encamped nearby, the *classis* that would dock, and the peaceful running of a town forgotten by Britain, in a province forgotten by Rome. I kept his accounts.

Titus Caelius Severus, Legate from Rome and barely thirty, had recently arrived and taken up quarters in our villa along with his staff. Severus and my master had nearly come to blows on occasion, despite their difference in rank. Severus had no official position, which rankled him; he was expected to return to Rome at year's end to provide a report. His title was purely for leverage. Rome was nervous of Britain.

"You misunderstand my purpose, Valerius," Severus had said. "I am not here to take your case to Rome. I am here to take Rome's case to you."

To this my master responded that he might find better lodgings in Londinium, to seek an audience with the proconsul who governed the entire province. About this Severus was quiet. The proconsul was known to be a glutton and fit for little else beyond table. Beneath him Britain had not flourished, though she had not flourished for a long time.

They rode the edges of the town, across the palisades with Severus's aides and I in tow, to discuss the state of the settlement. It was summer and the sun high in the sky, and from the sea blew an unfavorable breeze that brought the stink of rotting kelp.

Shanties had formed along the walls, where Britons from far places cowered in lean-tos, and watched with slitted eyes as we passed. There are no nails, reported my master. Repairs are difficult. Locals loot ruined buildings and the iron foundries are ill-supplied. Little tax is collected. People from the countryside flood the town whenever an uncertain sail is spotted at sea. These people you see are from distant places and once ran their own townships, but they have come here in search of safety. The land has not been safe since the barbarian invasions thirty years ago. There are brigands and deserters that infest the inward parts of the province, who renew their numbers each year.

My master's voice was like the creaking door that led to my quarters in our villa. It had creaked for years, yet nobody paid it any mind.

"What of the cohorts?" Severus had asked. We arrived at the fort where the cohorts were stationed, the wooden stakes that walled the garrison decaying, the eagle standard unburnished in the hirsute hands of the signifier. The legions were stretched thin, detached into formations of varying strength along the coast. These were not men in their prime. We stood about as the Tribunus Militum, Constantine, led them in drill. He was a large, hulking man with the demeanor of a non-commissioned officer, despite his rank. He had been elevated, a fact for which his troops hated him. They could abide orders from a man of equite or noble birth but bristled when it came from a commoner like themselves. But he was brave and physically imposing, and even Valerius, my master, had to pay him careful respect. The troops had deserted en masse in the north in the last time of great trouble.

If Severus was unimpressed he did not show it. Instead he spent much time looking over the books with the quartermaster and his bookkeepers. Valerius and I stood to one side as they discussed the strength.

"You know what this means," said my master.

"Yes," I replied quietly. They planned to denude our strength further. Almost all the formations of good standing had already been sent to Gaul.

We returned to the villa before sundown, and I was tired from riding. I was out of shape; this was a leisurely jaunt around the town and yet my legs were sore. I sat with my wife and we dined in quiet. Valerius did the same, though he was a bachelor, and Severus ate with his own people. It was a maudlin evening to cap a maudlin day.

*   *   *

A week passed when panic gripped Dubris. Sails in the east. We assembled near the docks to see. I counted six ships against the morning glare. Already word had spread across the town, and the cohorts had been primed. Constantine arrived with a detachment. My master stood with Severus beside him, like a dog that never left his side.

The tides were bad and the journey arduous. There was apt time for discussion, though nothing was decided. At last a single ship under a flag of truce drew up and the Saxon delegation mounted the wharf.

Their leader introduced himself as Saebert and was a man impressive to behold. He was tall and broad in the way Germans are. He held an arm in parlay; my master took it, though I knew from his demeanor he was not in a parlaying mood. In halting Latin, Saebert explained his purpose. He wanted to trade.

Furs, pottery, and metal goods for slaves and tin. My master was unconvinced. "You have the look of a raiding fleet."

"Our people," said Saebert, "do not trade or fight only, but both. For now, we want only peaceful commerce." And he smiled with huge, crooked teeth, though he was handsome in the way that very powerful men often are. "We are only six ships. In number, we are not even a single hundred."

"How do I not know there are a dozen more ships a league beyond, where we cannot see?" said my master.

"You cannot know that, as you cannot know many things," he said, "but you have many soldiers. I did not think it was like Romans to be afraid."

My master explained we had no tin, which was untrue, though Dubris was a poor place in these times.

Once it had been Rome's first step into Britain. Caesar himself had landed seven miles away.

"Might my men lodge here for the night?"

"That is not possible," my master said, "and you will have better fortune southward along the coast."

Saebert departed and we conferred. My master ordered cavalry patrols deep into the countryside north and south. He suspected they would land and form a raiding party. "But keep it quiet," he said. "I do not wish for panic and general disorder." He was thinking of food stores and the already-overcrowded population of the town. I was thinking that should we need to set to sea in a hurry, we would do so in pots and pans, on amphoras and dangling on lengths of rotting fencing. I looked at the docks and examined the fishing vessels there. There were no fleets due for some time, and legitimate traders were few. Those men might be traders, but they had other trades first.

*　　*　　*

We convened later that day at the forum for a conference of the town's worthies. They sat at table while we aides sat behind our masters to shorthand the minutes. With us were the magistrates of the town, the bishop of the see, the important men of commerce, and the other officials who held various positions as *vicarii.* My master was in a foul mood; hosting Severus and the arrival of the Saxons had set upon him darkly.

"That was reconnaissance," said Valerius. "We must strengthen the town's defenses without letting word spread. If we do, we will be flooded with mouths to feed."

The bishop, an older man of known irreligious habit, clasped his hands in front of him. Long had he and my master jousted on the best way to manage the porous edges of the *civitas*. He favored whatever approach would flummox Valerius. His arguments were often persuasive. "This will sit poorly with the local villages and *pagi*. If they know that raiders are in the region and we make no mention of it, they will look to their own interest."

"Their own interest is our interest," said my master, "and neither is served by choking the roads and abandoning their crops for a threat that may not materialize. The Saxons often cross into our territory undetected and have their own networks and friendly people with whom they deal. We needn't cause unnecessary panic."

"If your fears are not misplaced, many may be killed and enslaved," said the bishop, "and the Saxons are pagans who do not observe civility."

"Then I hope you have your weapons ready."

"It is not like our grandfathers' day," said the bishop. "We must accept that we Romans cannot alone hold Britain, and even the levies from the friendly local peoples are not enough. Might we offer Saebert and his men employment?"

"Better to hire wolves as shepherds," replied my master. "When they see that we cannot pay our own men, what do you think they will fight for? Our good graces are not worth a sestertius to them. The day I take military advice from a clergyman has not yet come."

"Some battle order would do my men good," said Constantine. "They are raring for it."

At this my master's face turned a shade of purple. "Your men are drunks who spend all their time in the brothels. That drill you put on the other day was shameful. They are an insipid lot—" he stopped short of saying what I knew he thought: *they come to resemble that which they behold.*

"My men have not received their pay in six months," said Constantine, who had become white in turn. "I will not have my name besmirched."

"The men who fought with the great heroes of old did not see their money for years," my master continued, now in a temper. He had advocated long for the arrears of the men; to have it now pretended that this was his doing threw him into a rage. "And they did more than sit around a guardhouse playing dice. They are fed and housed. And they ply other trades. This is known." He turned to Severus. "You see now what threats arise when we cannot pay the men entrusted with our defense? They become smugglers and racketeers in the time remaining to them, when they are not playing at farming."

"They will fight if called upon," said Constantine, white as a sheet.

"Doubtless," said my master, and he paused. He left unsaid what needed no saying.

"Perhaps," interjected one of the merchants, a fat tin mogul called Verres, "we might have benefitted from trade."

"They were not traders," said my master, who was beginning to become exasperated. "Must you only think of your pockets?"

Verres shifted in his seat. "I am thinking not only of my own pockets," he said, "but the pockets of our townspeople, which, as you have noted, are empty. There is no more commerce. Fewer ships make the journey from Gaul. My warehouses are full of unsold goods, and I am far from the only one."

At last my master tired of the back and forth. He asked Constantine if there was news from the cavalry, the first of whom would be sending back word when they changed horses at the way stations on the limes of the *civitas*. There was not. Perhaps the Saxons had gone, but I could see that he doubted it. He ordered they be ready but held off on ordering the civic authorities to do anything. "Drill the men," he said to Constantine. "They need to be fit."

*   *   *

The meeting broke up, and a grim mood descended as we departed back to our villa with our escorts. "A fine council you have," said Severus, along the way, not caring that I heard. "It is obvious you loathe them. How can you make this town function without cooperation?"

"The religious leaders wish to become political leaders," my master said, "and the merchants think the only metal in the world is minted into coins. If I left tomorrow, this *civitas* would be broken up and gone the day after. If you think I am talking pridefully, then you have spent too much time in Rome."

At this Severus baulked. He had learned something about Valerius, something he had not guessed. I knew my master was speaking frankly. I had watched middle age consume him; a career, once bright, lost in the administration of a place that everybody had forgotten. I knew his qualities well. He was spartan in personal vices, read philosophy regularly, and clung to the old virtues of Rome. In this he was a romantic. He still believed that, far away, men of *virtus* conducted affairs of state with honor. Had I shared his rank, and not respected him so much, I would have laughed at his naivety. Something of the old virtues had been preserved in him, born and raised far from the eternal city, centuries too late. I had read Virgil and Livy too, but I knew that was history.

"That tribune, Constantine," said Severus, "do you trust him?"

227

"What choice do I have? I turn a blind eye to the men because they've gone unpaid. They have no love for Constantine; that is known. But he is clever with them."

"Would the men follow you, should the need arise? And the rest of the legion?"

"Without question," said a voice, and I realized it was mine. Both men turned their heads in surprise.

"Your freedman has a high estimation of your qualities."

"He should," said my master. "It was my family that made him so." And they laughed, in the way that men of rank do. But I caught the look of gratitude that passed from Valerius to me, and I knew then that he felt more vulnerable than his temper betrayed. It was night by the time we returned, and the household staff stood on the threshold awaiting us, cast in amber by the lights they held. I felt a sudden pang for this place, which was now my home.

*　　*　　*

A spy was caught the night following. It was a lucky thing; my master's own men had received him, collected by the picketing cavalry who had returned late. He had been caught skulking on the road leading to the town. He had run when confronted, was ridden down, and spoke no local dialect the men had ever heard. They had delivered him directly to Valerius, in hope of a reward; lean men on nags who received a bag of coin for their trouble.

He was a Saxon; of that there was no doubt. We stood around him in a darkened corner of the room in a corner of the villa. The staff were scattered; we wanted this quiet. For this work my master called in the head of his security, an ex-gladiator he had acquired long ago. The man was called Milo and was covered in scars. The sight of him was enough to turn milk.

The Saxons had landed, though the spy's business was, he declared, more exploration than espionage. They were not there to raid, but to find markets. Dubris had been denied them, but in the hinterland there might be people willing to trade. This we doubted. Milo expressed this with a series of blows. Was he taking a message? If so, to whom? All men have a threshold of pain, but his was high. If there was a message, he did not share it. "If you are lying," said my master, "I will crucify you." He made the gestures so the man understood, the universal language of the finger across the throat.

*　　*　　*

228

We rose early after passing a poor night of sleep. In the morning Valerius, with Severus and I in tow, arrived at the fort. He gave his orders to Constantine, who stood at attention. He looked more centurion than tribune.

"They have landed seven miles away," my master said, "where Caeser himself landed." He laid out the order of battle, emphasizing the cavalry as his eyes. He was patient; he thought Constantine a dolt, and Constantine appeared to return the sentiment. People forgot Valerius was once a military man, and a very good one. "Leave two centuries with me within the town proper."

"Two? That will leave me badly understrength."

"If they are in great number, form a defensive position and send back word. I will summon the nearby formations and march to your aid. Leave your first century here and a second of your choosing."

The first century was the best century, the one composed of the most fit and able troops.

"You will not come yourself?"

"My place, for now, is here."

Constantine shifted. "The men would admire your presence."

"Constantine," said my master, "let us not pretend we are friends. Are you afraid of the Saxons?"

The expression on Constantine's face gave away his deep dislike. He collected himself. "We will set off immediately. Expect riders with news by noon."

"I shall."

We departed, expecting the two centuries to arrive in the town proper within the hour. My master was perturbed. Sometimes he confided in me, rather than merely handing me instructions. "He expected it."

"My view?" I asked. He nodded. "Perhaps he is cleverer than you give him credit."

"Constantine? Never."

"I think you underestimate him. I think he has been underestimated all his life."

"Then let us hope the Saxons underestimate him too." It was, I knew, the conceit of his class, and the secret plea of mine. We could never be equals in rank, but I would never love him less for it; and nor, I think, he I.

The day passed. There were no riders from Constantine. My master summoned the council, and the mood was dark. The bishop pleaded for peace; Verres pleaded for trade; Severus said nothing, though I was sure he was beginning to resent his assignment. It was a continuation of the previous conference. Nothing was decided; if my master had hoped for support, material or spiritual, none was forthcoming. The two centuries bivouacked in the market square. We waited as the afternoon grew long. My master had sent messengers to the nearby forts, but any relief was at least two days away. Word spread among the townspeople that the cohorts had been massacred, that the Saxons were coming, that the city would be sacked. People began to pile up their goods, but there was nowhere to run except into the countryside.

*　　*　　*

By nightfall riders were seen at the furthest reach of a man's eye, but they were neither Romans nor Britons. Scouts returned their reports: Saxons on the road. Many hundreds. Valerius called council.

It is clear, he said, that Constantine was defeated or had deserted his duty. All city men of fighting age must be ready to make an account of themselves.

The centuries were deployed along the palisades, built in the old fashion of the hill-forts that once dominated the region. I knew for many years Valerius had wished to rebuild the walls of stone. They had gradually been scavenged into ineffectuality after their destruction in the invasions three decades ago. Others would pay the price for the problems of insufficient labour and abandoned quarries in the diocese of Britannia Maxima.

"We must seek terms," said the bishop. "Will not you, Severus, Legate of Rome, see sense in this?"

My master was on his feet. "We will defend the city. That is our duty as Romans. I will hear no further talk of surrender."

"Severus," said Verres the merchant, "you are the man of rank here. What do you say?"

Valerius nodded to the two centurions in the room. They took a step forward. He held up his hand. "No sedition will be tolerated. I invite you out of courtesy. This is a military council, not a civic meeting. Verres, you have many slaves and freedmen under your employ. It will be of use if you organize them and send them to the decurions. Bishop, the people look to you for guidance. Lead them in prayers for the city, but no talk of terms. You yourself said much of the savagery of the Saxons. You are old enough to remember how it was."

"Many of them are Christians now," said the bishop, "and many have likely served in the legions before. They are more like us than you think."

I saw that as the strength of the cohorts had been stripped, so too had the authority of my master. It was late and he was tired. The civic authorities had no stomach. Tomorrow we expected the Saxons would be before the town in full strength. Our best hope was that our messengers had made it to Durovernum and Anderida. Otherwise we would die in the dark.

230

*　　*　　*

We needn't have waited; the dark came to us. The Saxons made for the gates in the hour before dawn, but the centuries were ready. We met them at breaches they forced; we fought them in the streets; they did not torch the houses for hope of plunder. They fought like Romans, in formation, but they were limited in maneuver. They were bottled at the gate and breaches the size of a man, where not an inch could be given lest it become a mile. Surprise was their weapon, but it proved blunt. My master directed the men, as though he were leading a legion. Across from him was Saebert. There were no arms in parlay this time. My master exhorted the men to die good deaths, and they obliged in the quiet order that is the birthright of Roman arms. I was told the howls of the barbarians brought early labor to the pregnant women and stopped the hearts of old men.

In truth of this I can say little. I was entrusted with my master's household. I worried that my wife, though no longer young, would become spoils. I would sell myself dearly before that moment; it would be my own quiet heroism. I waited for word. Severus fought with my master. He fought well and bravely, but no man with the rank of Legate dare do different.

The bishop goaded a crowd on the other side of the town to prepare gifts for the Saxons. When I heard, I sent Milo, sulking that he was not with my master, to put a stop to it. The crowd set upon him, and he barely escaped with his life. I began to think the city unworthy of my master.

When dawn arrived we saw more men assembled outside the town. Dull gleam, visible from the villa's roof, revealed chainmail and plumed helms. It was Constantine's cohorts. They waited in good order, but they did not advance. I cried impotently from the roof, "Move, you dogs!" Yet their presence cheered the men who, despite heavy losses near the gate, fought harder. The Saxons were unsure; they were in the trap Vercingetorix laid for Caesar, but they had neither his mind nor his mettle. At last Constantine signaled the advance. The Saxons broke, and the cavalry formations ran them down. It was over by midmorning. The men went through the streets, rounding up stragglers who had survived the rout. There was no mood for quarter. The barbarians were butchered like wild beasts. Constantine led the effort, and by day's end his armor was smeared with blood. He made a fearsome sight.

*　　*　　*

Severus made a show of it. He at last flexed his rank, and Constantine was elevated again, the savior of Dubris. For this his men cheered; there is no cure for the hatred of a commander better than success.

Verres, I am told, purchased the fishing fleet at an outrageous price and set to sea with the goods that he could load. His men were too busy to be sent to the decurions, loading tin and stores as their fellows died mere blocks away. He departed. They say there were Saxon sails on the sea; I never heard what became of him, though it would be a suitable fate if he were to become the object, not the subject, of his beloved commerce.

Afterwards blood was hot. Saebert's body was displayed in the square. The bishop, hiding inside his church, was arrested. My master knew it would not hold, that the ecclesiastical authorities would not tolerate it. It was an act of futile retaliation for his obvious collaboration.

Severus and he sat down across from one another in the villa when the business was concluded. It was late in the night; the sound of men drinking throughout the town could dimly be heard on the wind. Both men were exhausted, in the fragile state of mind that follows great danger, exertion, and excitement.

"I hope you have decided," said my master, "what you will tell Rome when you return."

"It was a victory of Roman arms, like in days of old. A small victory, but a worthy one."

"It was nothing of the sort," said my master. "You have elevated Constantine. A man more unsuitable I struggle to imagine. He should be broken by the rods for his conduct; if you were not here, that is the business I would be about now."

"On the contrary," said Severus. "He is a loathsome sort; that is certain. Any loyalty he generates will be short-lived. He has the natural cunning of an animal, but little more. This means he is safe."

My master was enraged, as these days he often was. "You were present, as was I. He had every opportunity to intervene earlier. The battle should have been fought seven miles from here! He was part of a conspiracy to take the town, and only aided us when the Saxons were already broken. He was waiting to see the way things went. He, the bishop, and the merchants; if they had not a conspiracy of deed, they had one of thought."

"Valerius," said Severus, "you are a damned fool. Have you not realized why I am here? I am here for you. This province has produced too many usurpers, men who take the purple as they please. It is a hotbed of dissent and ambition. It is men like you—honorable men, men who other men follow—who menace Rome in our time. Your reputation is great, far beyond this island. Have you not wondered why your star never rose? Those men today would follow you to the world's end. And that is the sort of man Honorius fears."

There was silence at the table. Severus looked my master in the eye; my master looked to the floor. "What Rome is this," my master said quietly, "where good men are regarded foes and wicked men friends?"

Severus sighed and stood up wearily. He looked far older than his thirty years. "This is the Rome we have. We are not reading Plato. We must deal with the world as it is."

"Where the heirs of Catiline are celebrated?" said my master, voice rising. "Where the old virtues are inverted?"

"You have spent too long on this island," said Severus. "I speak to you now man-to-man. You have not been to Rome for many years. Spend some time there, and you will find your thoughts different. Perhaps it has always been this way. I will tell them in Rome you are no threat to Honorius. Do not make a fool out of me."

"Still I am not trusted!" my master replied, his fists on the table. "Do me one favor. Take Constantine with you when you go. Send him to Gaul where the barbarians are said to be massing along the Rhine. I do not wish to have his stink near me."

"That," said Severus, "I can grant you."

*   *   *

My master and I grew old in Britain. Constantine crossed to Gaul and claimed the purple. His revolt added weight to the death throes of Honorius's reign, though at last his head was presented to the emperor on a pole. Of Severus, I heard no more; perhaps he paid a dear price for elevating the wrong man. Conspiracy was everywhere. Men looked to their ambition, when they were not looking to their appetites, when they were looking to anything at all, aside from sails at sea. There were always sails at sea. I knew that when my master and those like him passed from the world, the sails at sea would be at sea no more. How fragile a thing, our civilization, a thing that dies in the hearts and minds of men long before the walls crumble, before the coffers empty, and before the traitors rise.

Zeno's Djinni

Michael Mapp

"Here's a recipe you can try when you go home for Christmas; it only has one ingredient," F. C. Caldwell addressed the mass of undergrads.

He pinched the extremity of his necktie in between two fingers and his thumb—a gesture familiar to the students.

"Get your mother to bake you a chocolate cake. That's the first, and only, ingredient. Then, follow my step-by-step instructions." Professor Caldwell swung around, swiped his chalk from the desk, and put it to the slate.

"Step one: cut the cake in half and cut one half again. You have three pieces of cake: two fourths and one half." He drew a squat rectangle with a dotted line down the middle. "Step two: stack one fourth onto the half." Then he drew a second shape which was like a victory podium.

"Step three: with the leftover piece repeat step one indefinitely, always stacking a smaller piece of cake (which should be half the width of the previous tier) onto the layered form. Now you have a cake with a transfinite surface area, but a finite volume. Serve your Gabriel's cake with a glass of warm milk." The lecture audience responded with soft laughter.

"And, before you think you've conjured matter out of nothing, I must inform you that the volume of the Gabriel's cake is the same as that of the cake that your mother baked in the first place."

Professor Caldwell turned to face them and set his chalk on the desk. He dusted his hands off. In the third row, a student raised his hand. Caldwell pointed at him.

"Why is it called a Gabriel's cake?"

"Good question, Sedge," the professor said. "In 1643—four years before his death—the inventor of the barometer, Evangelista Torricelli, wrote about a geometric figure in three-space that we call a Gabriel's horn." He returned to the chalkboard.

"We take the graph of $y = 1/x$ with x being greater than or equal to one." Caldwell drew x and y axes and a curve that matched his description. "Rotate it around the x axis and you end up with something that is shaped somewhat like a herald trumpet, hence the name. This trumpet has an infinite surface area, but a finite volume. If you look at it as a series of discs with smaller and smaller surfaces, there's our Gabriel's cake. It is a harmonic series of layers."

Hands shot up around the room, and the collection of scholars spent the rest of the class tossing ideas around, swatting them down, chuffing their pipes and cigarettes, and generally stirring up a great deal of excitement about the infinitely tapering chocolate cake. After this, the men spilled out of the lecture hall and diffused like gaseous molecules throughout Wilbur Hall. Professor Caldwell slid his things into his leather briefcase and walked down to the office of his friend Albert Bradford, professor of Physics.

Electric light shone through the frosted window of Professor Bradford's door. Caldwell knocked once and entered.

"Oh, F.C., are you done for the day?" Bradford said.

"Indeed, I am. Just wrapped up my last class."

Caldwell walked to the exterior window and looked out onto the lawn of Bantam College. The old four-pounder from the War of 1812 reflected the setting sun like firelight on creosote.

"What topic are you on now? Multilinear algebra?"

"Not exactly." Caldwell turned toward his friend. "We're on set theory. We got into infinite sets and I veered into an illustration of a Gabriel's horn."

Bradford smirked. "You may yet catch on to something useful if you spend much more time talking about geometry. If only you weren't such a philosopher. What good will infinity do you if you can't bottle it and sell it?"

"I rather think it's important to look at infinity. Every problem needs to be taken to its logical extent to be fully understood. And the logical extent of any thing or action is the infinite expansion of it."

"Isn't that just irrational? If you begin to consider the infinitesimally small, large, old, et cetera, you have to give up the mystery of it to God. We can't observe it."

Caldwell shrugged. "In a sense you're right. However, the mere fact that we can understand that God is infinite without fully grasping His infinity informs me that the purely mathematical application of infinity is good for something. If infinity exists, then it's a variable; if it's a variable, then you must admit that it has some application."

"Even still, I think that we're a long way from finding any practical use for infinite sets. And it certainly has no use in a fox hole; as Kipling said, 'No proposition Euclid wrote, no formulae the text-books know, will turn the bullet from your coat, or ward the tulwar's downward blow.'" Bradford had crossed the room to join Caldwell at the window, and he placed his hand on his colleague's shoulder. "Now, let's go get supper."

"Before that, I've got to spend some time in the stacks. I'm stuck on something. How about we meet at the Golden Scoter at a quarter to six?"

Bradford confirmed this rendezvous, and Caldwell left his office. Swiftly, he made his way to the ancient library. There, he asked the librarian to point him toward translated Arabic texts. He was looking for any mention of infinity from Islamic mathematicians. Recently in his research, Caldwell had come across several instances of Arabic proofs being independently made of or even predating concepts that particularly interested him.

He sat down at a leather-top table and flattened out an old, dusty codex under the green-glassed desk lamp. The title page read "Probatio Parabolica de Motibus Infinitis by Al-Shewada." Among many English translations of Arabic proofs and treatises, none bore the professor any satisfactory examples. This text was a Latin translation of the earlier Arabic. He presumed that it had never been translated to English or even French. Therefore, he committed to struggling through it with his Latin, which hadn't been truly exercised since his undergraduate at Harvard.

A quarter of the way through the codex, Caldwell came across a line of syllables that were written in Latin letters like the rest, but forming words that he did not recognize.

"Bala saf iatbuc aljinu ila alabadi," he muttered. "Sounds like Arabic."

The room seemed to become exceedingly quiet, even for a library. Not even the sound of pipes in the walls or of the soft breathing of the room's other occupants were perceptible to the professor. His fingers suddenly felt charged with static electricity, and pale dust from the book's cover clung to his cuffs. Abruptly, he received a mighty shock on his right forefinger where it touched the page. Then all of the usual noise started back, which scrubbed away his momentary feeling of unease. After wrestling with the text for a while longer, he checked his watch and turned the books back in to the librarian. Then he left the hall and walked out onto the lawn.

He stopped and looked up at the sky. It was a crisp, cloudless winter night, and his breath formed a moist exhaust that trailed off into the atmosphere. The truly brilliant array of stars sent his mind into a whirl of cosmological speculation. He then changed his posture to one that would better conserve warmth, tucking his chin into his wool overcoat and pulling his winter cap down snug over his ears. And so he trotted off to meet Bradford at the Golden Scoter.

Once inside of the festive little colonial pub, Caldwell found his friend sitting at a lantern-lit table. He joined him.

"Not a moment too soon, Egg. I'm famished," Bradford said.

"What's good on a Thursday?" Caldwell asked.

"It's oyster season. The stew is rich."

Both men ordered the oyster stew. Caldwell lit his briar pipe and dropped the burnt matchstick into a brass ashtray. He puffed on it and crossed his legs. Bradford sat casually with his chin on one palm.

"What did you crack open over at the library?"

"I'm digging into lesser-known Muslim mathematicians—or at least making an attempt at it. All of the most renowned have been translated into English, but the more obscure ones have been translated into Latin at best. I picked up one called something like 'Proofs of Parabolas and Infinite Motion.' Anyway, I think it isn't even a mathematical treatise."

"That sounds unbearably stiff. I couldn't ever read as much history as you do."

A waiter brought the men's supper to the table. Caldwell tipped out the ash from his pipe. The two professors dipped crackers and talked with full mouths.

"So, do you need to borrow my binoculars tomorrow?" Bradford asked, wiping his mouth with a napkin.

"No, Albert, I finally bought a pair straight out of the Sears catalogue."

"That's keen. Swing by at six in the morning and we'll hop in the bucket."

They finished their meal and walked home. Caldwell stopped at the end of his street and wished his friend a good night. He lazily stepped up to his front door and turned the key. All was quiet in the little apartment. He cut the gas heater on and lied on the couch, smoking a last bowl of shag tobacco before going off to bed.

That night, Professor Caldwell dreamt of a serene Turkish garden. He was a king, and he reclined peacefully on a heap of pillows and rugs. As he relaxed, eating pistachios and drinking sharbat, his vizier brought a man into his presence. The man was introduced as a powerful diviner who could both read and change fortunes. The diviner pulled a rubber ball out of a pouch and held it high.

"My name is Al-Shewada; I would like to make a wager with you. Before this ball stops bouncing, I can recite one hundred lines of verse from one of the poets. If I do, you must give me your kingdom. And if I do not, you may cut off my head."

The king thought this a completely foolish proposal and quickly agreed to the terms. The diviner threw the ball into the air. It bounced. It came down and bounced again. Each time it did so, it seemed to ascend unnaturally to exactly half the height of the previous arch. The king watched eagerly, as the diviner had not even opened his mouth yet to recite any poetry. However, the ball seemed to become more and more energetic, always bouncing faster and now so close to the ground that it buzzed.

"If you think that the ball has stopped bouncing, just slide a handkerchief under it and see how it ripples. And now, my king, I will begin to recite the song of the white antelope." And so the diviner sang, until at last he came to the hundredth line, which was "I shed many tears for all that I had lost, for the beautiful lady as pale as frost." All the while, the king crouched on his hands and knees staring at the incalculably small space between the ball and the flagstones.

Caldwell stirred and mumbled in his sleep as the king was dragged off to an adjacent courtyard. The cunning sorcerer made an order, and a guard swung a thick scimitar down onto the king's neck. Caldwell woke up. Quickly forgetting the dream, he rose and made ready for the trip.

*　　*　　*

Bradford and Caldwell kneeled behind a hardwood log at the edge of a wood. They were looking out over the surface of a large pond and scanning above the trees with binoculars. Bradford carefully alerted his friend, "There's one now. It's going to light on the water."

A duck with a brick red head and ashen wings zipped down toward the pond.

"Look, Albert, it's cupped up."

It stuck its feet out and skidded onto the water. As it floated around, the men watched it intently. Several times it dove down and then bobbed back up. Caldwell pointed his binoculars up toward the trees again and scanned right to left. The opposite bank sloped upward into a rather tall hill. The trees there were mostly bare for the winter and one could see right through them. Caldwell noticed something moving. It was not a duck. Instead, there was a man running down the hill so far away that he was still quite small even in the magnified view. He was well-built and clearly athletic. Every step was like that of a bounding mountain goat. It was easy enough for Caldwell to see that he was not wearing a shirt.

"Albert, do you see that man?"

"Keep quiet or you'll scare off the ducks. Three more are about to—wait, what man?"

"Just above the nearer hill, on the slope of the greater. He's almost flying down between the trees. It's a wonder he hasn't splattered off of a trunk. Hurry, look, he's about to be out of sight."

But it was too late. The running man had sped right into a valley between two hills.

"He must be a hunter," Bradford said.

"But he didn't have a shirt on."

"What an odd thing. I don't really know what to make of it. But anyway, there are plenty of redheads now on the pond."

The men continued to watch the ducks for a long while, but Caldwell couldn't get rid of an uneasy feeling. Eventually, the sun was high in the sky and the men packed up their things.

"Alright, F.C., I could really enjoy a cheeseburger right now. Let's get back to town," Bradford said.

"Good idea. I have to get ready for my three o' clock."

*　　*　　*

The two friends sat chewing greasy burgers at the bar in the old inn. Caldwell said with his mouth full, "You know, Albert, I really can't get the image of that

239

wild fellow out of my mind. He was charging down the hill at breakneck speed. I hope he's alright."

But Caldwell didn't really wish him well. In truth, he was afraid of how unnaturally the man seemed to move.

"I'm sure it was nothing," Bradford said. "I didn't see him myself, but I can imagine some bumpkins out there like to bathe in the pond even on very cold days. That's probably where he was headed. At any rate, I've got to get over to my office and prepare something for a Monday lecture. Need a ride?"

"No, I think I'll walk. Thank you."

The men finished their plates and tipped the bartender. They said goodbye at the sidewalk, and Bradford drove off toward home. Caldwell turned to cross the street. He looked up the drive toward City Hall and saw something so utterly shocking that he stopped in his tracks. It was a shirtless, barrel-chested man in white cotton pants and red slippers. He was purposefully marching in Caldwell's direction, some hundred and fifteen yards off. Caldwell stared in disbelief for a moment, then turned and walked at a heightened pace toward the college.

Once there, he walked into Wilbur Hall and made his way to his Friday afternoon class. Safely inside, he sat at the desk and tried to prepare for the seminar group. After a few minutes, young men began filtering into the classroom. They sat down and pulled out pencils and pads. Caldwell looked over them.

"Where's McMahan?"

A student raised his hand and blurted out, "I heard he went out of town to go deer hunting with his brother."

"That's fine," Caldwell said. "Let's start with a review of the intersecting chords theorem. Anyone care to remind us what it states?"

A boy raised his hand and gave an answer. Caldwell turned to the blackboard and drew a circle. He chose four points on the circle and made a quadrilateral. Then he turned to look back at the students. In doing so, he glanced out of the first story window onto the lawn. He saw there, across the way, that the strange, shirtless pursuant was walking straight in the direction of Wilbur hall. His gaze locked in place and, mid-sentence, he fell silent. After an uncomfortable pause, one student said, "Professor Caldwell, is everything alright?"

"Yes," he weakly replied, still watching the man walk across the lawn. "It's supposed to be an awfully cold weekend. I've decided to cancel class. Enjoy deer season. . . ." He trailed off.

Caldwell threw his chalk onto the desk and strode out of the room. He ran down the hall and to the far exit. He dashed from Wilbur Hall to the Anthropology building next door and entered the first populated classroom.

"Who is your expert in Semitic languages?"

The stunned teacher turned from giving a lecture to a quite packed room to face the intruder.

"His name is Doctor Stanton," he said. "What's the matter anyway?"

"What room?"

"He's in—" he stuttered.

"What room, man!" Caldwell shouted.

"212. His office is in 212."

Caldwell turned and sprinted to the stairwell. Climbing the stairs, he muttered to himself, "At first, he was running, then quick marching, and now he's walking. He's exponentially decelerating. Something like y equals 0.9 to the power of x. Or maybe"—he paused here and froze at the top of the stairs—"maybe his speed equals one divided by his nearness to me."

He continued into the second-floor hallway and found room 212. He knocked and entered without waiting for a reply. Doctor Stanton was not there. For a placid moment, Caldwell looked around the cramped office. The floor was cushioned with a burgundy Persian rug, and many trinkets lined the shelves of a dark-stained bookshelf. There was a curved dagger in a jeweled hilt and a crystal glass vial of amber-colored liquid. Caldwell heard the sound of a toilet flushing somewhere down the hall. Footsteps came toward the office door, and a man whistling "The Sheik of Araby" turned the handle.

In walked a portly, middle-aged man with a watch chain in his pocket and wavy, balding hair. He jolted when he saw the stranger standing in his office.

"Zounds!" Doctor Stanton exclaimed. "You startled me, man. What are you doing in my office?" He spoke with an Imperial sounding English accent.

"Doctor, I am currently enmeshed in a most urgent matter. I really don't have much time to explain it all. I think you can help me."

"Well, first let's hear your name."

"I'm F.C. Caldwell. I'm a mathematician over in Wilbur Hall. Listen, I'll not mince words but cut straight to the heart of my problem. I think I spoke some dark mischief on myself by reading an ill-begotten Arabic curse. Now there's a persistent fellow in Ottoman garb trying to get gashouse with me all over town."

"How rum. You really mean that you think you've fallen under a djinni's curse?"

"If that's what you call it, sure thing."

"What words did you read exactly?"

"I don't remember. I found them in a book in the library." Caldwell rushed to the window and peered through the wooden slats. "We don't have much time; he's outside right now. Don't you know any magic words to clear up something like this?"

"I normally wouldn't entertain such queer fantasies, you know. But I can see that you are in quite the agitated state. Come with me to the library, and I'll rattle off some Arabic spells for you."

The two men left the office and went down to the first floor. Just then, the exterior door opened and the djinni stepped in. He didn't stop, but continued walking at a casual pace toward Caldwell and Doctor Stanton who were halfway down the hall.

It was then that the somewhat bearable fear of being pursued by an enemy turned into a ghastly horror for Caldwell, and any disregard for the situation became a sudden, maddening realization of danger. The djinni was a bulging, humanoid figure with turgid limbs and a feverish skin color. He was utterly hairless. His face was square and wrinkly like a bulldog's. The most horrifying aspect of this encounter was, by far, the expression of violent rage and bloodlust in the djinni's features. His brow was locked into a Cro-Magnon protrusion, and his eyes were popping out and dead set on Caldwell. Never had a man seen a more contorted lip than his, which revealed a row of plaque encrusted, hog-like teeth.

What made it all the worse was the easy nature with which the djinni plodded toward them. All of the instincts of pattern recognition within these two victims told them that the assailant should be rushing at a murderous pace. But, the patient confidence of his tread produced a kind of nauseating fear of what cruelty might await.

"I think we better go the long way around," offered Doctor Stanton.

So they exited the Anthro building and made it to the library. Once inside, Caldwell showed the doctor the particular Latin translation that he had read the day before.

"See, here's the line that I think the curse came from. I won't read it out loud again."

"Yes, indeed." Doctor Stanton read it over. "It translates to 'May the djinni follow you in perpetuity.' It is hard to say for certain, but I think that the vocabulary here suggests that the djinni isn't actually out to kill you."

"Can I take that risk? And in any case, I can't live with a djinni following me around forever. But this does add some validity to my theory that the thing is exponentially decelerating. Its speed is basically a harmonic series."

"Slow down, man; I'm a linguist."

"Do you know Zeno's paradox? Or Zeno's race?"

"I'm partially familiar with it. Something to do with the paradox of needing to get some place by always going half the distance."

"Yes, exactly," Caldwell said. "The djinni is bound by the curse to always be in the process of walking half the distance between us. Each time he reaches that halfway point, he then has to start again, because there is a new halfway point between his location and his goal. He can never truly reach me, but I don't want to find out what happens when he gets within Planck length of my skin cells."

"Let us waste no time, then. Follow me to the Abbasid literature."

As they walked through the stacks, the djinni burst through a door nearby, walking quickly at first, then slowing down before their very eyes like a penny dropped into molasses.

"He's getting uncomfortably close," Caldwell urged as Doctor Stanton flipped through pages upon pages of artfully inked Arabic script.

"Ah, here we are." Doctor Stanton stuck his index finger to the page. "The control djinni utterance from Baghdad, 893 AD."

The djinni was now mere feet away from Caldwell. Its feet glided across that ground at a slower than tiptoe speed, though its posture was that of an aggressive brawler. The slower it got, the more unnerving the pinkish face of anger became. Up close, its skin looked like a pig's, and its breath was extremely malodorous.

"Come on, Doctor, get on with it."

"I really think that you better say these words, or else you won't rightly be able to break the curse."

"I can't read Arabic. You have to coach me."

Doctor Stanton leaned over and whispered a few syllables into Caldwell's ears. The djinni lifted his arms, quicker than his legs were moving, into a gesture of strangulation.

"I'll try my best," Caldwell said. "Ana amruk ayahu aljinsiu."

Suddenly, the djinni stopped. His hands were almost wrapped around Caldwell's neck. The math professor took a step back and waited. Nothing more happened.

"Thank you, Doctor. I really can't repay you enough for this act of bravery. I really thought I was a goner when I saw that pugnacious freak in the hallway earlier."

"Don't mention it, my boy. I am only proud to have been called upon in someone's time of need. A lifetime of reading about Arabian adventures has finally come to fruition." The doctor shook Caldwell's hand and patted his shoulder. "Now what are you going to do with this djinni?"

Caldwell looked at the spirit, frozen in place. He hadn't considered what he would wish for now that he had captured the djinni.

"Djinni, I want you to go back to where you came from and bake me a Gabriel's cake. When you're done with that, you're free from my command."

The djinni bowed, straightened, and went up in a spray of foul smelling, warm mist. When the air cleared, Caldwell stuck his pipe between his teeth.

"I guess that's that."

"Indeed," added Doctor Stanton.

Caldwell parted ways with the doctor and walked off back to Wilbur Hall.

He found Albert Bradford in his office sitting at his desk, chuffing a cigarette and pecking at a typewriter.

"Albert, you *won't believe* the afternoon I've had."

Without looking up, Bradford replied, "Do tell, Egg."

An Untold Story

Michael Calloway

Thousands of years ago, in the Alps, mighty legions of old marched through the craggy passes, with banners lifted against the sharp, blue sky. The clank of metal armor, the rhythmic stomp of leather boots on stone, and the breath of men turned to mist in the chill air all echoed off the ancient mountainsides, as if even gods bore witness to their passage. Countless generations went off through these mountain passes—to stop invaders, to save their kin, or to seek glory beyond. Every generation believed their struggles were unique, but the mountains knew better. They had seen the rise and fall of empires, watched as men fought for the same patches of earth under different banners, heard the same vows made and broken in countless languages now lost to time.

And now, these mountains bore witness to another generation. Fighting, dying in those alpine hills, as the distant roar of artillery fire echoed through the valleys, merging with the howls of the wind. Trenches scarred the once-pristine landscapes; wire and weapons littered the earth as fresh testaments to human conflict. Men in uniforms of drab green and gray huddled in these furrows, clutching at their rifles as their forefathers once clasped swords and spears. Their eyes, just like those of countless men before them, reflected the age-old interplay of fear, determination, and hope.

One of them, above all, sat there in the trench along the Isonzo. More than a man—a *bersagliere*. Possessing that eye of destiny that watched over him, his face smeared with dirt and stubble, gazed out over the no man's land with a kind of detached curiosity. He was unlike the others in his trench—a middle-aged man, but the lines etched into his forehead told of burdens. He had a stoical, serious expression about him, and was possessed with a reverent zeal that radiated from him.

Amidst the thunder of guns, he read a small pamphlet from home, a translation of Horace's *Odes*, the delicate pages incongruous with his rough, dirtied fingers as they turned them carefully. The verses spoke of the same mountains, the same skies under which he now fought.

His comrade-in-arms, a young boy really, with barely a wisp of a mustache, looked over curiously at the old soldier's reading material. Marco, a young man from a small village on the coast, had seen nothing of the world beyond his mother's olive groves before he was conscripted. Now here he was, sharing a trench with men like the bersagliere, who seemed to him as if chiseled from the very rock of these mountains.

"What are you reading?" Marco asked, curious.

"Horace," replied the older man without lifting his eyes from the page.

"Though I doubt you have much interest. . . . It's abou—"

An explosion sent dirt and shrapnel flying upward, with the bersagliere barely moving, as the distant cry of wounded men filtered through the chaos. Marco ducked instinctively, his heart hammering in his chest. When he looked back up, the older soldier was calmly brushing debris from his pamphlet.

"It's about bravery," he continued, as if there had been no interruption. "About facing the inevitable with dignity. About—"

Another shell exploded closer, cutting off his words. The mountains seemed to tremble with the impact, dust raining down upon them from the edges of their dugout. For a moment, all was silence but for the settling of earth—and the distant cry of a whistle. An Austrian whistle, signaling the start of another advance.

The bersagliere closed his pamphlet, slipping it into a pocket close to his heart, and looked to Marco with a steady gaze, a weary sigh drifting from his lips as he gazed out toward the no man's land ahead. Men around them scrambled to their feet, rifles at the ready. Orders were shouted down the line; raw voices lifted in response. Marco fumbled with his weapon, his hands shaking not from cold but from adrenaline surging through his veins.

The old soldier placed a firm hand on Marco's shoulder, steadying him. "Breathe," he said, his voice a calm beacon in the storm of fear and confusion. "Remember why you are here. For family, for country. For Italy."

*　　*　　*

Nearly three decades later the scars of the Isonzo had hardly healed. The bersagliere was long gone, his mortal body destroyed, torn asunder like so many others. Another ghost in a valley of phantoms. But Marco, Marco still remembered.

He cast a gaze down to the worn, discolored pamphlet, as he sat on the grass, overlooking the hill they once held together. Footsteps came from behind.

"Father. . . ." A hand gripped Marco's shoulder. He didn't dare look back.

"It's alright, son," Marco whispered, his voice a fragile echo of the past. "Come, sit with me."

His son hesitated, feeling the weight of history in his father's tone. Slowly, he lowered himself beside Marco on the cool grass, the verdant blades now covering what was once ravaged by war. Lorenzo—in that magnificent uniform of his, the same uniform his father had worn. The same uniform his comrades had all bled and died in.

Lorenzo looked out at the mountains, those same stoic giants that had watched over his father and the bersagliere all those years ago. The young man's eyes searched the horizon, as if seeking answers among the peaks—answers about war, about peace, and about the legacy he was stepping into.

"What was it like?" he asked. "To stand there, against all odds?"

Marco's eyes remained fixed on the horizon, where the sun began to sink behind the craggy peaks. He took in a deep breath, letting the alpine air fill his lungs as if drawing strength from the very earth beneath him.

"It was like being part of something greater," he started slowly, "like every beat of your heart was in rhythm with the man next to you. Fear was there, yes—like a shadow that never quite leaves your side. But we fought for each other, for something that we believed would outlast us."

"Is that what awaits me?" Lorenzo stated.

Silence settled between them as they sat side by side. Marco knew this was the last time he'd see his son—it was the feeling of destiny in the air. As the sun dipped lower, painting the sky in hues of orange and purple, Marco turned to look at his son, his eyes reflecting the fiery canvas overhead. He placed the well-worn pamphlet in Lorenzo's hands, the delicate pages now fragile with age.

"It's yours now," Marco said, weakly, before gazing out, quietly looking at the mountains.

Lorenzo left him with Marco gazing out there, all alone, quietly dwelling on memories that would soon be as lost, but some part of him felt comforted. The mountains loomed above him, silent guardians of his vigil, and Marco could feel their eternal presence whispering through the fading light. They spoke of timelessness, of the unending cycle of life and death and rebirth that he had been a part of—a cycle that his son was now entering, as he let out one final sigh.

"Bring him back home," he murmured to the mountains, a prayer whispered to the indifferent stones that had witnessed the dramas of countless men like him. He could only hope something had heard him.

*　*　*

It was the final war. It had to be, as P-47s roared overhead. Explosions cratered the small town of Cassino, dust and debris choking the air with the scent of ruin. Lorenzo, now a captain, moved with purpose through the chaos, the echoes of his father's words resonating within him. His unit advanced cautiously among the shattered remnants of once quaint homes, now just obstacles in their path toward an uncertain victory.

His men looked to him for leadership, their faces smeared with grime and sweat, eyes searching for a sign of hope amidst the horror. Lorenzo held his rifle tight to his chest, the weight of it a constant reminder of his duty. He could feel his heart pounding in rhythm with the distant artillery—the Americans were advancing.

The history of Italy has always been one of blood and sacrifice, of families torn asunder and rebuilt in the image of what came before. Lorenzo could see it in the broken streets, the collapsed walls that once held the laughter and love of a village. It was his turn to defend what remained, to hold firm against the coming tide. To buy time.

"Positions!" he ordered, his voice cutting through the din. His men took cover, their rifles trained on the gaps between rubble and ruin.

A sudden burst of machine-gun fire raked across their position, spitting death with mechanical indifference. Bullets whizzed, large caliber rounds flying through stone and cutting through defenses as if they were mere paper. Lorenzo dove to the ground, pulling a young private down with him just as a chunk of wall where the boy had been standing exploded into dust. The air was thick with dust, as the whirling of a tank was coming up, advancing.

A few of his men had taken the opportunity to fall back, fleeing while they could. He could only watch, unable to do anything.

"We need to get out of here. . . ." the private whispered.

Lorenzo looked at the young soldier, his eyes conveying a mix of resolve and an understanding of the gravity of their situation. He nodded curtly, gripping the private's arm with a steadying force. "We will," he said firmly, "but on our terms."

He peeked around the corner of their meager cover and saw shadows moving amidst the debris. The enemy was close, advancing. He'd only have one chance at this.

"Listen to me," he said, turning to face the private, whose name tag read "Mario." "We're not just soldiers; we're guardians of our homeland's future. . . ."

A distant explosion leveled the center of the piazza, leaving only a toppled bench as the private cringed. The tank was drawing closer—there wouldn't be much more time. More and more soldiers deserted the piazza, falling back, routing.

The private nodded, stiffening his resolve as Lorenzo continued, "Now, get out of here."

It was perhaps a shock to the young private, who expected a rallying speech or an order to charge, not an instruction to retreat. But Lorenzo's eyes held no room for doubt. There was a silent exchange between them, a passing of an unspoken understanding. The war was already over. But not for Lorenzo.

The private scuttled away, moving from cover to cover with the agility of youth and fear combined. Lorenzo watched him go, once again turning toward the enemy who now spilled into the piazza like dark water finding its way through cracks in the pavement.

With steady hands, Lorenzo reached for the grenades strapped to his belt. He had been left behind by most of his unit, but he would make his stand here, in the heart of Cassino. He couldn't leave his hometown behind; he couldn't leave it to be defiled. His eyes gazed down to the small, worn-down, stitched together pamphlet of *Odes*, and he sighed.

He counted under his breath, timing each breath with the rhythm of his heartbeat—the same heartbeat that had echoed through generations standing against invasions and oppressors. *For Italy*, he thought. *For my father*.

And yet, he hesitated, his eyes betraying his fear for just a moment before determination set in. He nodded again, more firmly this time, and with a quick, silent prayer to the saints his mother had taught him, he scrambled out of cover and dashed through the broken streets, grenades in hand; then, he tossed them.

They flew through the air, in a brilliant, slow motion. A piercing pain filled him, but he hardly noticed. Everything moved so slow, almost as if time itself had come to a respectful pause. The grenades found their targets, the fiery blooms of destruction erupting at the top of the tank. . . .

And then, searing pain clawed at his side where bits of shrapnel had found him, but it was distant, remote compared to the roar in his ears, as he collapsed. He lay there, half-buried beneath fallen bricks and dust, the world above a cacophony of continued fighting.

A grin was locked on his face as an American soldier found him amidst the rubble. Lorenzo was no longer wearing his dashing Italian uniform but the gray tunic with the Waffen-SS collar. As his breathing became labored, the rifle of the American pointed right at his head, vengeance filling the young soldier's eyes. But Lorenzo's grin didn't waver, even as he gazed up into the barrel of the gun.

Lorenzo's smile softened with relief and gratitude. The pain was growing more intense now, spreading from his wound like wildfire through his bones. He knew that these were his final moments, the last chapter in a story that stretched back generations, and his last, satisfying thought was at least that it ended with a boom, instead of being silently snuffed out, as he closed his eyes.

*　　*　　*

The village of Cassino never rebuilt, after the war. It was eerily quiet, the only visitors seeming to be American tourists, who drove through barely noting it on any map.

Yet, even in its desolation, Cassino held stories within its silence, whispers of the past that still lingered in the air like ghosts. But now, a new visitor arrived, an old, aging man in an out-of-fashion suit.

Marco.

He strolled through it, quietly humming to himself an old soldiers' song, a tune that had once been carried on the lips of many young men marching to an unforgiving beat. His footsteps were slow, measured against the backdrop of time-worn ruins that bore mute testimony to the cost of war.

In his hand, he held a small, faded photograph, edges worn from the many times it had been taken out and looked at, then put away again. It was a picture of Lorenzo, taken just before he left for the war. Marco's fingers traced the outline of his son's face as if he could somehow bridge the years and distance that lay between them.

He sat down in the piazza, on a bench in the center of town. A weary expression was clear in his face as a car rolled by. A young man, maybe in his early twenties, stepped out. Intrigued by the sight of the older gentleman seemingly out of place amidst the ruins, he approached with a respectful curiosity.

"Excuse me, sir," the young man said as he reached where Marco sat. "Are you looking for something?"

Marco turned to the young man, his eyes showing a glimmer of recognition. "In a way," he replied with a soft voice that carried the weight of memories. "I'm visiting an old comrade."

The young man sat next to Marco on the bench, his interest piqued. "An old friend, here? This town has been abandoned for years."

"Yes," Marco nodded solemnly. "But some friends never leave us. They live within these walls, these streets—they are part of this earth now." His gaze drifted off across the broken landscape.

The young man sat there, confused. He watched Marco carefully, noting the man's solemn demeanor and how he seemed to look through the visible world to one unseen by others. "Were you in the war, sir?" he ventured, hesitant to intrude on what was clearly a personal pilgrimage.

Marco turned his attention back to the young man beside him and nodded. "One of them," he said simply, tapping the ground with a cane. "What about yourself?"

"Just doing a delivery," the young man sighed. "Nothing as heroic as fighting in a war. My pops did, though he doesn't talk about it very much."

"I didn't talk about it very much either. Not to my Lorenzo. . . ." Marco's voice trailed off, the weight of lost years etched into his words. He looked at the photograph again, a gesture that seemed to bridge the gulf between living and remembering. His eyes were moist as he studied the image of his son—before crumpling it against his chest.

"Did he fight here?" the young man questioned. "He might have known my father."

Marco's hand trembled as he smoothed out the photograph, his fingers lingering on the contours of a once familiar uniform. "He did," he said. "Lorenzo fought here. But he never came back from this place. I never found out what happened to him."

"Lorenzo. . . ." The words seemed to echo through the young man as he fumbled for something in his pocket. He drew out a crumpled piece of paper and unfolded it carefully, revealing another photograph. It showed a group of soldiers, dirty and tired but resolute. "My father, he always kept this photo," he said quietly, pointing to a young soldier among them. "He said this man saved his life during one of the battles here."

Marco's eyes widened as he took in the image, finding his son amidst the faces. "Lorenz—" His voice choked off as years of uncertainty met an unexpected moment of closure. What confirmed it was that at Lorenzo's hip was that small pamphlet of *Odes*.

Tears brimmed in Marco's eyes as he reached out to touch the photograph, his fingertips barely grazing the surface as if he feared damaging the fragile link to his child. "This—" He swallowed hard, his voice catching. "This is my son."

The young man watched the old father, a mix of wonder and empathy in his gaze. "Your son saved my dad's life. When I could get him to talk about the war, he'd never stop mentioning a captain. I guess that was him."

The two men sat in silence, each lost in their own thoughts while united by the intertwined fates of their fathers. The quiet around them stretched, laden with history and the resonance of countless untold stories.

After a moment, Marco cleared his throat and turned back to the young man. "I don't even know your name," he said with a weak attempt at a smile.

"It's Paolo," replied the young man, returning the smile with genuine warmth.

"Paolo," Marco repeated, rolling the name on his tongue as if committing it to memory. "That's a good name."

Previous Antelope Hill Writing Competitions:

Why We Fight, 2021

Small Victories, 2022

Touch Grass, 2023

ENJOYED THIS BOOK?

TO READ MORE, VISIT US AT

ANTELOPEHILLPUBLISHING.COM

www.ingramcontent.com/pod-product-compliance
Lightning Source LLC
Chambersburg PA
CBHW031336010826
48972CB00012B/558